STRANGER THINGS™ and DUNGEONS & DRAGONS®

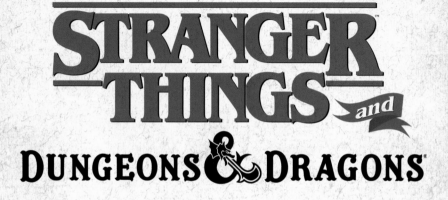

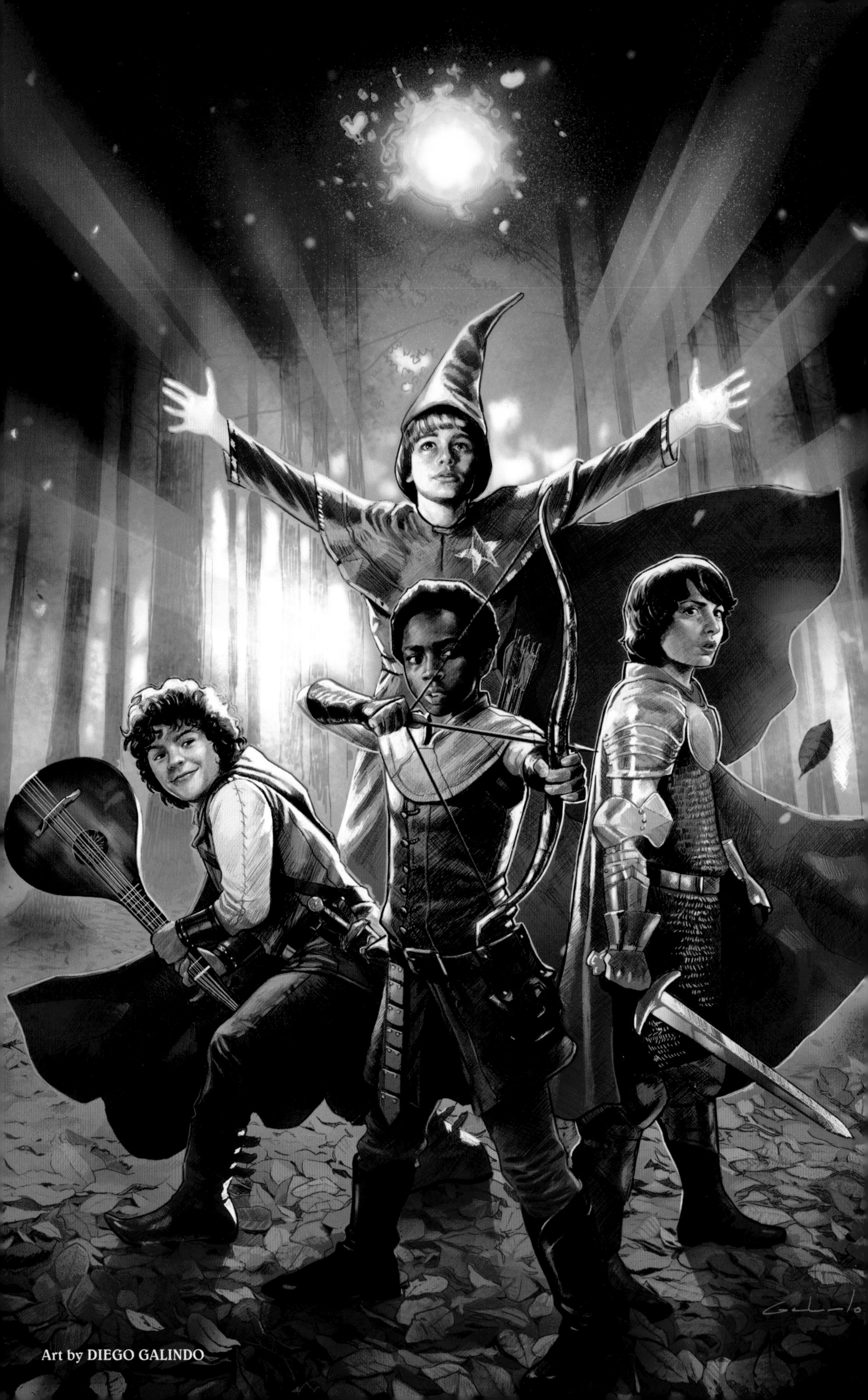

Art by DIEGO GALINDO

STRANGER THINGS and DUNGEONS & DRAGONS

script
JODY HOUSER AND JIM ZUB

line art
DIEGO GALINDO

colors
MSASSYK

lettering
NATE PIEKOS OF BLAMBOT®

front cover art by
KYLE LAMBERT

chapter break art by
E.M. GIST

Dark Horse Books

president and publisher
Mike Richardson

editor
Spencer Cushing

assistant editor
Konner Knudsen

collection designer
Patrick Satterfield

digital art technician
Samantha Hummer

Special thanks to Kyle Lambert, Shannon Schram, NETFLIX including Joe Lawson, the D&D team at Wizards of the Coast, and Megan Brown and John Barber at IDW.

This volume collects issue #1 through #4 of the Dark Horse and IDW comic book series *Stranger Things and Dungeons & Dragons.*

Published by Dark Horse Books
A division of Dark Horse Comics LLC
10956 SE Main Street • Milwaukie, OR 97222

Advertising Sales: (503) 905-2315
To find a comics shop in your area, visit comicshoplocator.com

DarkHorse.com • Netflix.com
idwpublishing.com • dnd.wizards.com

First edition: June 2021
eBook ISBN 978-1-50672-108-8
Trade Paperback ISBN 978-1-50672-107-1

1 3 5 7 9 10 8 6 4 2
Printed in China

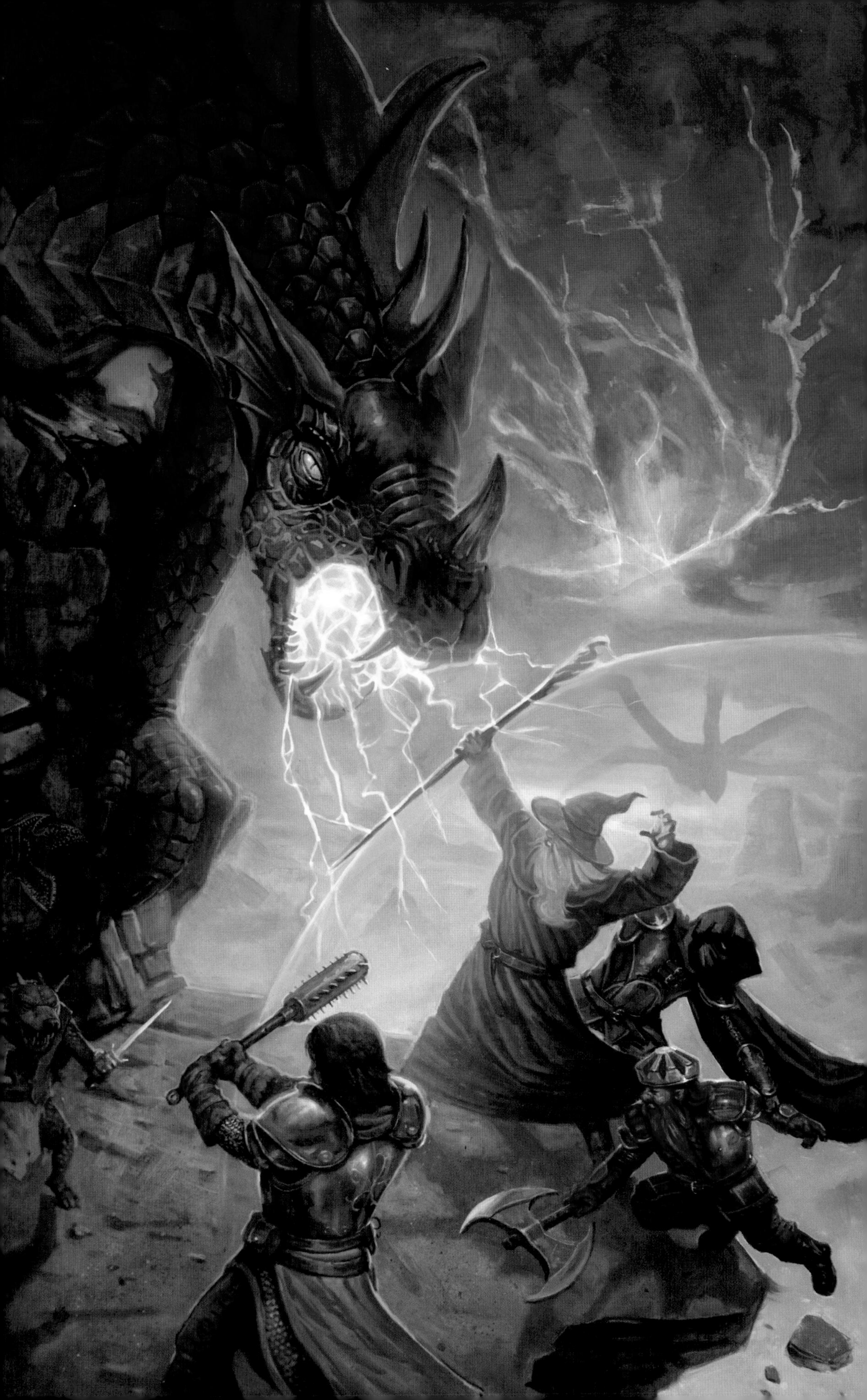

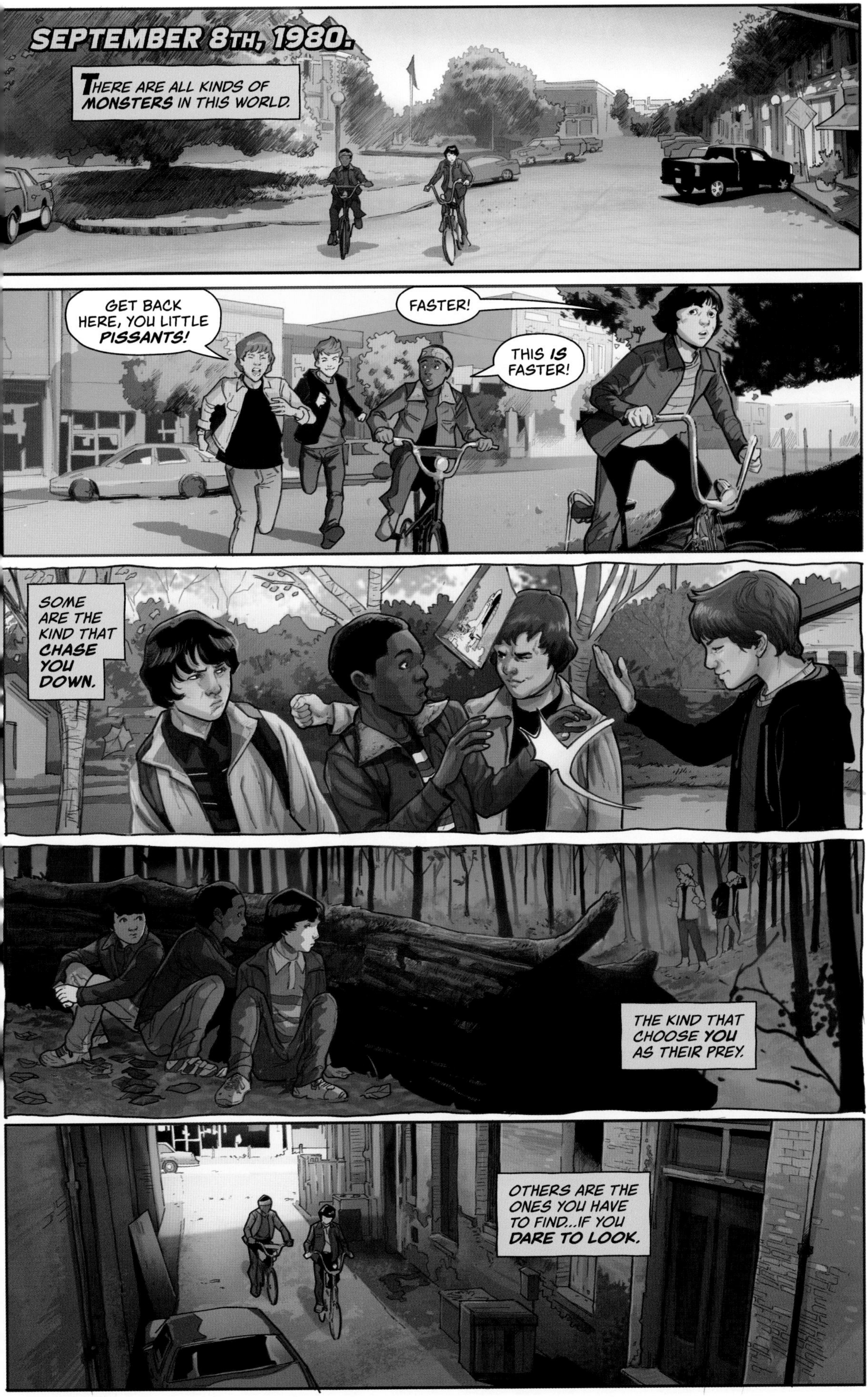
SEPTEMBER 8TH, 1980.
THERE ARE ALL KINDS OF MONSTERS IN THIS WORLD.
GET BACK HERE, YOU LITTLE PISSANTS!
FASTER!
THIS IS FASTER!
SOME ARE THE KIND THAT CHASE YOU DOWN.
THE KIND THAT CHOOSE YOU AS THEIR PREY.
OTHERS ARE THE ONES YOU HAVE TO FIND...IF YOU DARE TO LOOK.

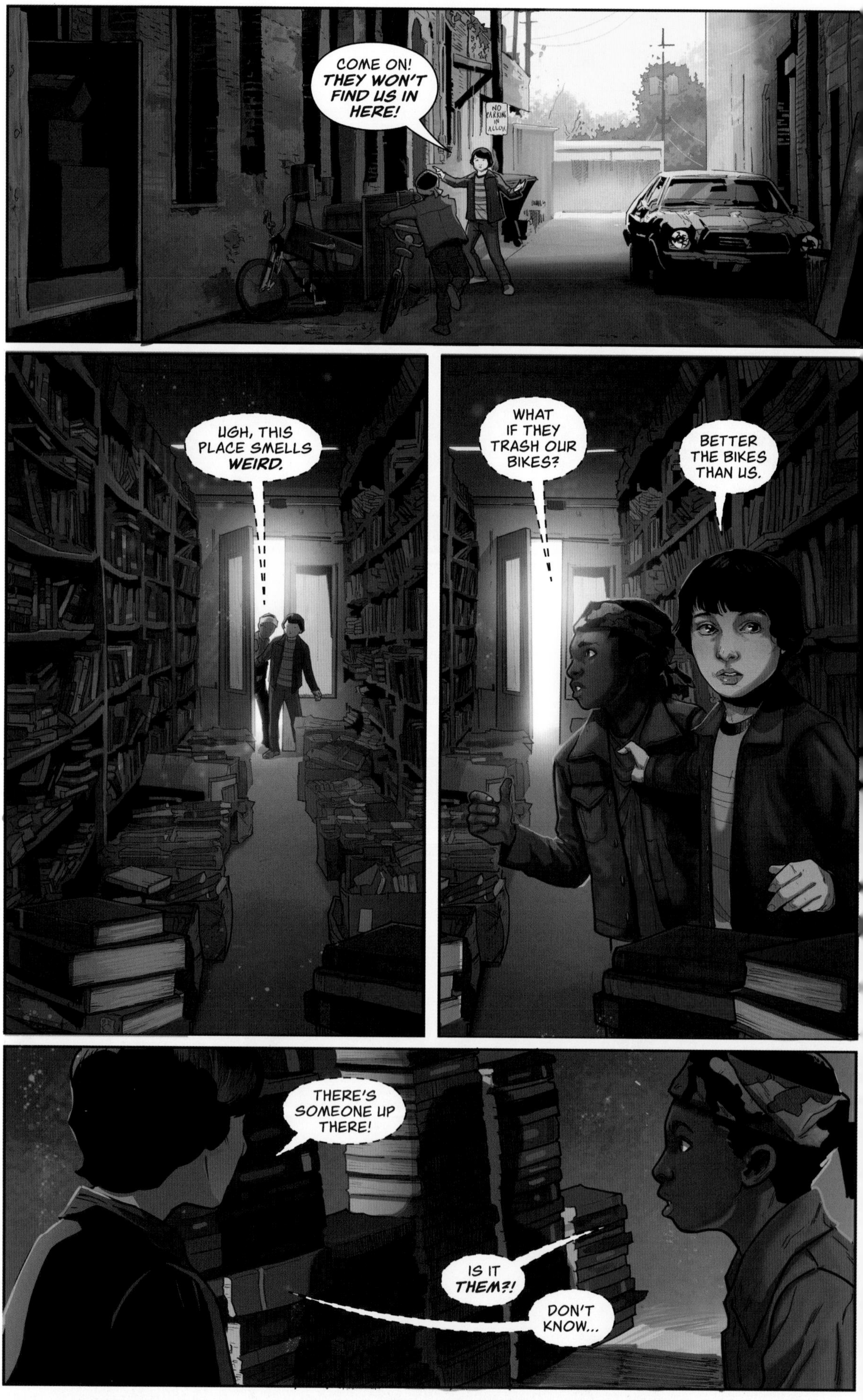
COME ON! THEY WON'T FIND US IN HERE!
UGH, THIS PLACE SMELLS WEIRD.
WHAT IF THEY TRASH OUR BIKES?
BETTER THE BIKES THAN US.
THERE'S SOMEONE UP THERE!
IS IT THEM?!
DON'T KNOW...

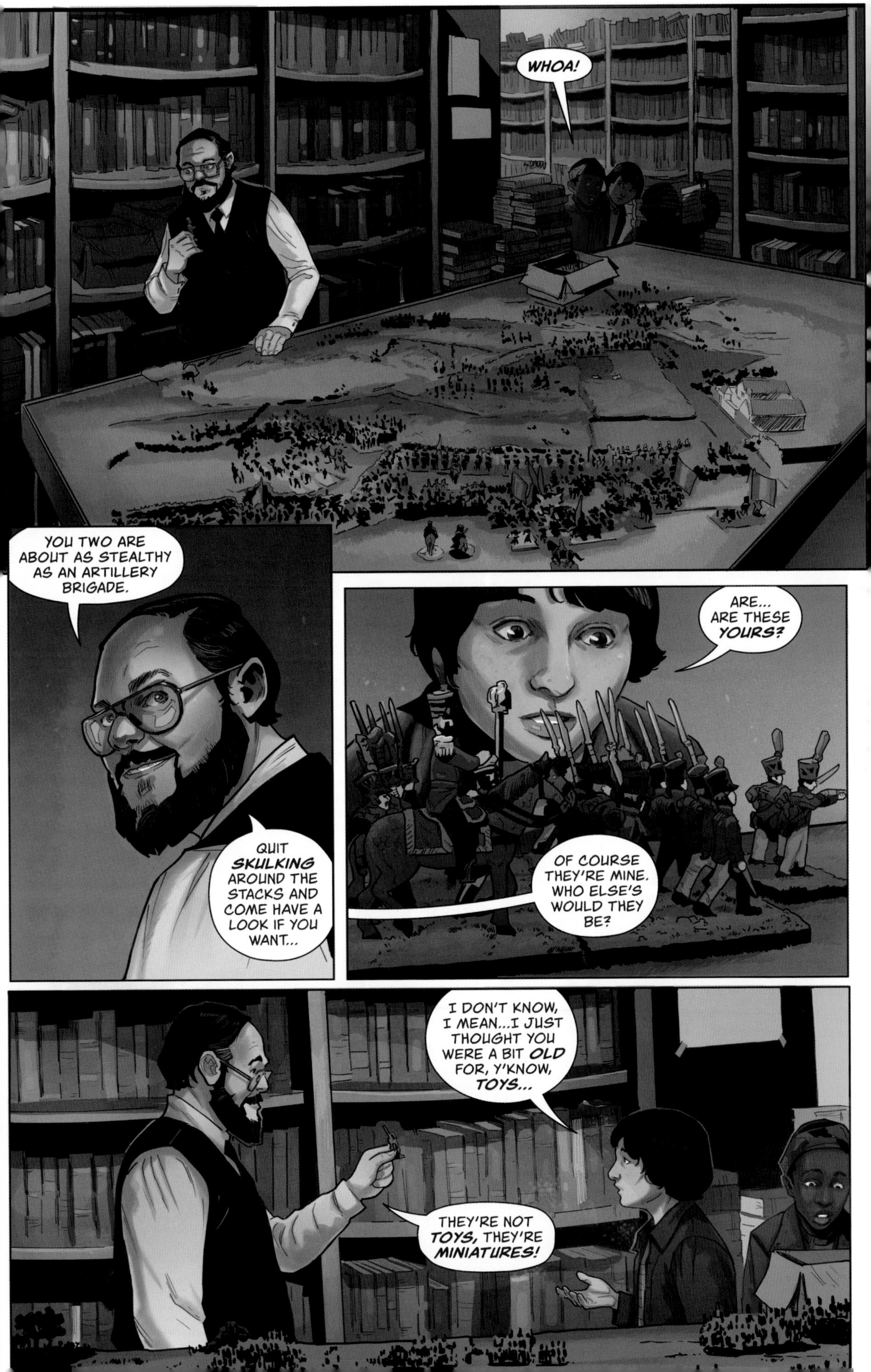
WHOA!
YOU TWO ARE ABOUT AS STEALTHY AS AN ARTILLERY BRIGADE.
QUIT SKULKING AROUND THE STACKS AND COME HAVE A LOOK IF YOU WANT...
ARE... ARE THESE YOURS?
OF COURSE THEY'RE MINE. WHO ELSE'S WOULD THEY BE?
I DON'T KNOW, I MEAN...I JUST THOUGHT YOU WERE A BIT OLD FOR, Y'KNOW, TOYS...
THEY'RE NOT TOYS, THEY'RE MINIATURES!

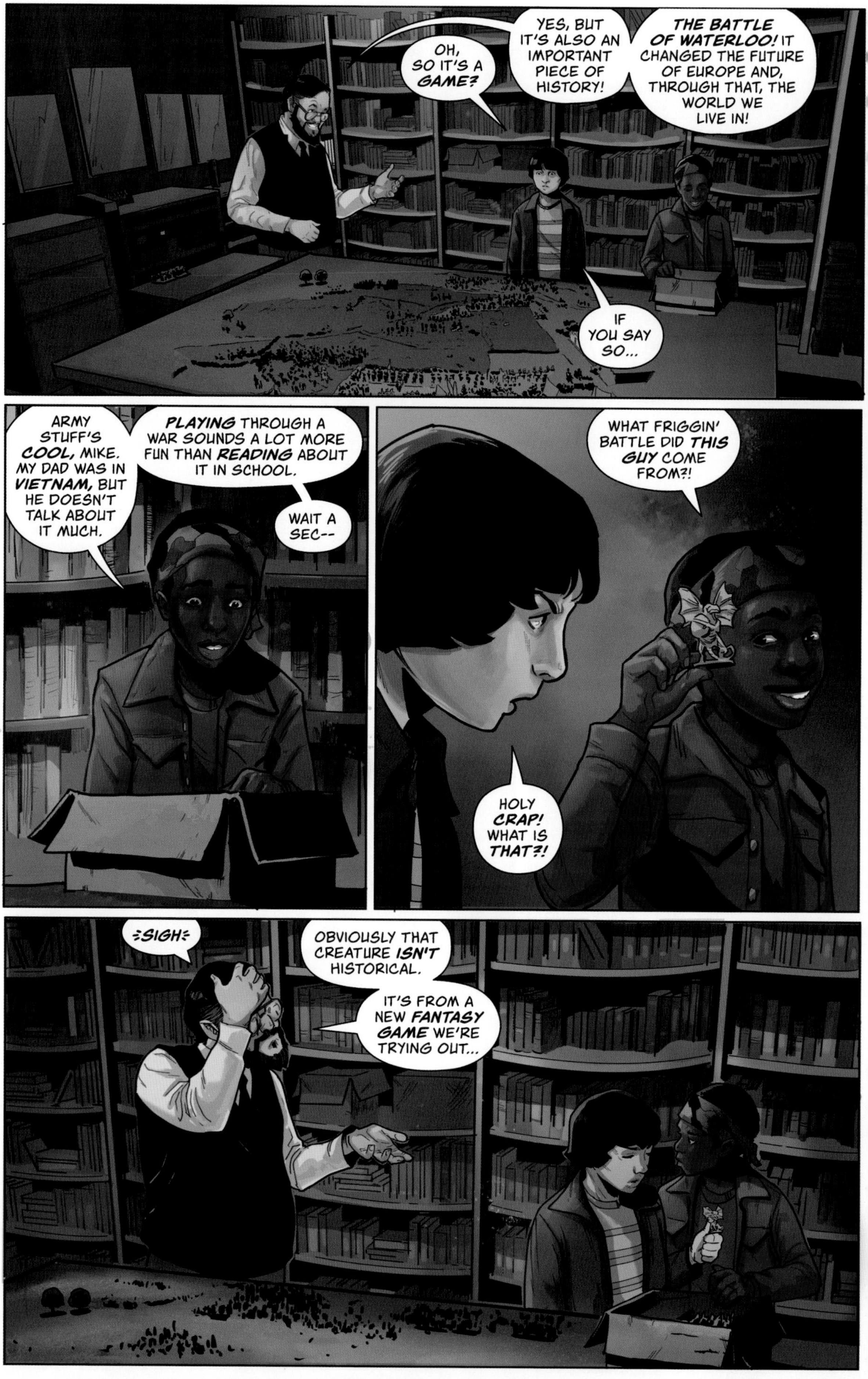
OH, SO IT'S A GAME?
YES, BUT IT'S ALSO AN IMPORTANT PIECE OF HISTORY!
THE BATTLE OF WATERLOO! IT CHANGED THE FUTURE OF EUROPE AND, THROUGH THAT, THE WORLD WE LIVE IN!
IF YOU SAY SO...
ARMY STUFF'S COOL, MIKE. MY DAD WAS IN VIETNAM, BUT HE DOESN'T TALK ABOUT IT MUCH.
PLAYING THROUGH A WAR SOUNDS A LOT MORE FUN THAN READING ABOUT IT IN SCHOOL.
WAIT A SEC--
WHAT FRIGGIN' BATTLE DID THIS GUY COME FROM?!
HOLY CRAP! WHAT IS THAT?!
SIGH
OBVIOUSLY THAT CREATURE ISN'T HISTORICAL.
IT'S FROM A NEW FANTASY GAME WE'RE TRYING OUT...

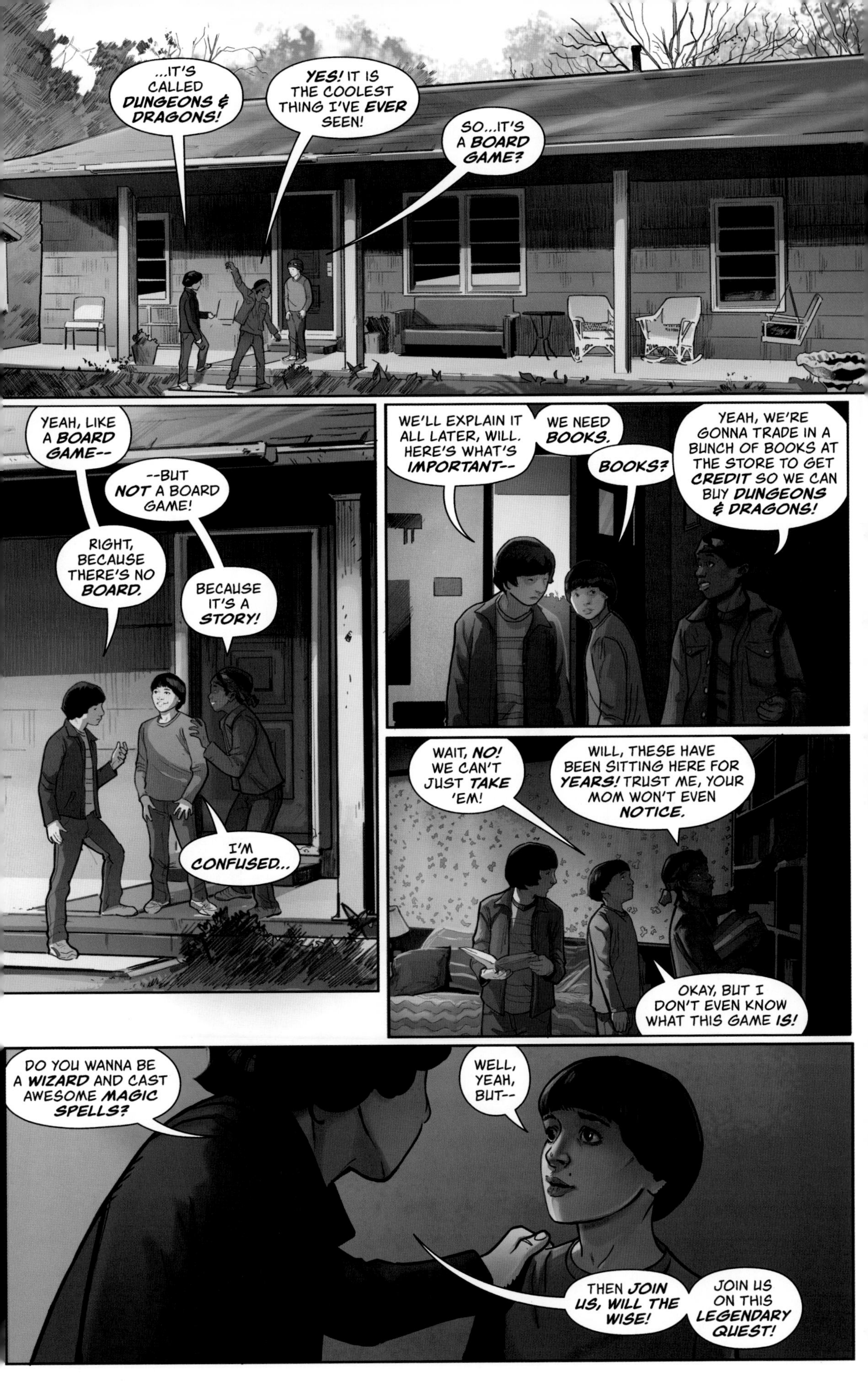
...IT'S CALLED DUNGEONS & DRAGONS!
YES! IT IS THE COOLEST THING I'VE EVER SEEN!
SO...IT'S A BOARD GAME?
YEAH, LIKE A BOARD GAME--
--BUT NOT A BOARD GAME!
RIGHT, BECAUSE THERE'S NO BOARD.
BECAUSE IT'S A STORY!
I'M CONFUSED...
WE'LL EXPLAIN IT ALL LATER, WILL. HERE'S WHAT'S IMPORTANT--
WE NEED BOOKS.
BOOKS?
YEAH, WE'RE GONNA TRADE IN A BUNCH OF BOOKS AT THE STORE TO GET CREDIT SO WE CAN BUY DUNGEONS & DRAGONS!
WAIT, NO! WE CAN'T JUST TAKE 'EM!
WILL, THESE HAVE BEEN SITTING HERE FOR YEARS! TRUST ME, YOUR MOM WON'T EVEN NOTICE.
OKAY, BUT I DON'T EVEN KNOW WHAT THIS GAME IS!
DO YOU WANNA BE A WIZARD AND CAST AWESOME MAGIC SPELLS?
WELL, YEAH, BUT--
THEN JOIN US, WILL THE WISE!
JOIN US ON THIS LEGENDARY QUEST!

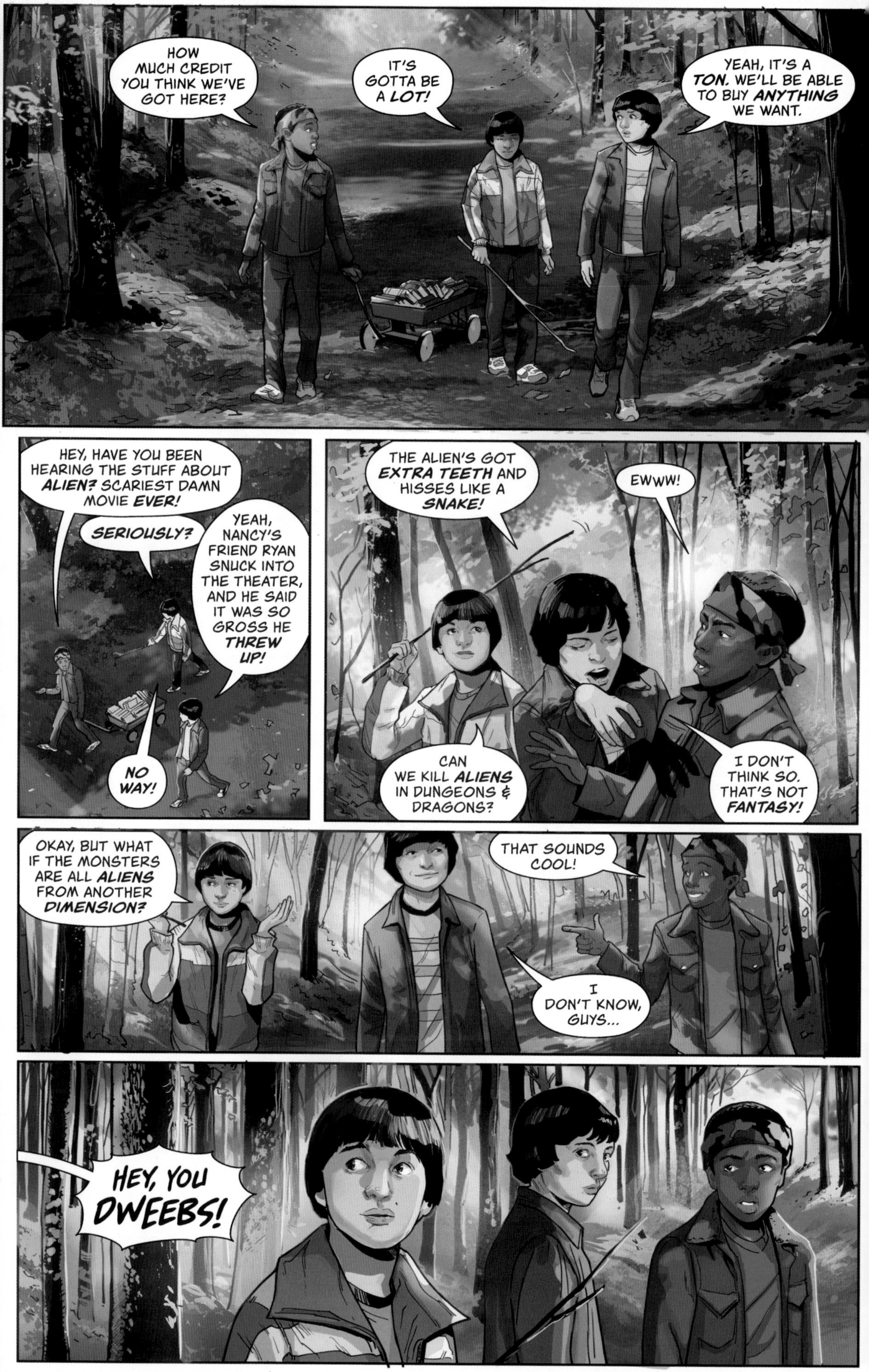
HOW MUCH CREDIT YOU THINK WE'VE GOT HERE?
IT'S GOTTA BE A LOT!
YEAH, IT'S A TON. WE'LL BE ABLE TO BUY ANYTHING WE WANT.
HEY, HAVE YOU BEEN HEARING THE STUFF ABOUT ALIEN? SCARIEST DAMN MOVIE EVER!
SERIOUSLY?
YEAH, NANCY'S FRIEND RYAN SNUCK INTO THE THEATER, AND HE SAID IT WAS SO GROSS HE THREW UP!
NO WAY!
THE ALIEN'S GOT EXTRA TEETH AND HISSES LIKE A SNAKE!
EWWW!
CAN WE KILL ALIENS IN DUNGEONS & DRAGONS?
I DON'T THINK SO. THAT'S NOT FANTASY!
OKAY, BUT WHAT IF THE MONSTERS ARE ALL ALIENS FROM ANOTHER DIMENSION?
THAT SOUNDS COOL!
I DON'T KNOW, GUYS...
HEY, YOU DWEEBS!

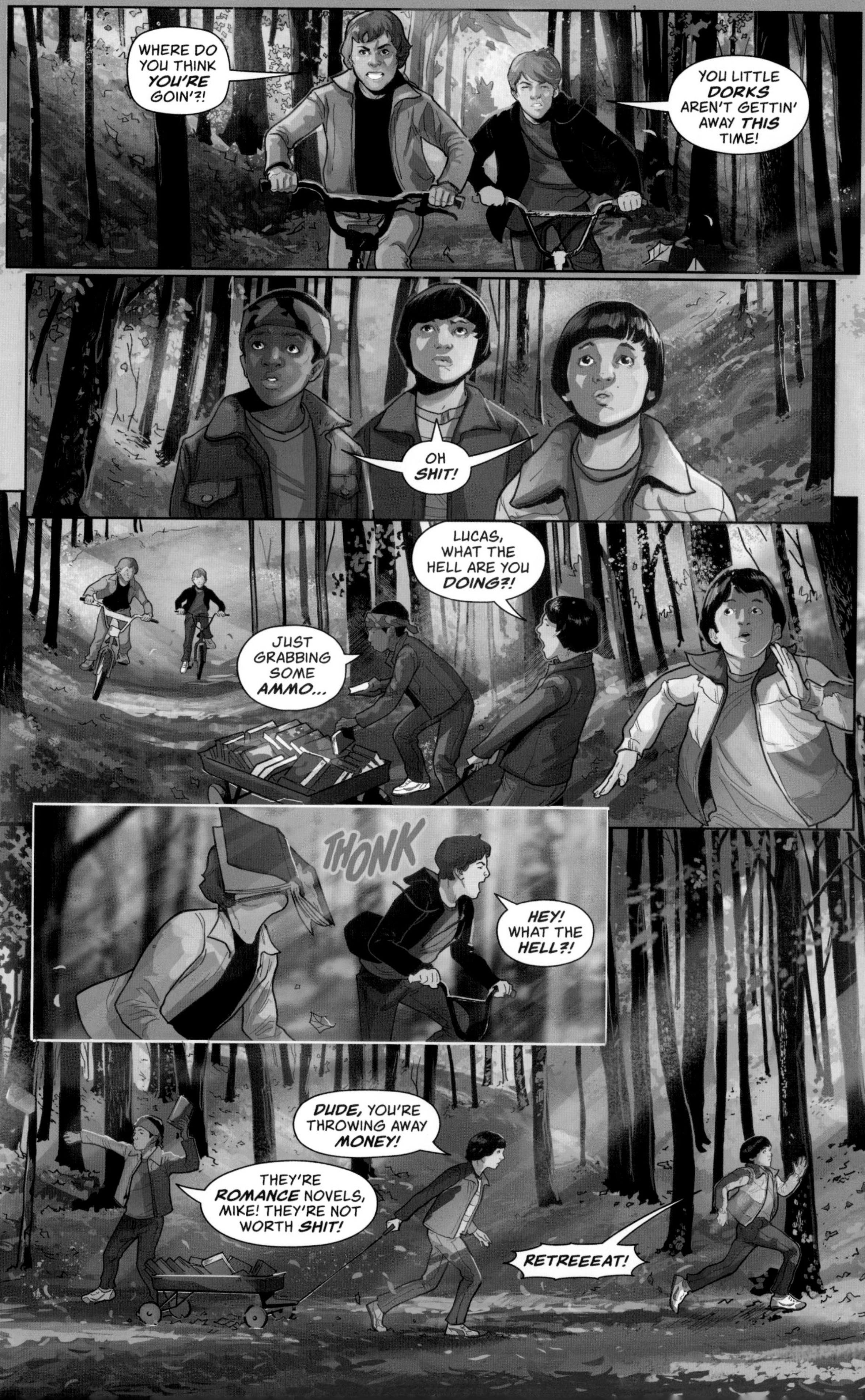

WHERE DO YOU THINK *YOU'RE* GOIN'?!
YOU LITTLE **DORKS** AREN'T GETTIN' AWAY **THIS** TIME!
OH **SHIT!**
LUCAS, WHAT THE HELL ARE YOU **DOING?!**
JUST GRABBING SOME **AMMO...**
THONK
HEY! WHAT THE **HELL?!**
DUDE, YOU'RE THROWING AWAY **MONEY!**
THEY'RE **ROMANCE** NOVELS, MIKE! THEY'RE NOT WORTH **SHIT!**
RETREEEAT!

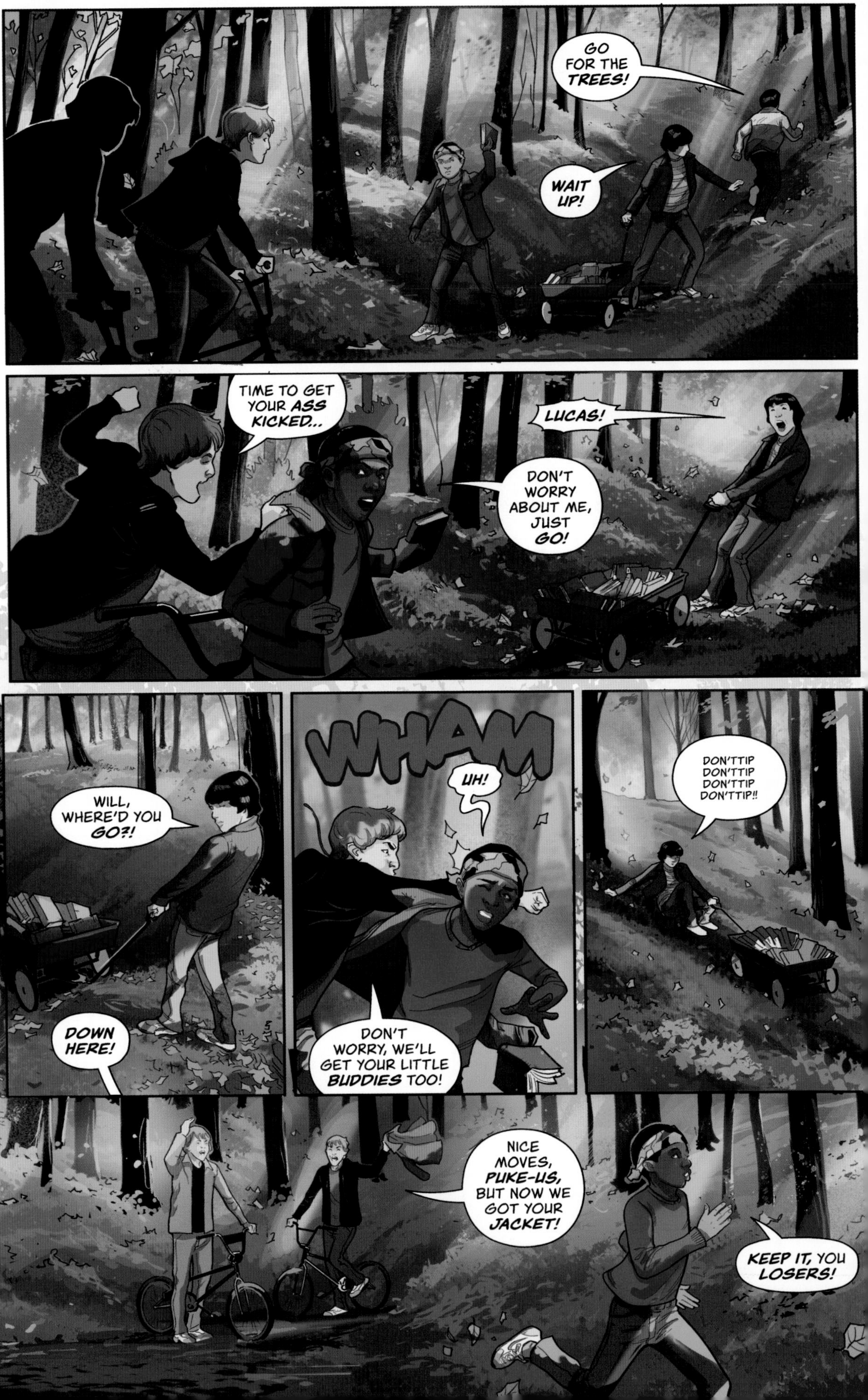
GO FOR THE TREES!
WAIT UP!
TIME TO GET YOUR ASS KICKED...
LUCAS!
DON'T WORRY ABOUT ME, JUST GO!
WILL, WHERE'D YOU GO?!
DOWN HERE!
WHAM
UH!
DON'T WORRY, WE'LL GET YOUR LITTLE BUDDIES TOO!
DON'TTIP DON'TTIP DON'TTIP DON'TTIP!!
NICE MOVES, PUKE-US, BUT NOW WE GOT YOUR JACKET!
KEEP IT, YOU LOSERS!

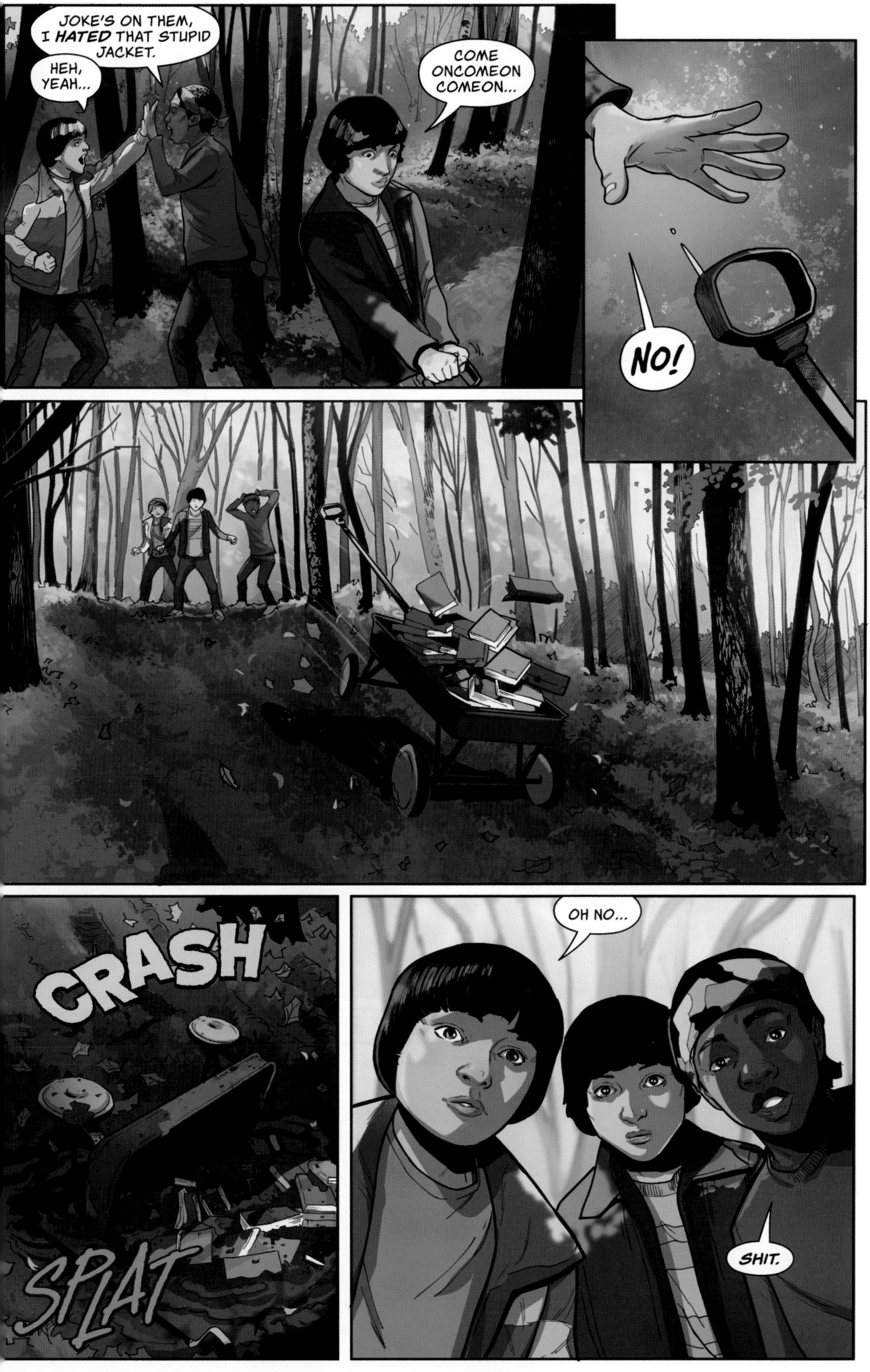

JOKE'S ON THEM, I **HATED** THAT STUPID JACKET.
HEH, YEAH...
COME ONCOMEON COMEON...
NO!
CRASH
SPLAT
OH NO...
SHIT.

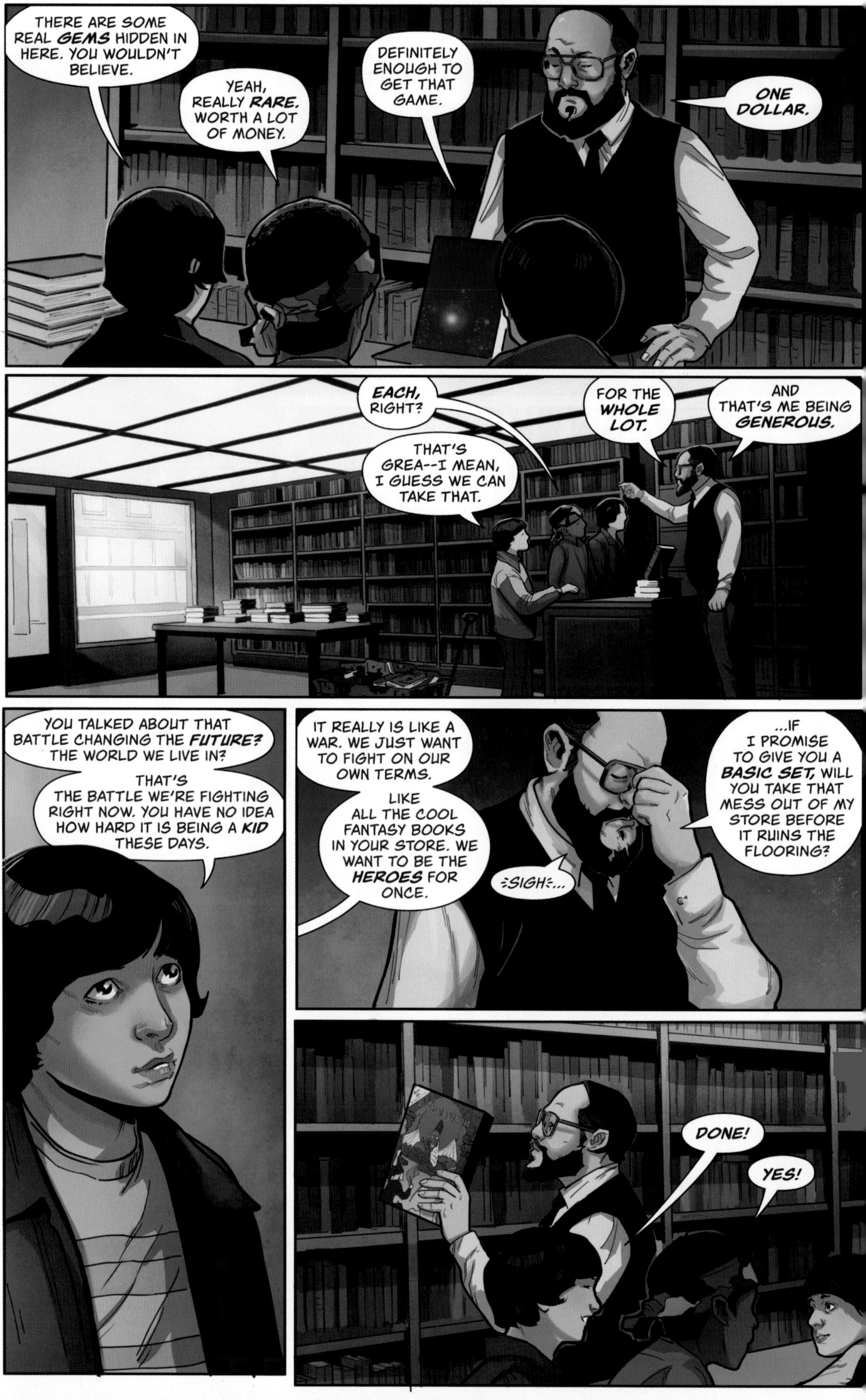
THERE ARE SOME REAL GEMS HIDDEN IN HERE. YOU WOULDN'T BELIEVE.
YEAH, REALLY RARE. WORTH A LOT OF MONEY.
DEFINITELY ENOUGH TO GET THAT GAME.
ONE DOLLAR.
EACH, RIGHT?
FOR THE WHOLE LOT.
AND THAT'S ME BEING GENEROUS.
THAT'S GREA--I MEAN, I GUESS WE CAN TAKE THAT.
YOU TALKED ABOUT THAT BATTLE CHANGING THE FUTURE? THE WORLD WE LIVE IN?
THAT'S THE BATTLE WE'RE FIGHTING RIGHT NOW. YOU HAVE NO IDEA HOW HARD IT IS BEING A KID THESE DAYS.
IT REALLY IS LIKE A WAR. WE JUST WANT TO FIGHT ON OUR OWN TERMS.
LIKE ALL THE COOL FANTASY BOOKS IN YOUR STORE. WE WANT TO BE THE HEROES FOR ONCE.
SIGH...
...IF I PROMISE TO GIVE YOU A BASIC SET, WILL YOU TAKE THAT MESS OUT OF MY STORE BEFORE IT RUINS THE FLOORING?
DONE!
YES!

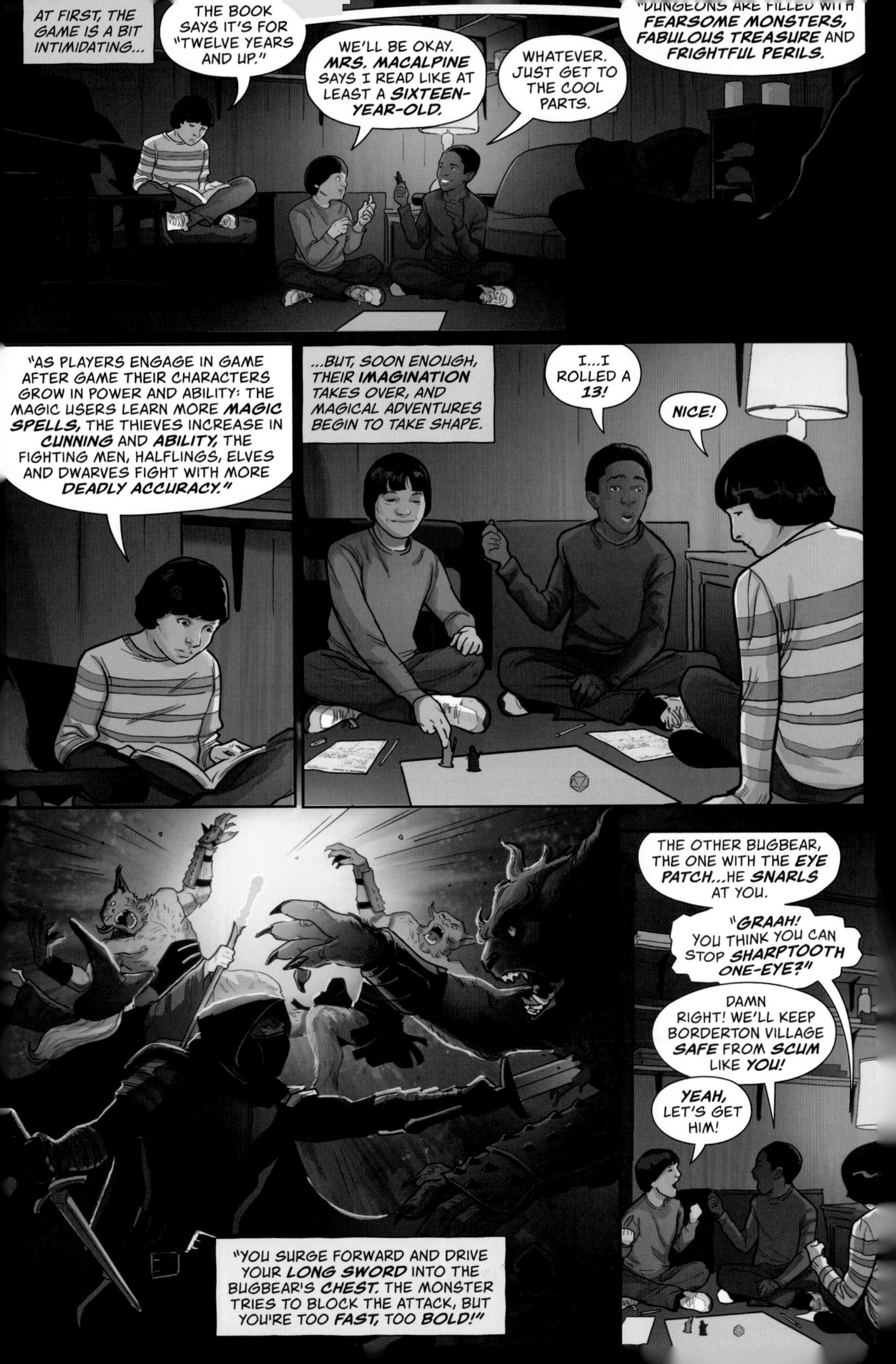
AT FIRST, THE GAME IS A BIT INTIMIDATING...
THE BOOK SAYS IT'S FOR "TWELVE YEARS AND UP."
WE'LL BE OKAY. MRS. MACALPINE SAYS I READ LIKE AT LEAST A SIXTEEN-YEAR-OLD.
WHATEVER. JUST GET TO THE COOL PARTS.
"DUNGEONS ARE FILLED WITH FEARSOME MONSTERS, FABULOUS TREASURE AND FRIGHTFUL PERILS.
"AS PLAYERS ENGAGE IN GAME AFTER GAME THEIR CHARACTERS GROW IN POWER AND ABILITY: THE MAGIC USERS LEARN MORE MAGIC SPELLS, THE THIEVES INCREASE IN CUNNING AND ABILITY, THE FIGHTING MEN, HALFLINGS, ELVES AND DWARVES FIGHT WITH MORE DEADLY ACCURACY."
...BUT, SOON ENOUGH, THEIR IMAGINATION TAKES OVER, AND MAGICAL ADVENTURES BEGIN TO TAKE SHAPE.
I...I ROLLED A 13!
NICE!
"YOU SURGE FORWARD AND DRIVE YOUR LONG SWORD INTO THE BUGBEAR'S CHEST. THE MONSTER TRIES TO BLOCK THE ATTACK, BUT YOU'RE TOO FAST, TOO BOLD!"
THE OTHER BUGBEAR, THE ONE WITH THE EYE PATCH...HE SNARLS AT YOU.
"GRAAH! YOU THINK YOU CAN STOP SHARPTOOTH ONE-EYE?"
DAMN RIGHT! WE'LL KEEP BORDERTON VILLAGE SAFE FROM SCUM LIKE YOU!
YEAH, LET'S GET HIM!

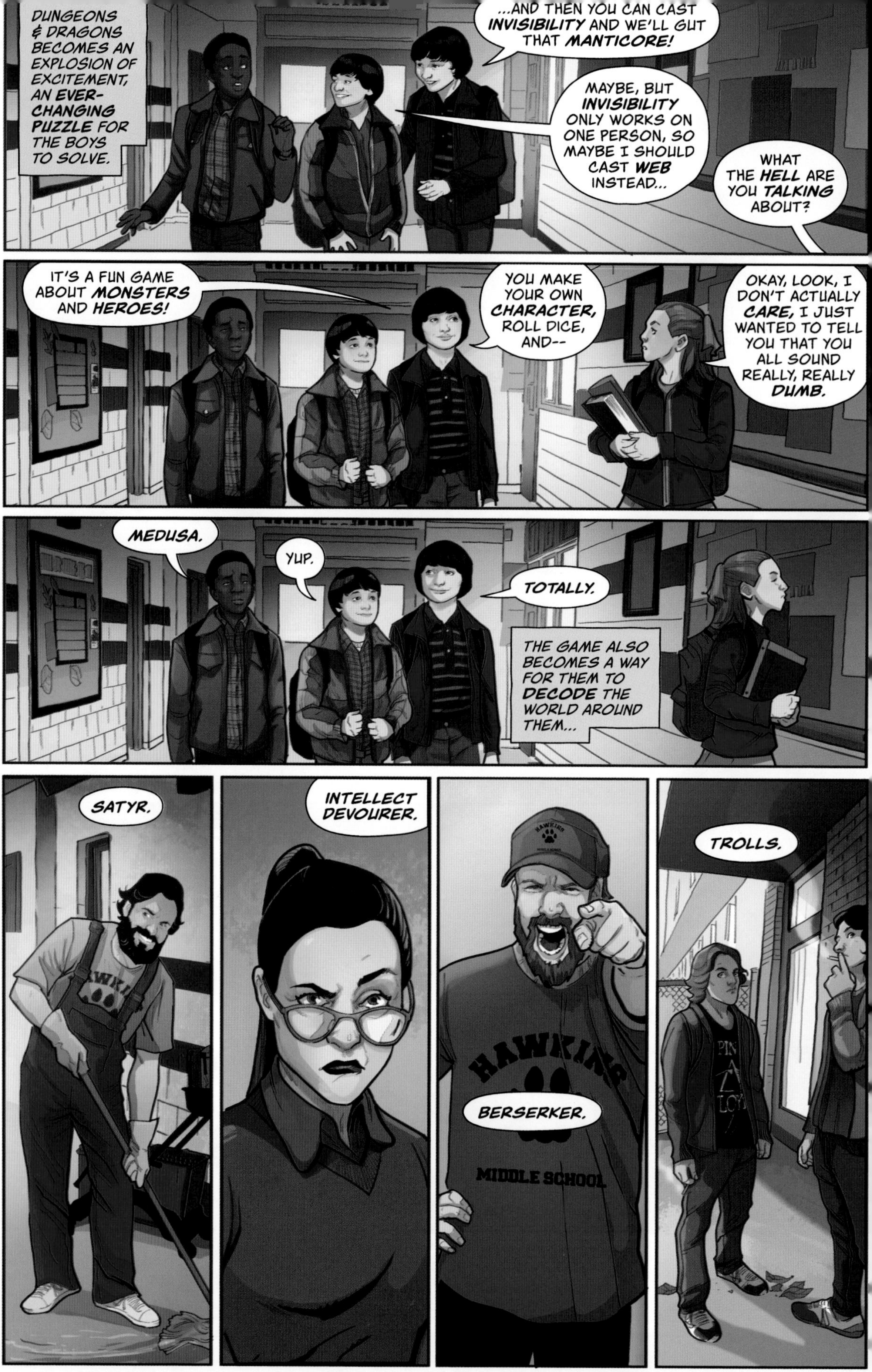
DUNGEONS & DRAGONS BECOMES AN EXPLOSION OF EXCITEMENT, AN EVER-CHANGING PUZZLE FOR THE BOYS TO SOLVE.
...AND THEN YOU CAN CAST INVISIBILITY AND WE'LL GUT THAT MANTICORE!
MAYBE, BUT INVISIBILITY ONLY WORKS ON ONE PERSON, SO MAYBE I SHOULD CAST WEB INSTEAD...
WHAT THE HELL ARE YOU TALKING ABOUT?
IT'S A FUN GAME ABOUT MONSTERS AND HEROES!
YOU MAKE YOUR OWN CHARACTER, ROLL DICE, AND--
OKAY, LOOK, I DON'T ACTUALLY CARE, I JUST WANTED TO TELL YOU THAT YOU ALL SOUND REALLY, REALLY DUMB.
MEDUSA.
YUP.
TOTALLY.
THE GAME ALSO BECOMES A WAY FOR THEM TO DECODE THE WORLD AROUND THEM...
SATYR.
INTELLECT DEVOURER.
HAWKINS MIDDLE SCHOOL
BERSERKER.
TROLLS.

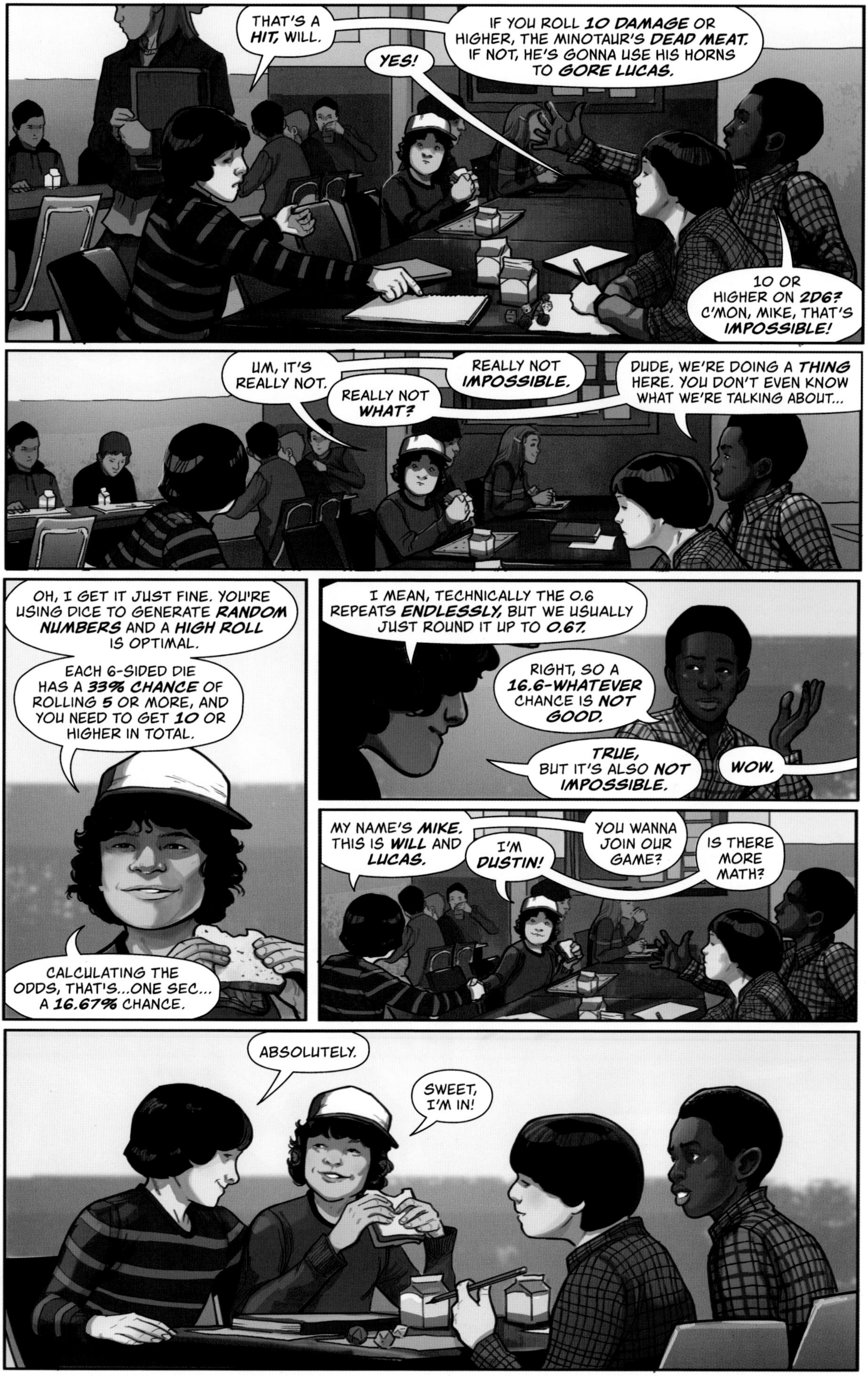
THAT'S A HIT, WILL.
IF YOU ROLL 10 DAMAGE OR HIGHER, THE MINOTAUR'S DEAD MEAT. IF NOT, HE'S GONNA USE HIS HORNS TO GORE LUCAS.
YES!
10 OR HIGHER ON 2D6? C'MON, MIKE, THAT'S IMPOSSIBLE!
UM, IT'S REALLY NOT.
REALLY NOT WHAT?
REALLY NOT IMPOSSIBLE.
DUDE, WE'RE DOING A THING HERE. YOU DON'T EVEN KNOW WHAT WE'RE TALKING ABOUT...
OH, I GET IT JUST FINE. YOU'RE USING DICE TO GENERATE RANDOM NUMBERS AND A HIGH ROLL IS OPTIMAL.
EACH 6-SIDED DIE HAS A 33% CHANCE OF ROLLING 5 OR MORE, AND YOU NEED TO GET 10 OR HIGHER IN TOTAL.
CALCULATING THE ODDS, THAT'S...ONE SEC... A 16.67% CHANCE.
I MEAN, TECHNICALLY THE 0.6 REPEATS ENDLESSLY, BUT WE USUALLY JUST ROUND IT UP TO 0.67.
RIGHT, SO A 16.6-WHATEVER CHANCE IS NOT GOOD.
TRUE, BUT IT'S ALSO NOT IMPOSSIBLE.
WOW.
MY NAME'S MIKE. THIS IS WILL AND LUCAS.
I'M DUSTIN!
YOU WANNA JOIN OUR GAME?
IS THERE MORE MATH?
ABSOLUTELY.
SWEET, I'M IN!

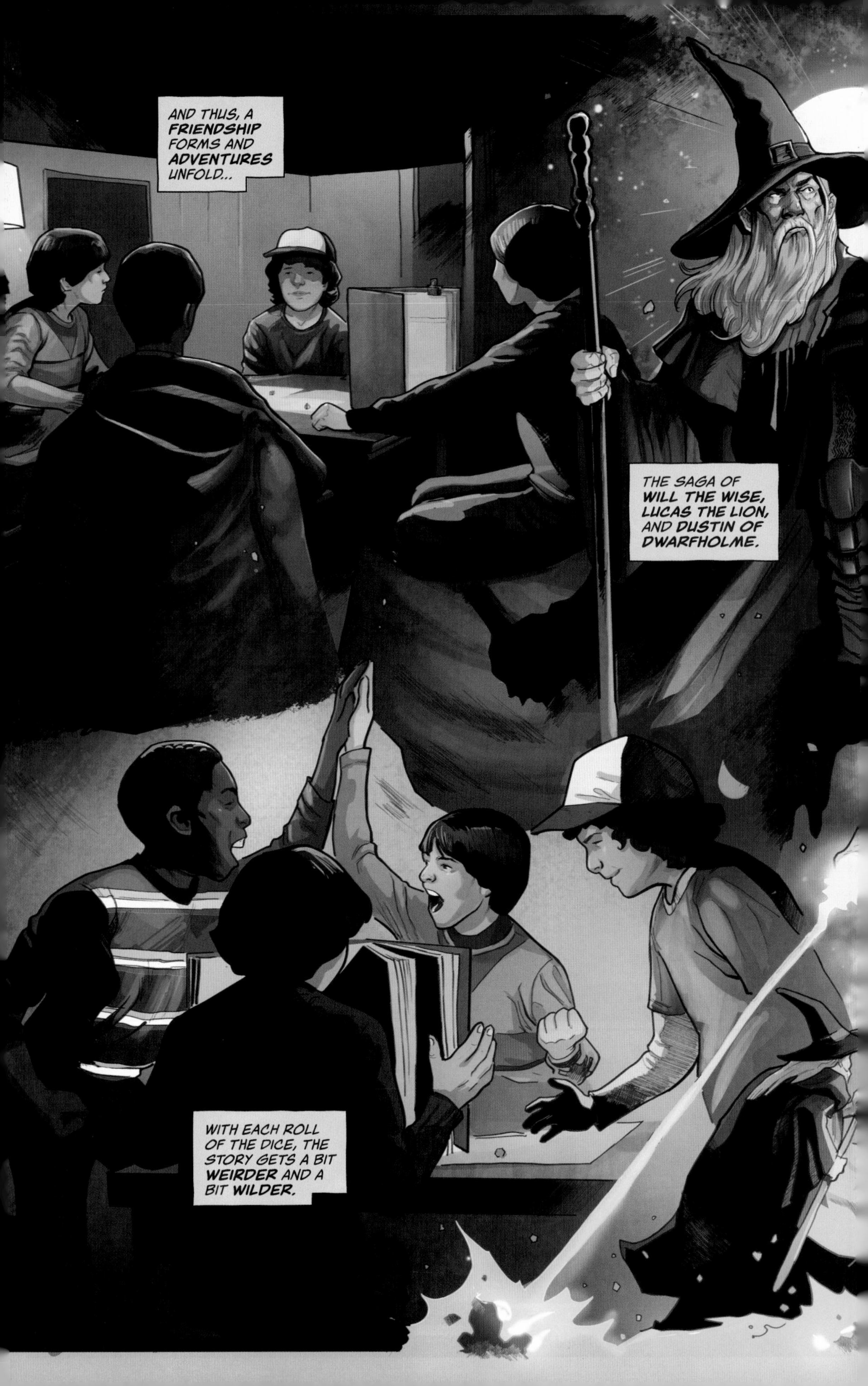
AND THUS, A FRIENDSHIP FORMS AND ADVENTURES UNFOLD...
THE SAGA OF WILL THE WISE, LUCAS THE LION, AND DUSTIN OF DWARFHOLME.
WITH EACH ROLL OF THE DICE, THE STORY GETS A BIT WEIRDER AND A BIT WILDER.

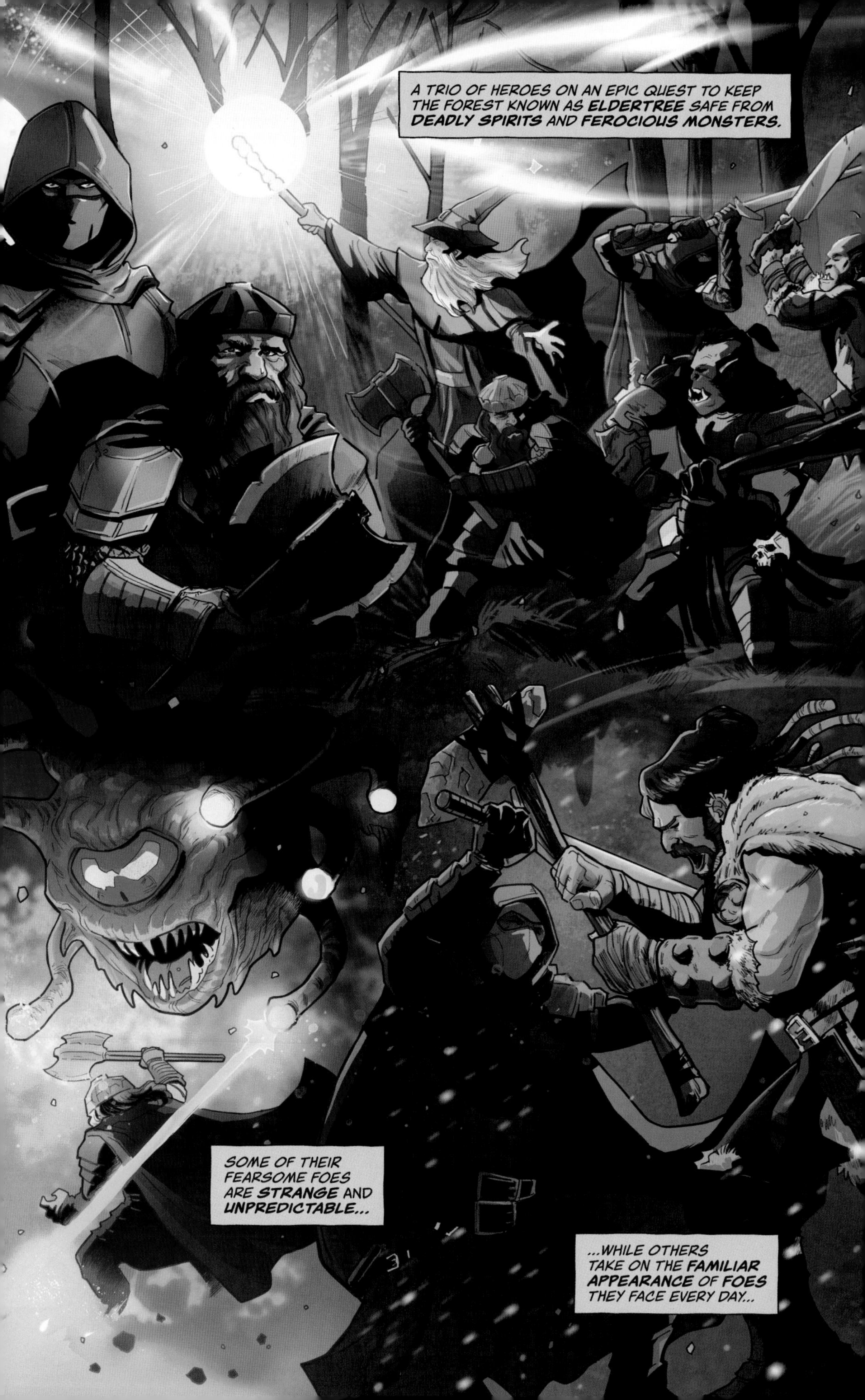
A TRIO OF HEROES ON AN EPIC QUEST TO KEEP THE FOREST KNOWN AS **ELDERTREE** SAFE FROM **DEADLY SPIRITS** AND **FEROCIOUS MONSTERS.**
SOME OF THEIR FEARSOME FOES ARE **STRANGE** AND **UNPREDICTABLE...**
...WHILE OTHERS TAKE ON THE **FAMILIAR APPEARANCE** OF **FOES** THEY FACE EVERY DAY...

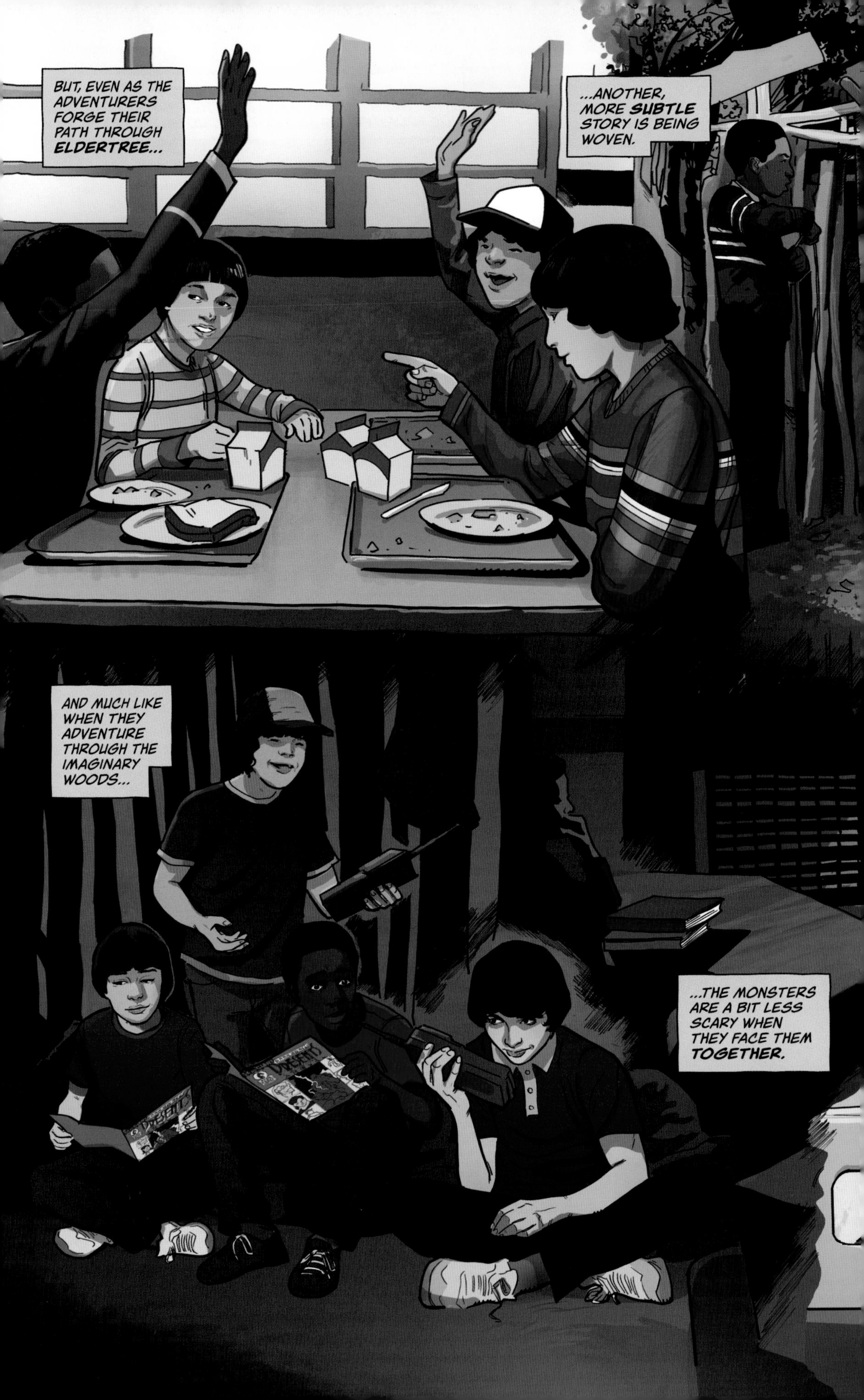
BUT, EVEN AS THE ADVENTURERS FORGE THEIR PATH THROUGH ELDERTREE...
...ANOTHER, MORE SUBTLE STORY IS BEING WOVEN.
AND MUCH LIKE WHEN THEY ADVENTURE THROUGH THE IMAGINARY WOODS...
...THE MONSTERS ARE A BIT LESS SCARY WHEN THEY FACE THEM TOGETHER.

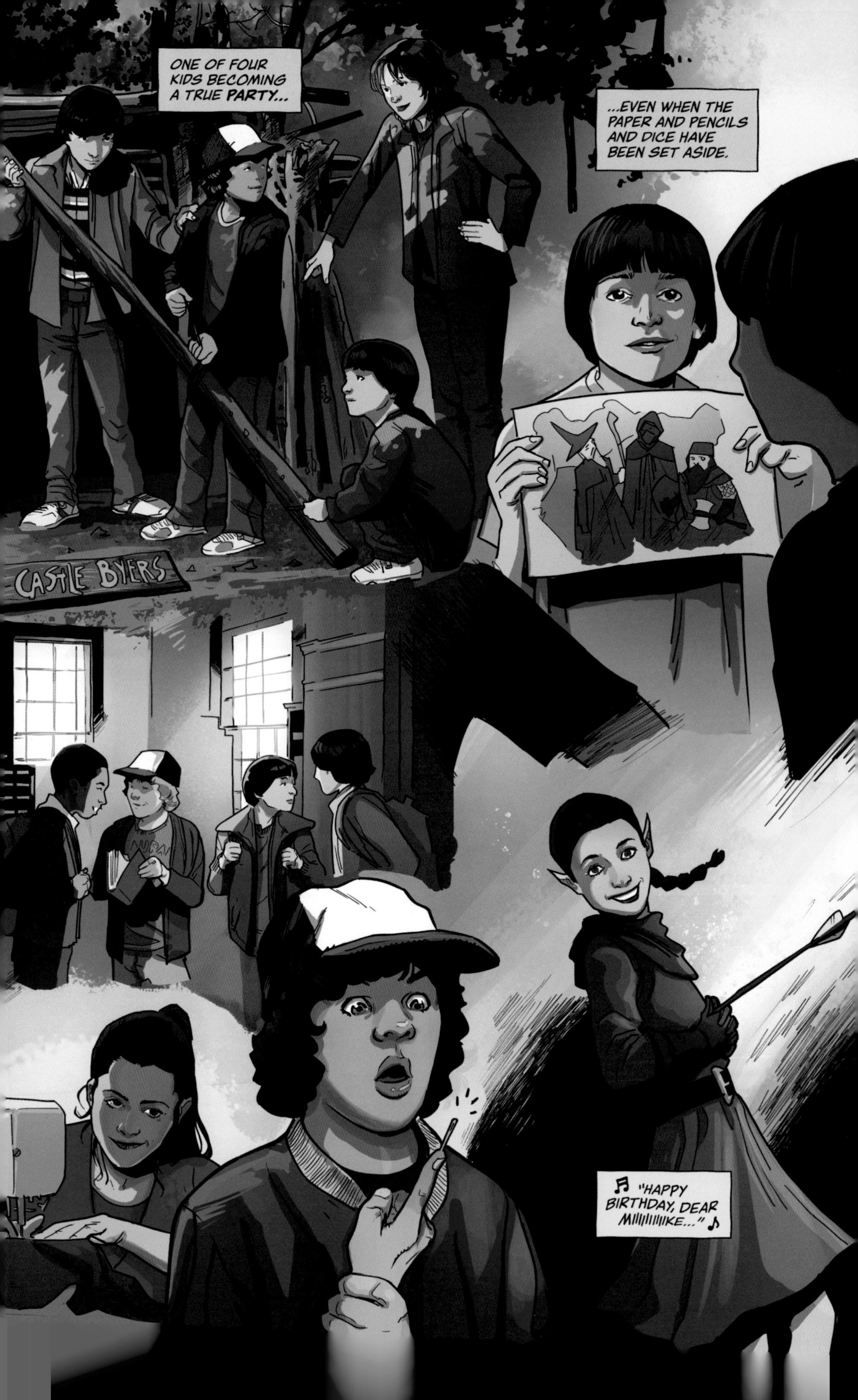
ONE OF FOUR KIDS BECOMING A TRUE PARTY...
...EVEN WHEN THE PAPER AND PENCILS AND DICE HAVE BEEN SET ASIDE.
CASTLE BYERS
"HAPPY BIRTHDAY, DEAR MIIIIIIIIKE..."

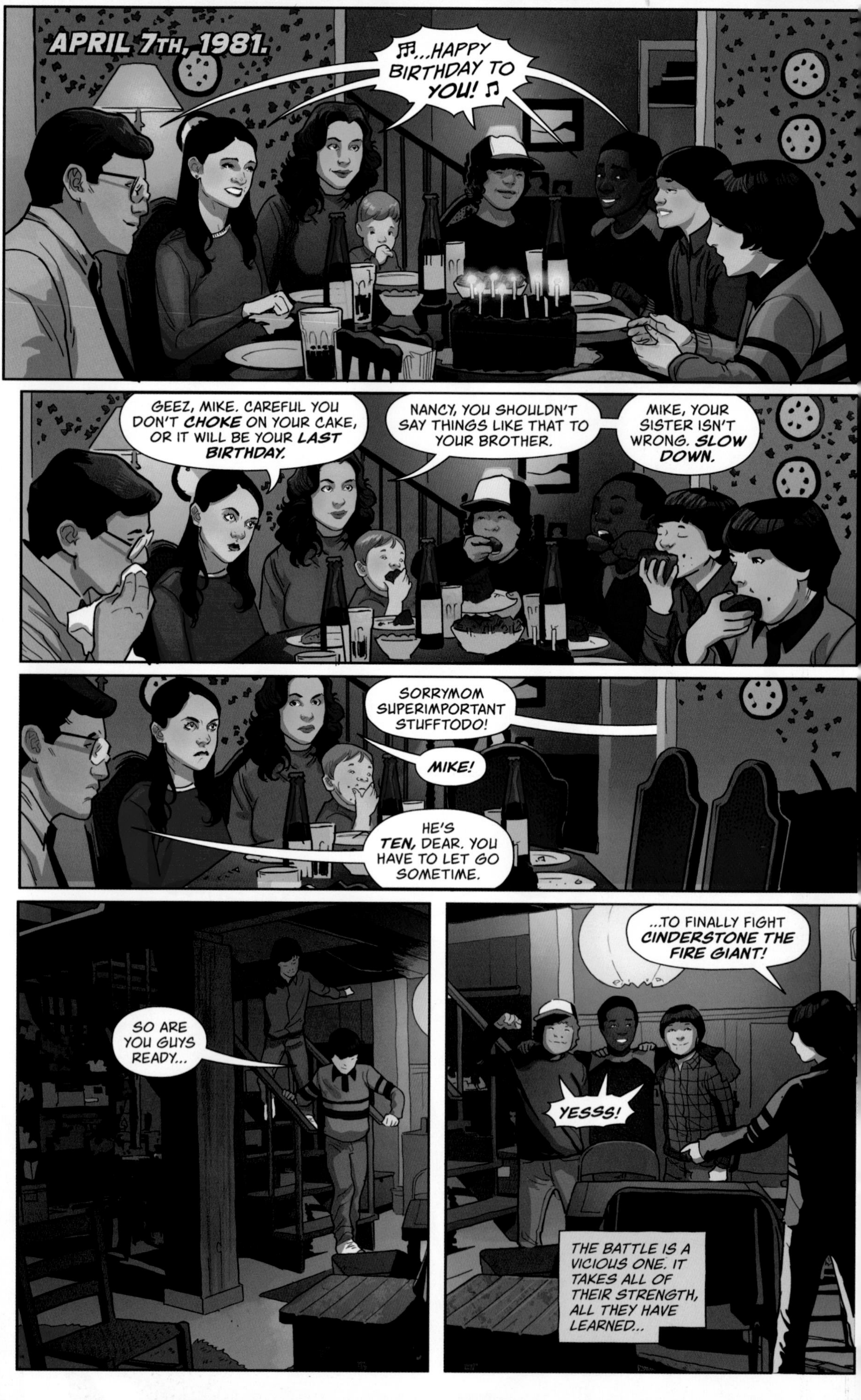

APRIL 7TH, 1981.
...HAPPY BIRTHDAY TO YOU!
GEEZ, MIKE. CAREFUL YOU DON'T CHOKE ON YOUR CAKE, OR IT WILL BE YOUR LAST BIRTHDAY.
NANCY, YOU SHOULDN'T SAY THINGS LIKE THAT TO YOUR BROTHER.
MIKE, YOUR SISTER ISN'T WRONG. SLOW DOWN.
SORRYMOM SUPERIMPORTANT STUFFTODO!
MIKE!
HE'S TEN, DEAR. YOU HAVE TO LET GO SOMETIME.
SO ARE YOU GUYS READY...
...TO FINALLY FIGHT CINDERSTONE THE FIRE GIANT!
YESSS!
THE BATTLE IS A VICIOUS ONE. IT TAKES ALL OF THEIR STRENGTH, ALL THEY HAVE LEARNED...

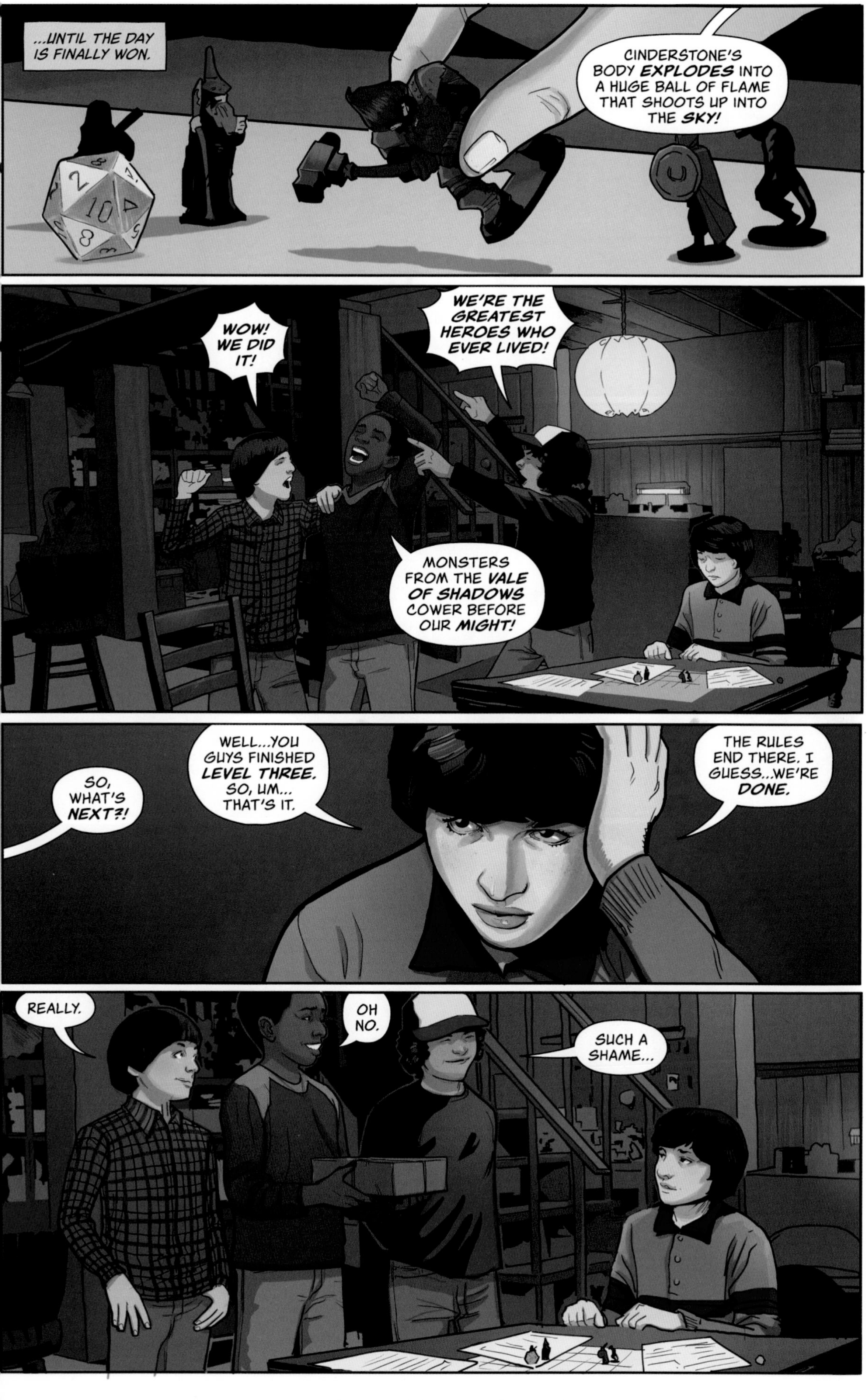

...UNTIL THE DAY IS FINALLY WON.
CINDERSTONE'S BODY **EXPLODES** INTO A HUGE BALL OF FLAME THAT SHOOTS UP INTO THE **SKY!**
WOW! WE DID IT!
WE'RE THE GREATEST HEROES WHO EVER LIVED!
MONSTERS FROM THE **VALE OF SHADOWS** COWER BEFORE OUR **MIGHT!**
SO, WHAT'S **NEXT?!**
WELL...YOU GUYS FINISHED **LEVEL THREE.** SO, UM... THAT'S IT.
THE RULES END THERE. I GUESS...WE'RE **DONE.**
REALLY.
OH NO.
SUCH A SHAME...

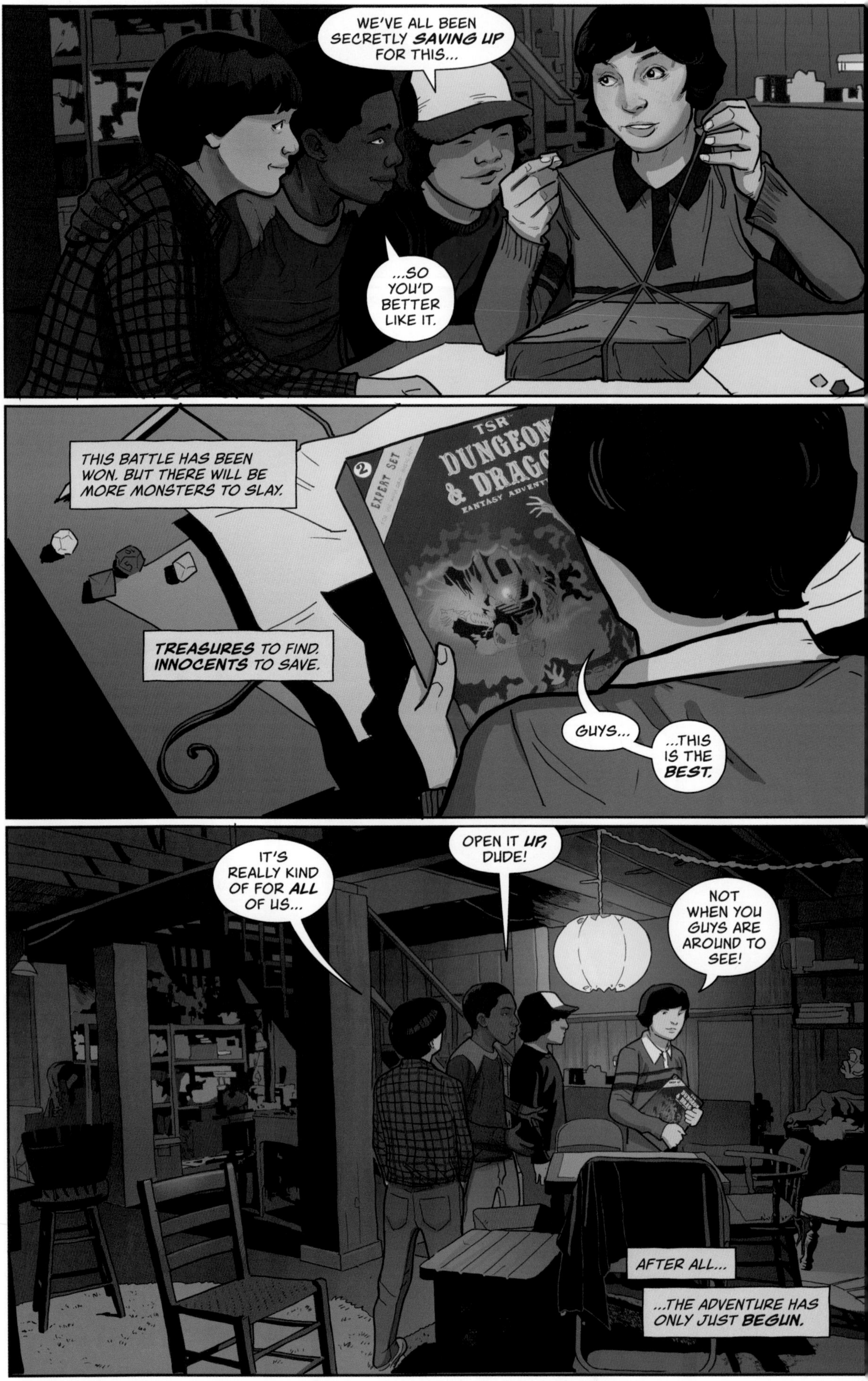
WE'VE ALL BEEN SECRETLY SAVING UP FOR THIS...
...SO YOU'D BETTER LIKE IT.
THIS BATTLE HAS BEEN WON. BUT THERE WILL BE MORE MONSTERS TO SLAY.
TSR DUNGEONS & DRAGONS FANTASY ADVENTURE
EXPERT SET
2
TREASURES TO FIND. INNOCENTS TO SAVE.
GUYS...
...THIS IS THE BEST.
IT'S REALLY KIND OF FOR ALL OF US...
OPEN IT UP, DUDE!
NOT WHEN YOU GUYS ARE AROUND TO SEE!
AFTER ALL...
...THE ADVENTURE HAS ONLY JUST BEGUN.

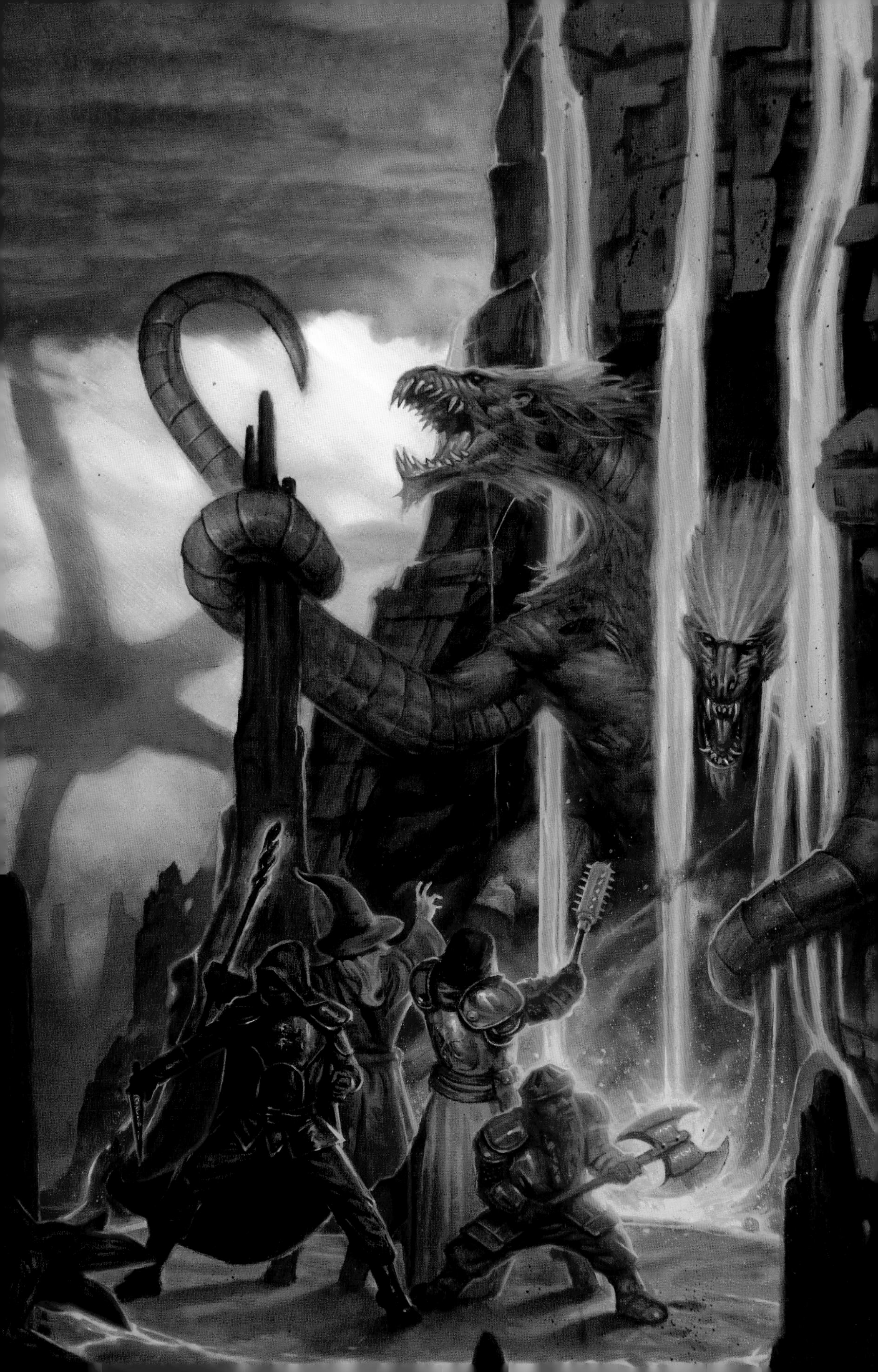

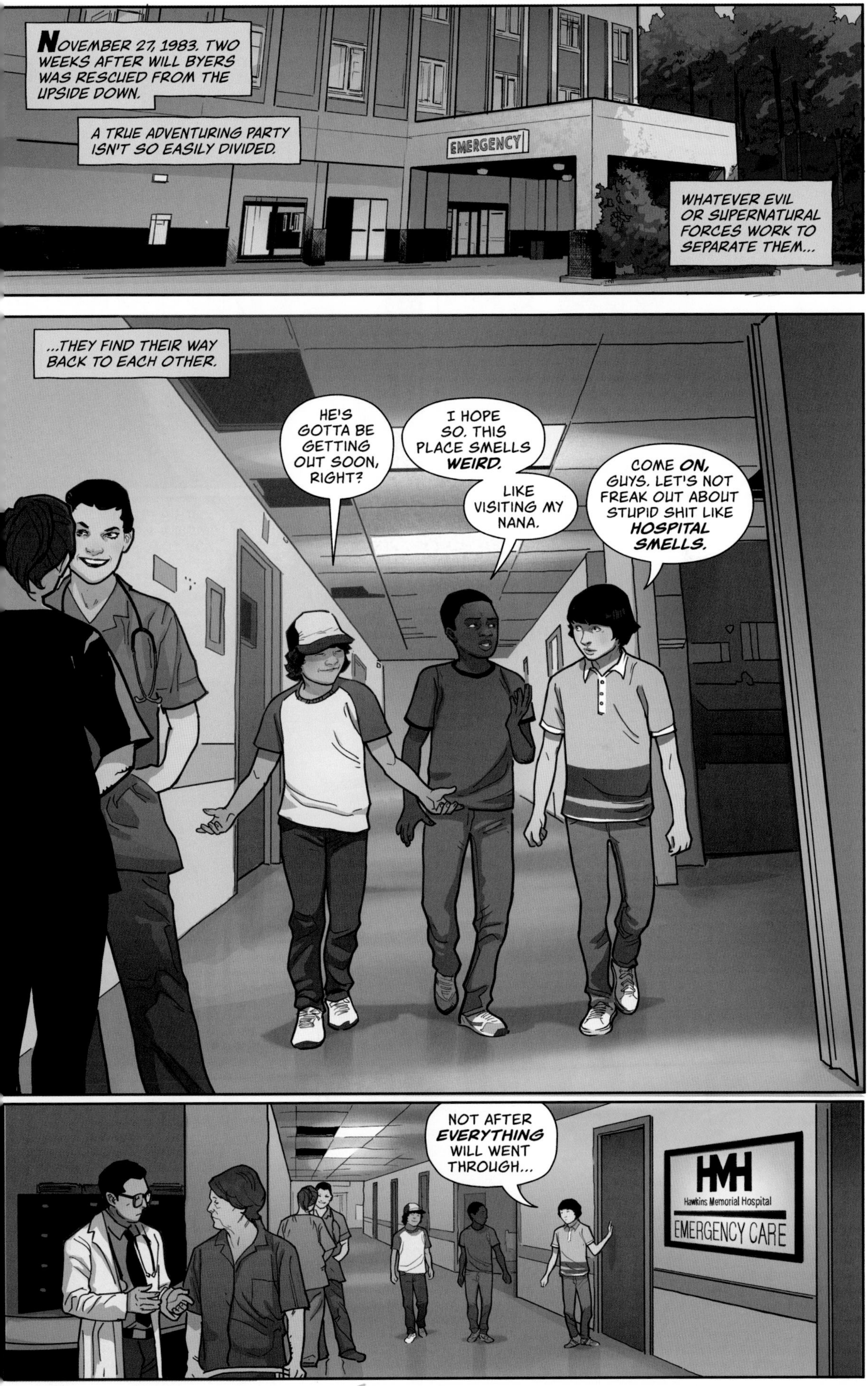
NOVEMBER 27, 1983. TWO WEEKS AFTER WILL BYERS WAS RESCUED FROM THE UPSIDE DOWN.
A TRUE ADVENTURING PARTY ISN'T SO EASILY DIVIDED.
EMERGENCY
WHATEVER EVIL OR SUPERNATURAL FORCES WORK TO SEPARATE THEM...
...THEY FIND THEIR WAY BACK TO EACH OTHER.
HE'S GOTTA BE GETTING OUT SOON, RIGHT?
I HOPE SO. THIS PLACE SMELLS WEIRD.
LIKE VISITING MY NANA.
COME ON, GUYS. LET'S NOT FREAK OUT ABOUT STUPID SHIT LIKE HOSPITAL SMELLS.
NOT AFTER EVERYTHING WILL WENT THROUGH...
HMH
Hawkins Memorial Hospital
EMERGENCY CARE

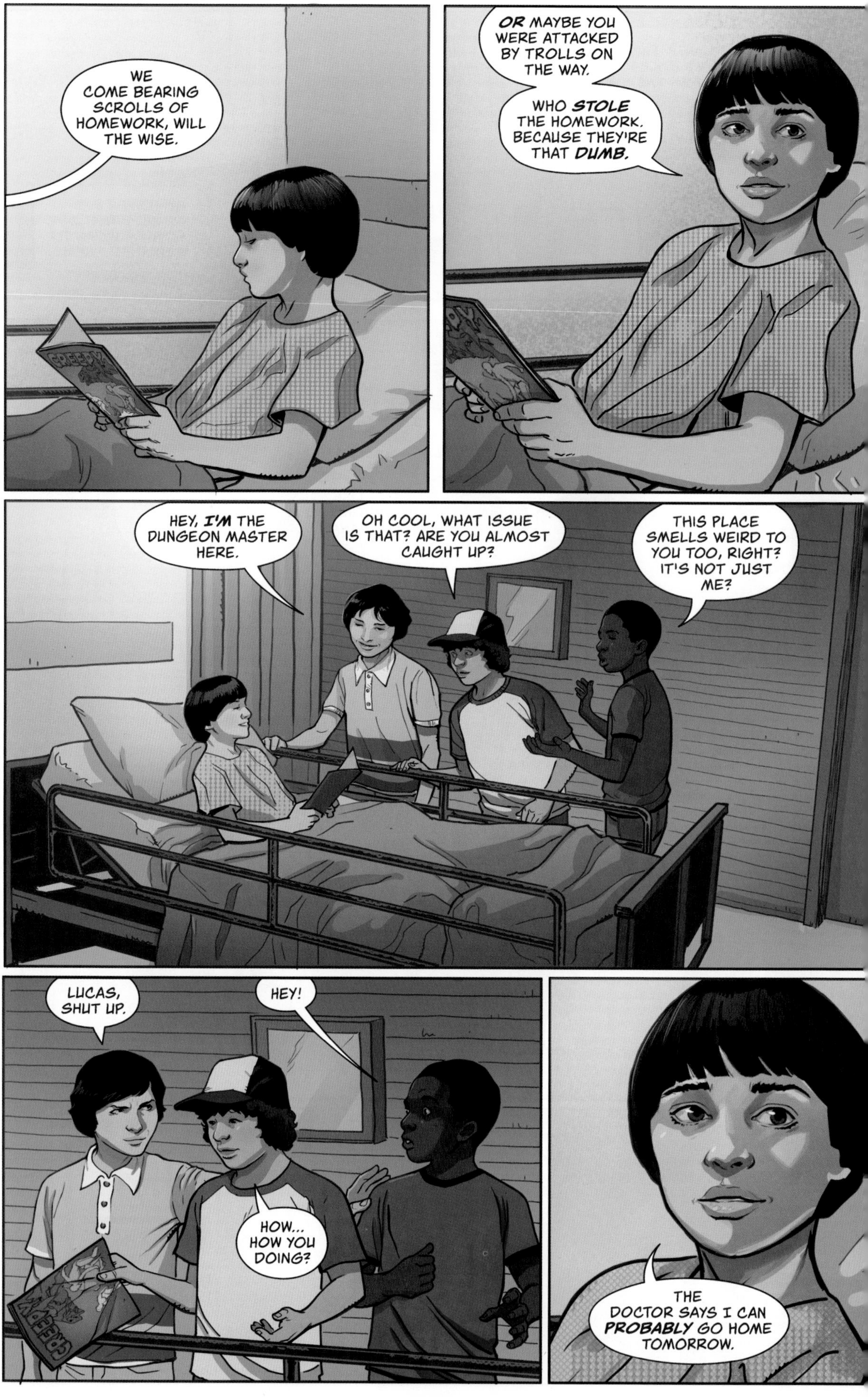
WE COME BEARING SCROLLS OF HOMEWORK, WILL THE WISE.
OR MAYBE YOU WERE ATTACKED BY TROLLS ON THE WAY.
WHO STOLE THE HOMEWORK. BECAUSE THEY'RE THAT DUMB.
HEY, I'M THE DUNGEON MASTER HERE.
OH COOL, WHAT ISSUE IS THAT? ARE YOU ALMOST CAUGHT UP?
THIS PLACE SMELLS WEIRD TO YOU TOO, RIGHT? IT'S NOT JUST ME?
LUCAS, SHUT UP.
HEY!
HOW... HOW YOU DOING?
THE DOCTOR SAYS I CAN PROBABLY GO HOME TOMORROW.

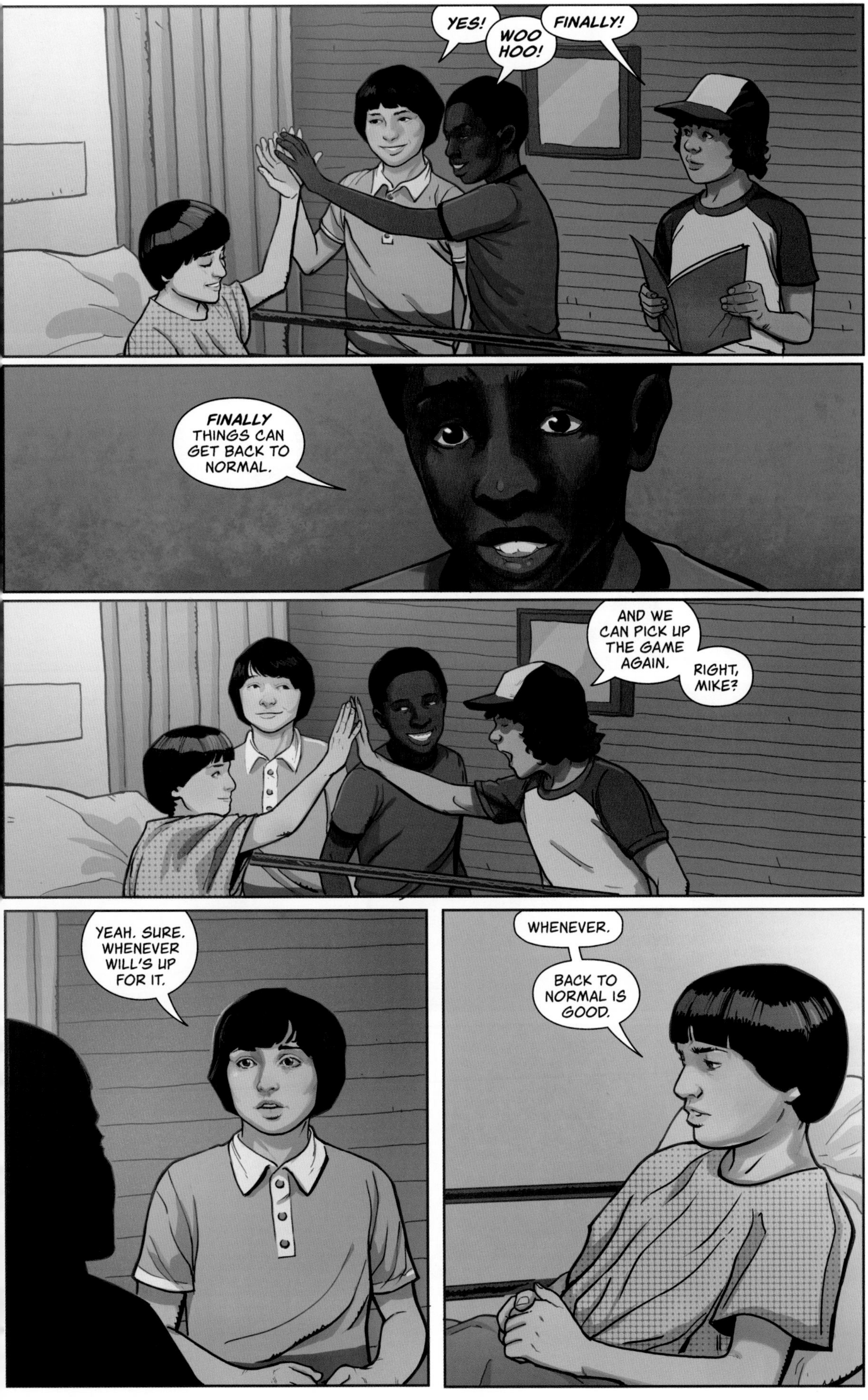
YES!
WOO HOO!
FINALLY!
FINALLY THINGS CAN GET BACK TO NORMAL.
AND WE CAN PICK UP THE GAME AGAIN.
RIGHT, MIKE?
YEAH. SURE. WHENEVER WILL'S UP FOR IT.
WHENEVER.
BACK TO NORMAL IS GOOD.

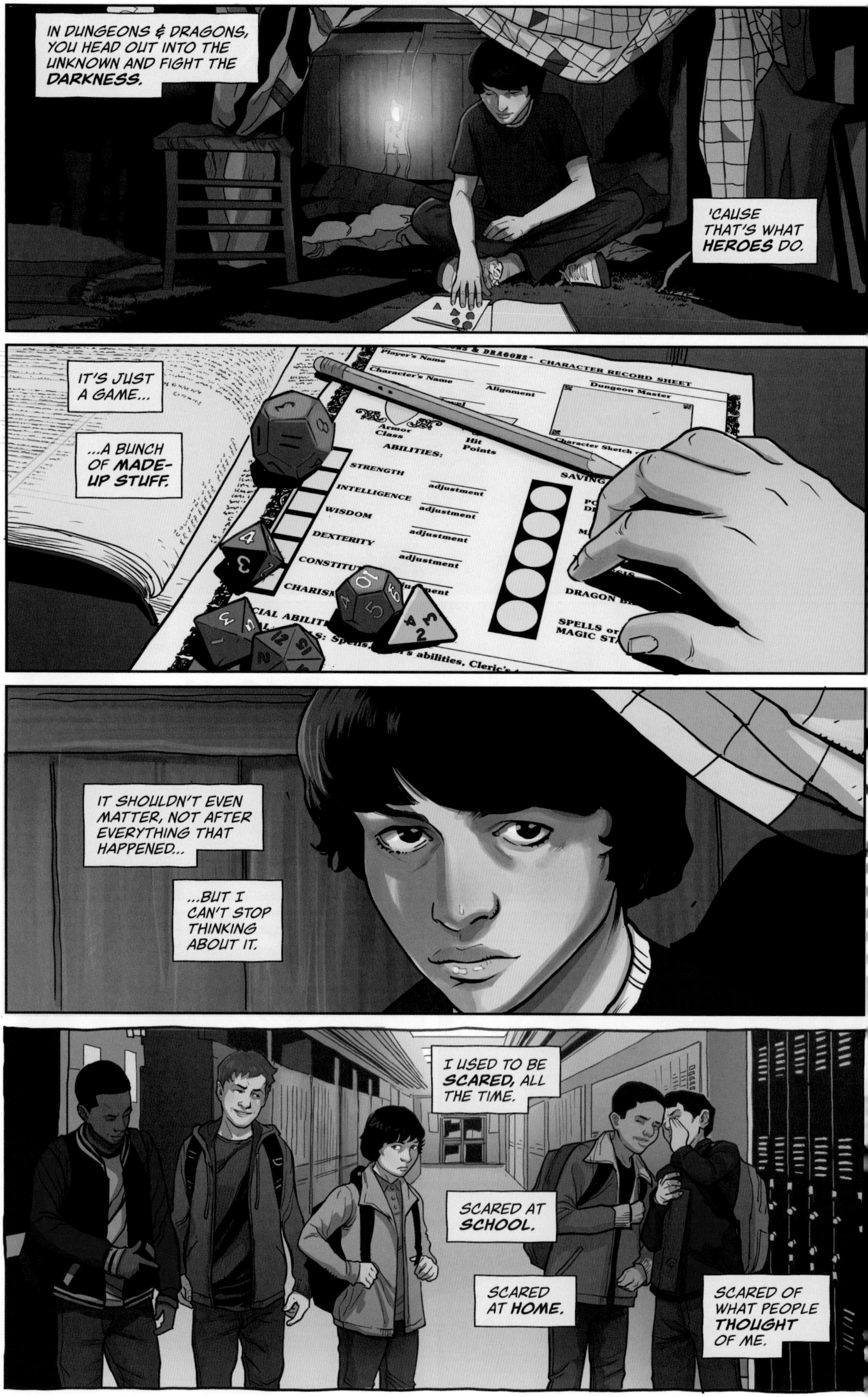

IN DUNGEONS & DRAGONS, YOU HEAD OUT INTO THE UNKNOWN AND FIGHT THE DARKNESS.
'CAUSE THAT'S WHAT HEROES DO.
IT'S JUST A GAME...
...A BUNCH OF MADE-UP STUFF.
CHARACTER RECORD SHEET
Player's Name
Character's Name
Alignment
Dungeon Master
Armor Class
Hit Points
ABILITIES:
STRENGTH
INTELLIGENCE
WISDOM
DEXTERITY
adjustment
Character Sketch
SPELLS or MAGIC
DRAGON
IT SHOULDN'T EVEN MATTER, NOT AFTER EVERYTHING THAT HAPPENED...
...BUT I CAN'T STOP THINKING ABOUT IT.
I USED TO BE SCARED, ALL THE TIME.
SCARED AT SCHOOL.
SCARED AT HOME.
SCARED OF WHAT PEOPLE THOUGHT OF ME.

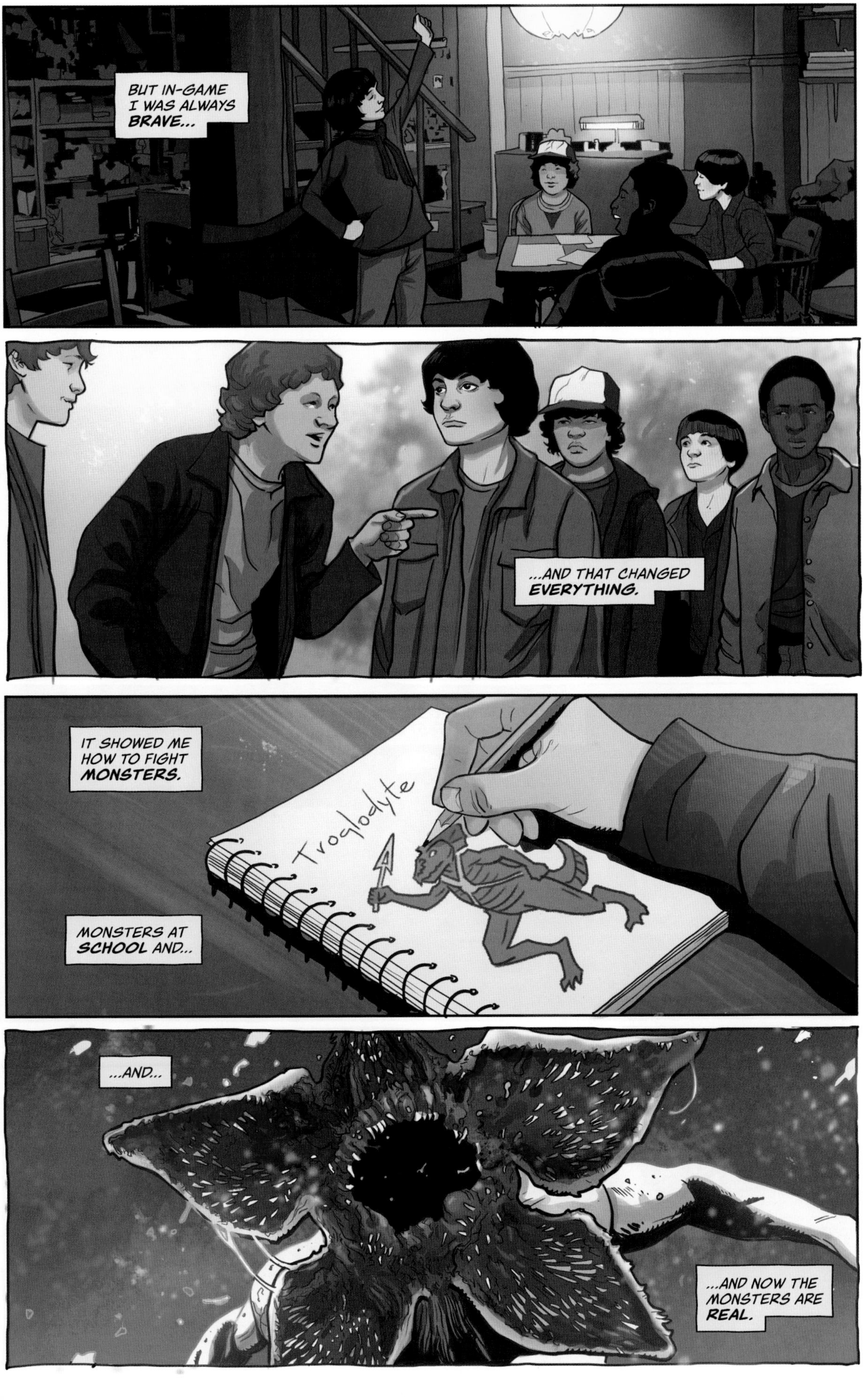
BUT IN-GAME I WAS ALWAYS BRAVE...
...AND THAT CHANGED EVERYTHING.
IT SHOWED ME HOW TO FIGHT MONSTERS.
Troglodyte
MONSTERS AT SCHOOL AND...
...AND...
...AND NOW THE MONSTERS ARE REAL.

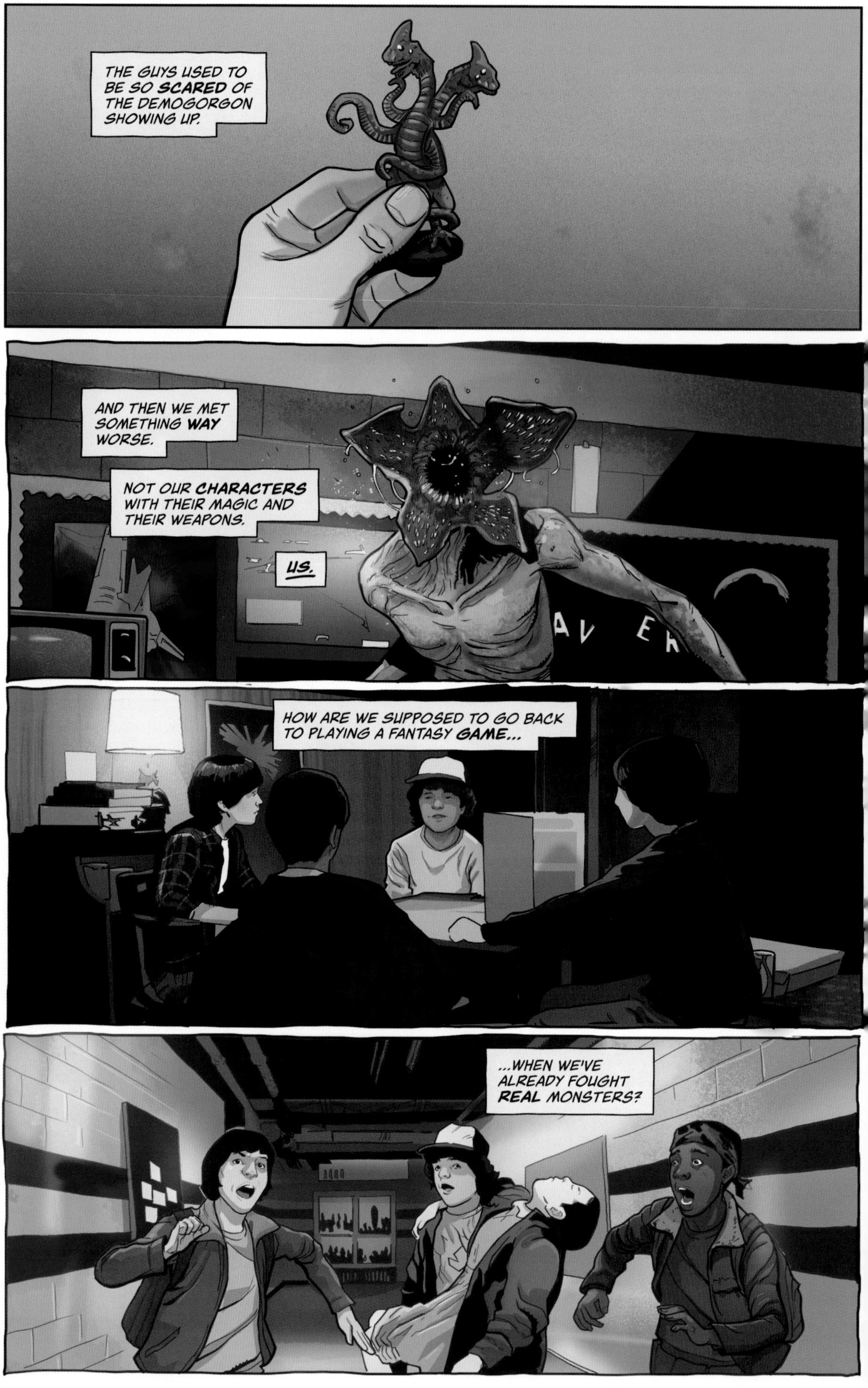
THE GUYS USED TO BE SO SCARED OF THE DEMOGORGON SHOWING UP.
AND THEN WE MET SOMETHING WAY WORSE.
NOT OUR CHARACTERS WITH THEIR MAGIC AND THEIR WEAPONS.
US.
HOW ARE WE SUPPOSED TO GO BACK TO PLAYING A FANTASY GAME...
...WHEN WE'VE ALREADY FOUGHT REAL MONSTERS?

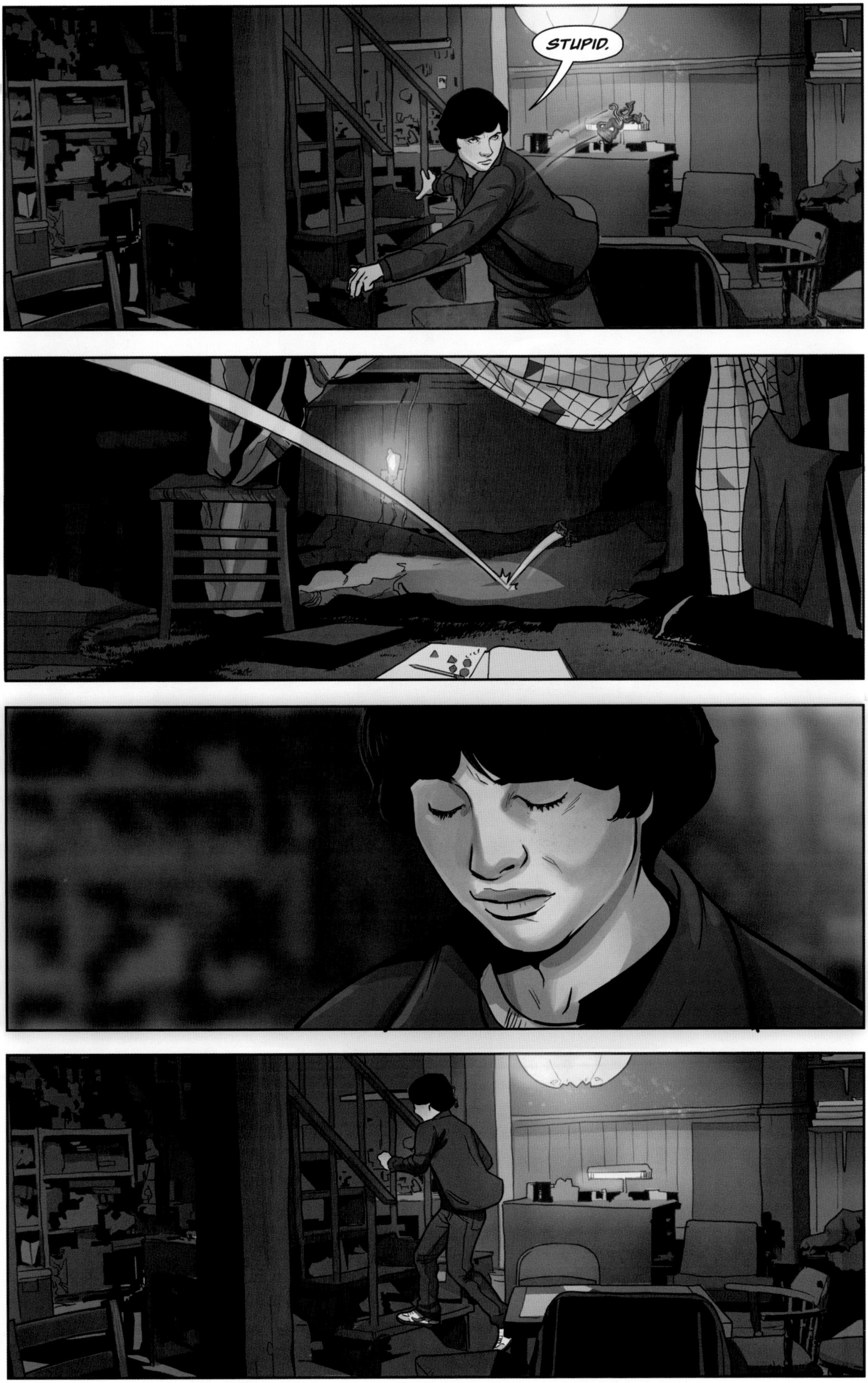
STUPID.

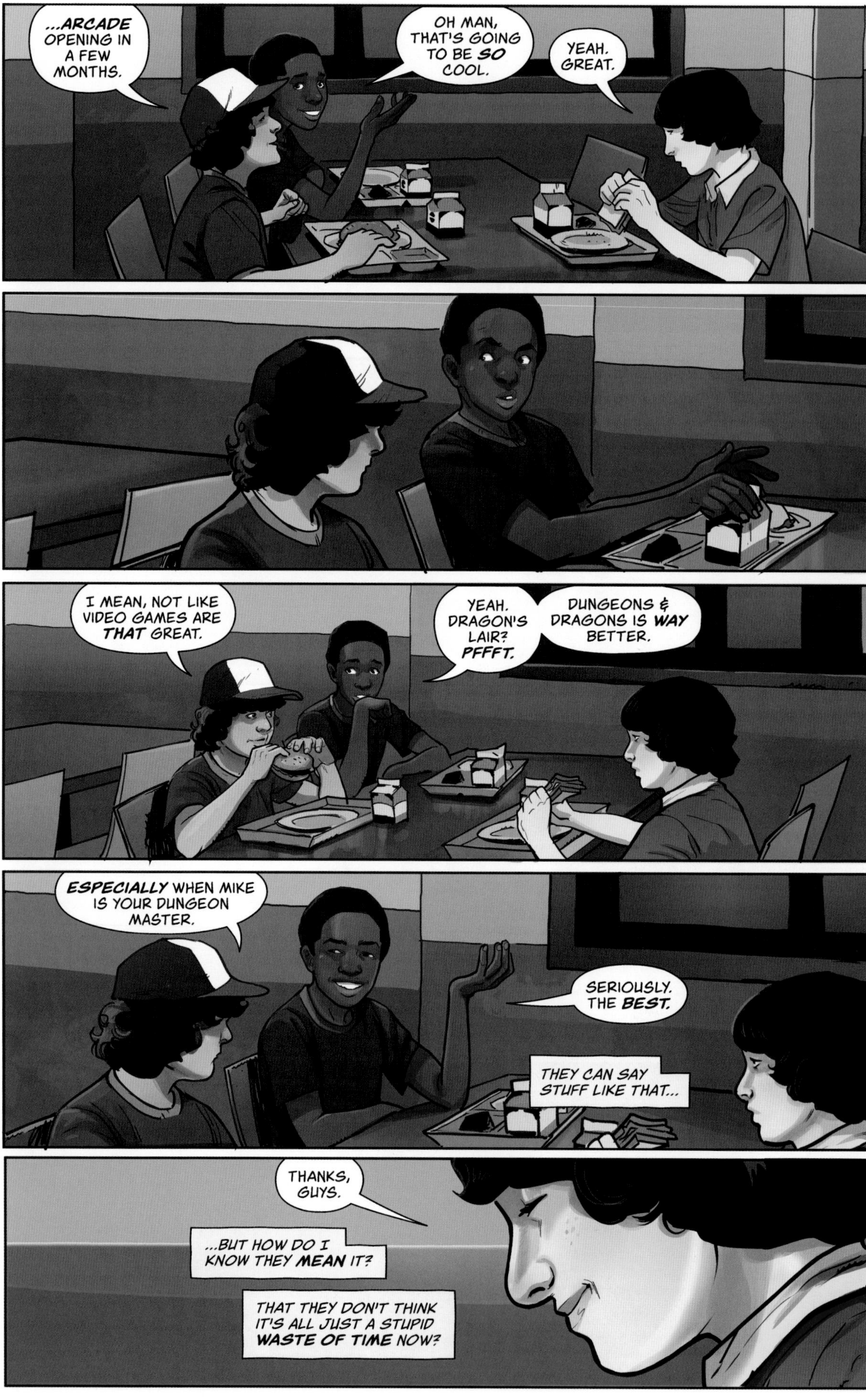
...ARCADE OPENING IN A FEW MONTHS.
OH MAN, THAT'S GOING TO BE SO COOL.
YEAH. GREAT.
I MEAN, NOT LIKE VIDEO GAMES ARE THAT GREAT.
YEAH. DRAGON'S LAIR? PFFFT.
DUNGEONS & DRAGONS IS WAY BETTER.
ESPECIALLY WHEN MIKE IS YOUR DUNGEON MASTER.
SERIOUSLY. THE BEST.
THEY CAN SAY STUFF LIKE THAT...
THANKS, GUYS.
...BUT HOW DO I KNOW THEY MEAN IT?
THAT THEY DON'T THINK IT'S ALL JUST A STUPID WASTE OF TIME NOW?

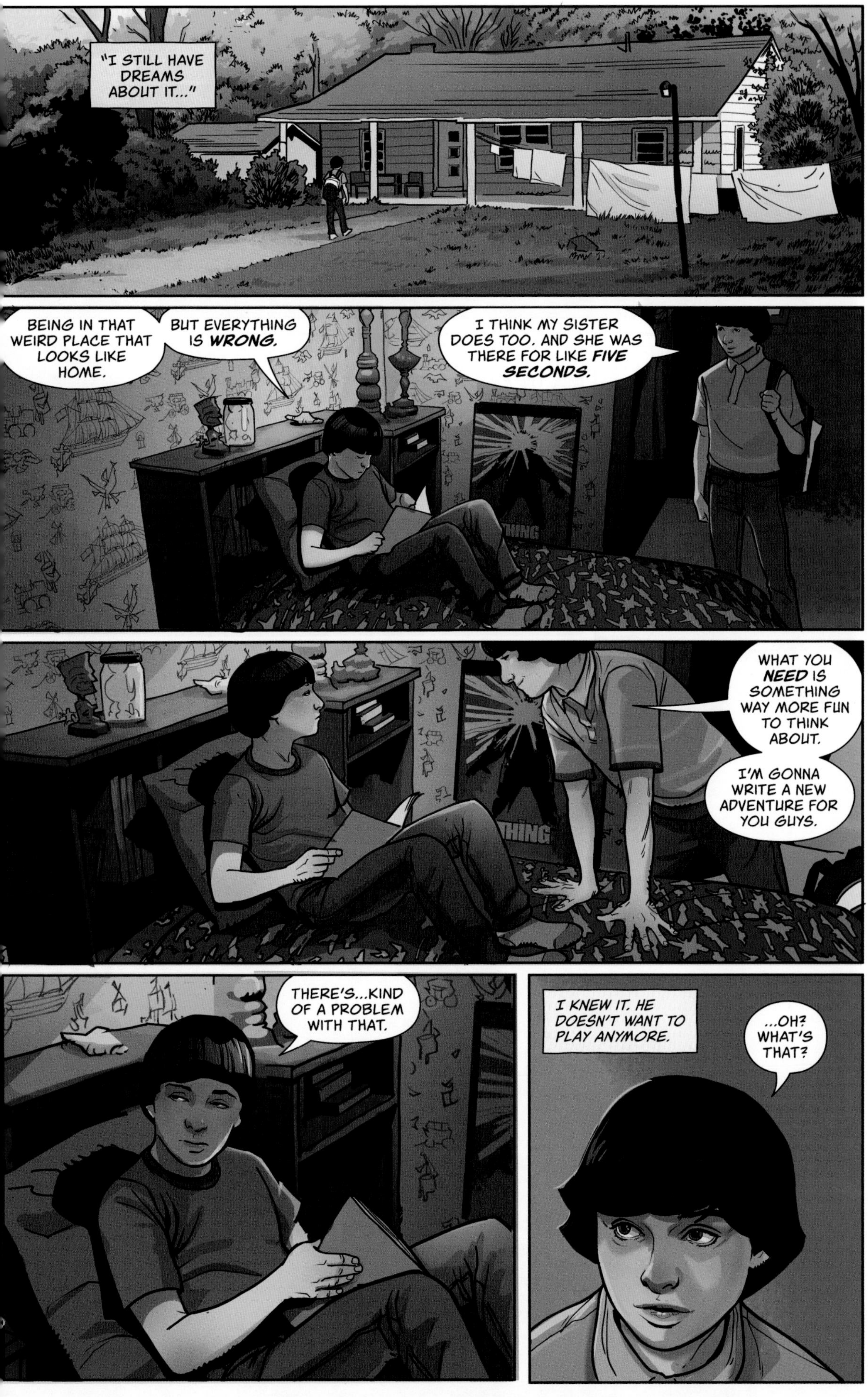
"I STILL HAVE DREAMS ABOUT IT..."
BEING IN THAT WEIRD PLACE THAT LOOKS LIKE HOME.
BUT EVERYTHING IS WRONG.
I THINK MY SISTER DOES TOO. AND SHE WAS THERE FOR LIKE FIVE SECONDS.
WHAT YOU NEED IS SOMETHING WAY MORE FUN TO THINK ABOUT.
I'M GONNA WRITE A NEW ADVENTURE FOR YOU GUYS.
THERE'S...KIND OF A PROBLEM WITH THAT.
I KNEW IT. HE DOESN'T WANT TO PLAY ANYMORE.
...OH? WHAT'S THAT?

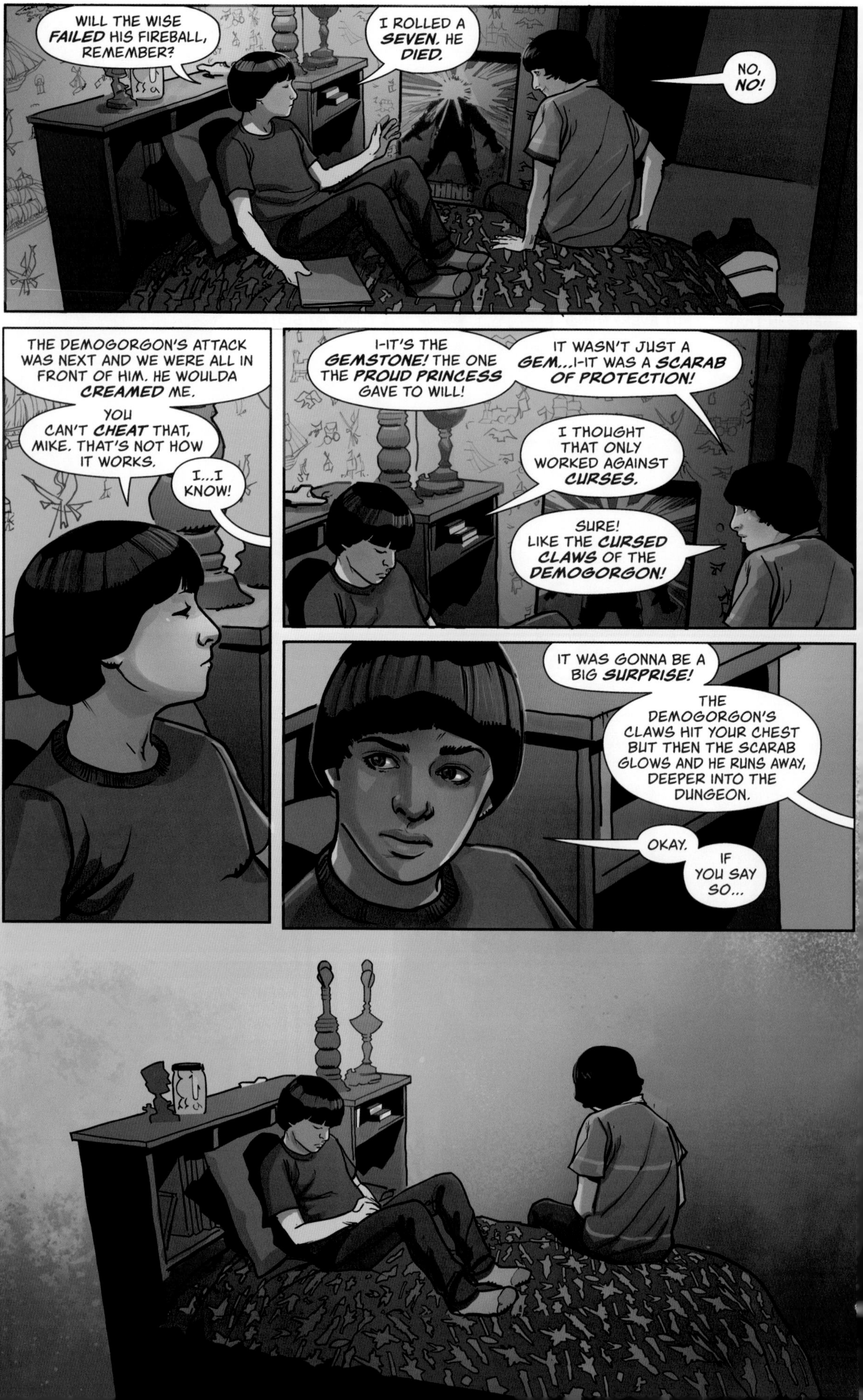
WILL THE WISE FAILED HIS FIREBALL, REMEMBER?
I ROLLED A SEVEN. HE DIED.
NO, NO!
THE DEMOGORGON'S ATTACK WAS NEXT AND WE WERE ALL IN FRONT OF HIM. HE WOULDA CREAMED ME.
YOU CAN'T CHEAT THAT, MIKE. THAT'S NOT HOW IT WORKS.
I...I KNOW!
I-IT'S THE GEMSTONE! THE ONE THE PROUD PRINCESS GAVE TO WILL!
IT WASN'T JUST A GEM...I-IT WAS A SCARAB OF PROTECTION!
I THOUGHT THAT ONLY WORKED AGAINST CURSES.
SURE! LIKE THE CURSED CLAWS OF THE DEMOGORGON!
IT WAS GONNA BE A BIG SURPRISE!
THE DEMOGORGON'S CLAWS HIT YOUR CHEST BUT THEN THE SCARAB GLOWS AND HE RUNS AWAY, DEEPER INTO THE DUNGEON.
OKAY.
IF YOU SAY SO...

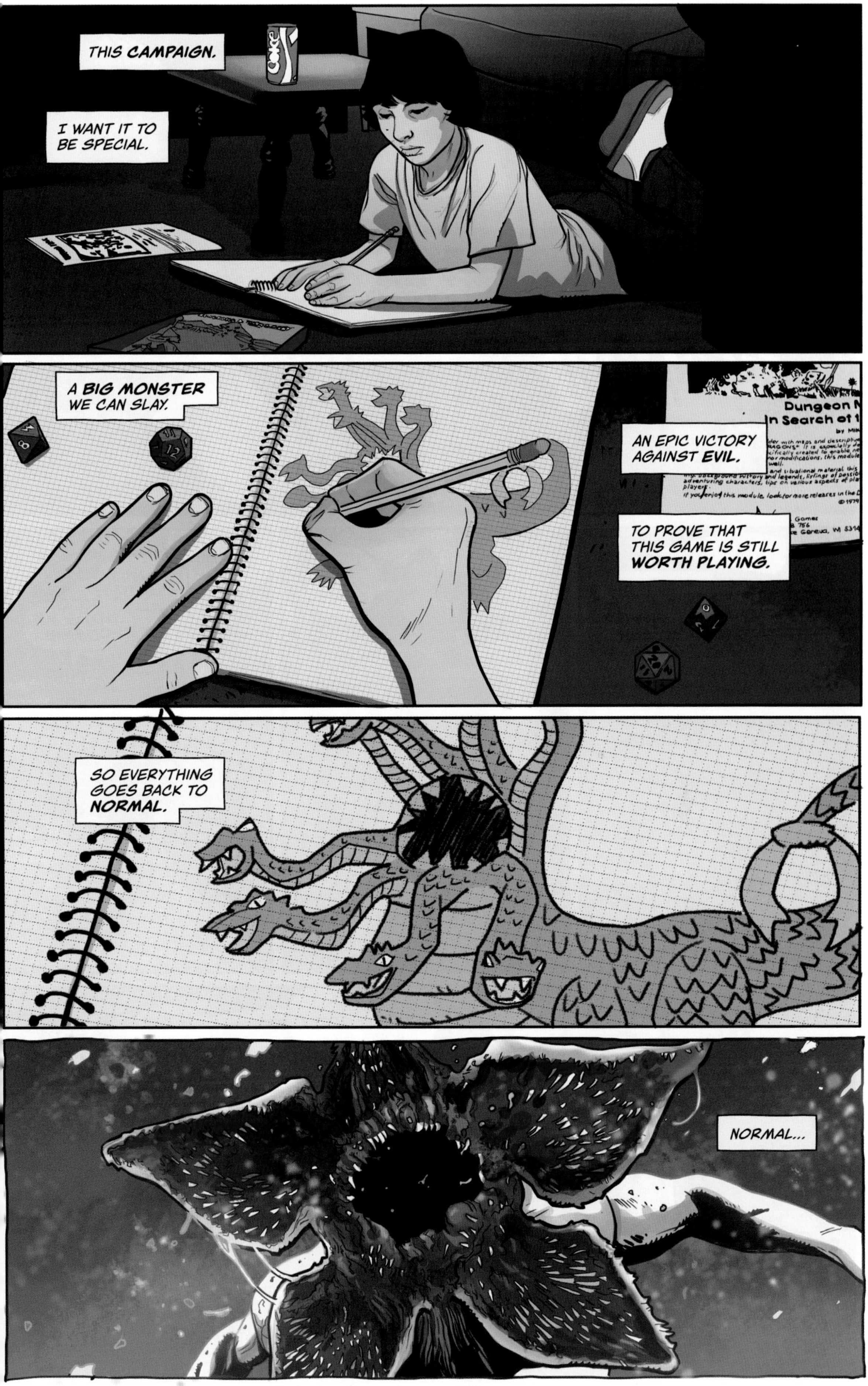
THIS CAMPAIGN.
I WANT IT TO BE SPECIAL.
A BIG MONSTER WE CAN SLAY.
AN EPIC VICTORY AGAINST EVIL.
TO PROVE THAT THIS GAME IS STILL WORTH PLAYING.
SO EVERYTHING GOES BACK TO NORMAL.
NORMAL...

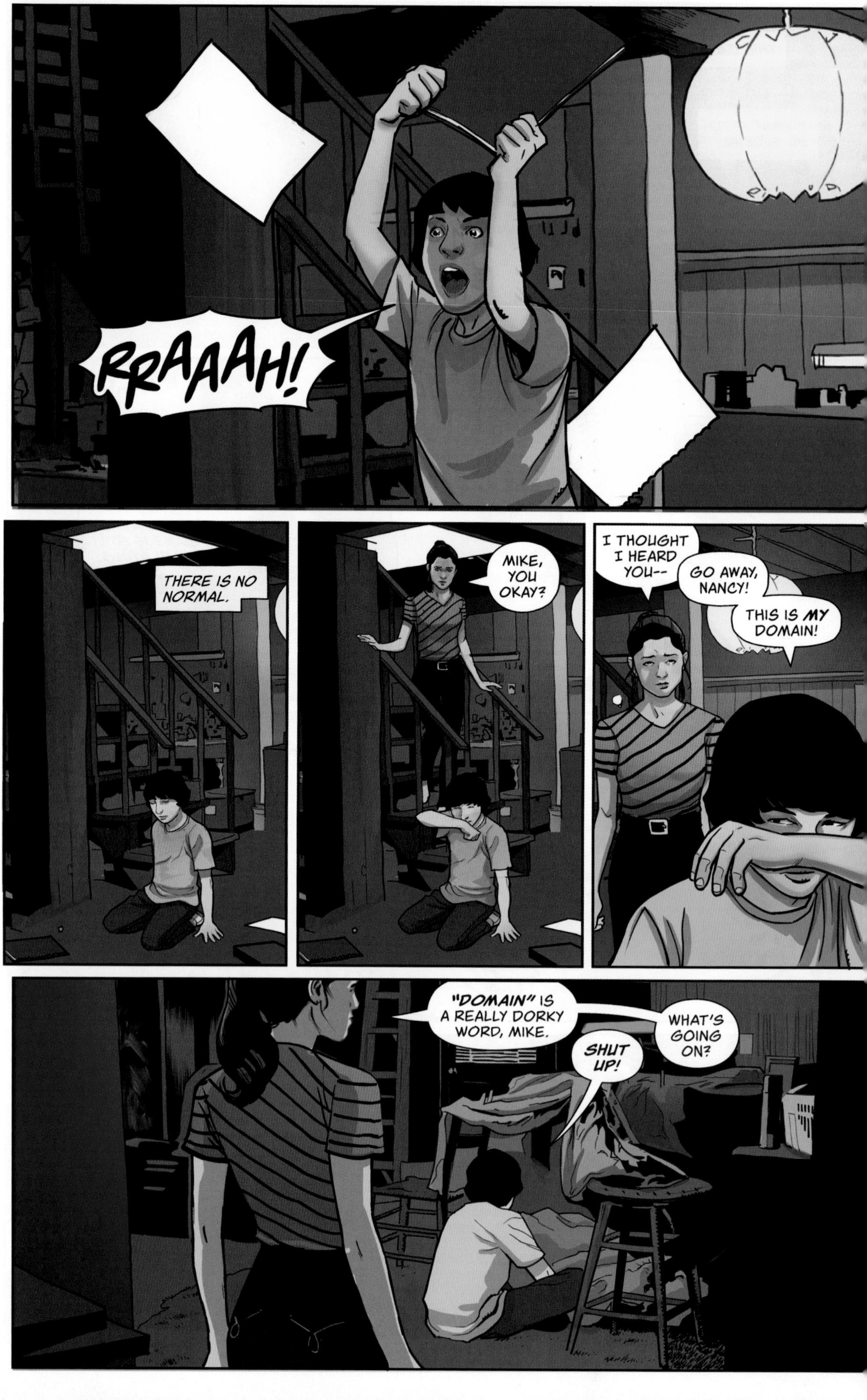
RRAAAH!
THERE IS NO NORMAL.
MIKE, YOU OKAY?
I THOUGHT I HEARD YOU--
GO AWAY, NANCY!
THIS IS MY DOMAIN!
"DOMAIN" IS A REALLY DORKY WORD, MIKE.
WHAT'S GOING ON?
SHUT UP!

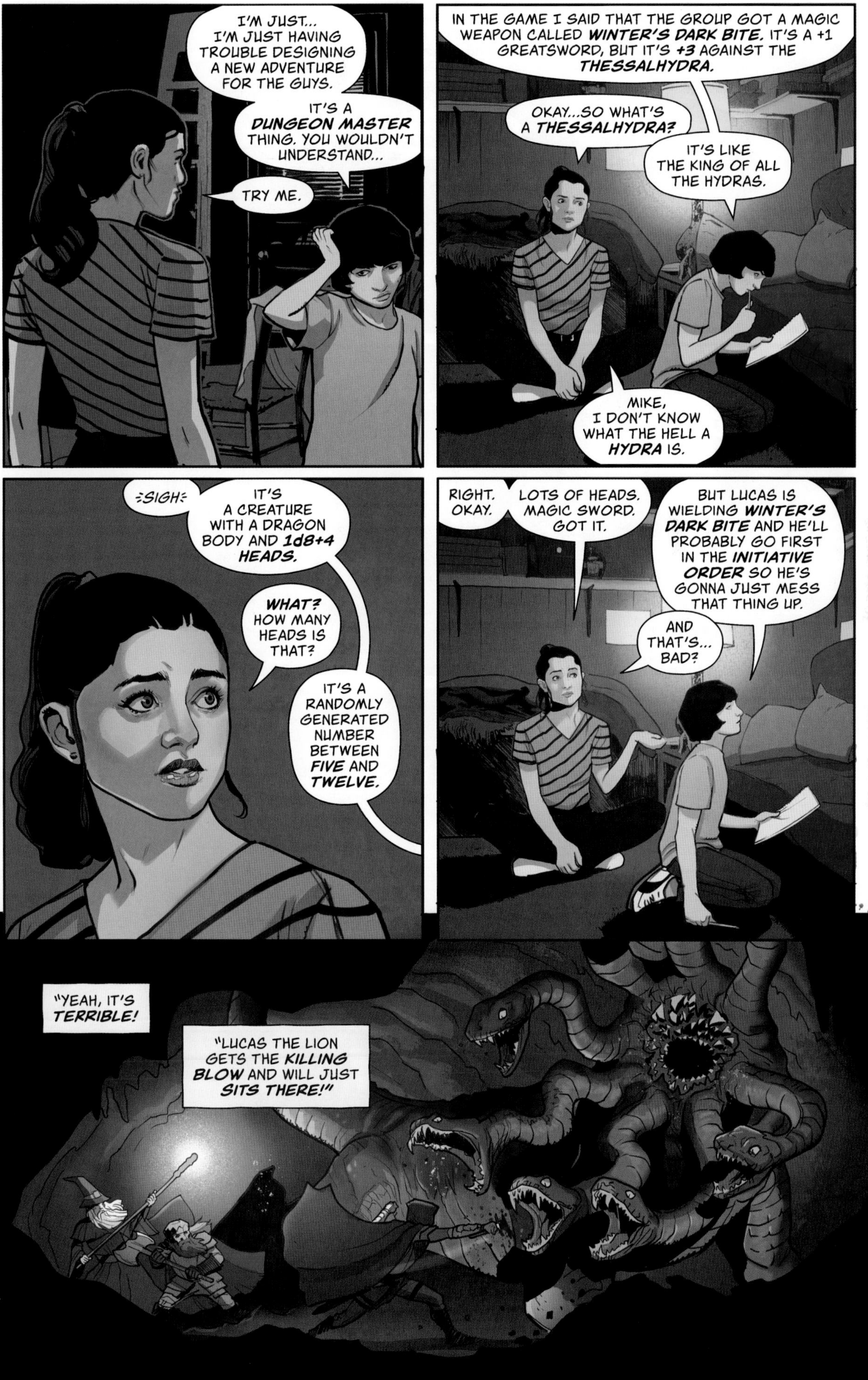
I'M JUST... I'M JUST HAVING TROUBLE DESIGNING A NEW ADVENTURE FOR THE GUYS.
IT'S A DUNGEON MASTER THING. YOU WOULDN'T UNDERSTAND...
TRY ME.
IN THE GAME I SAID THAT THE GROUP GOT A MAGIC WEAPON CALLED WINTER'S DARK BITE. IT'S A +1 GREATSWORD, BUT IT'S +3 AGAINST THE THESSALHYDRA.
OKAY...SO WHAT'S A THESSALHYDRA?
IT'S LIKE THE KING OF ALL THE HYDRAS.
MIKE, I DON'T KNOW WHAT THE HELL A HYDRA IS.
=SIGH=
IT'S A CREATURE WITH A DRAGON BODY AND 1d8+4 HEADS.
WHAT? HOW MANY HEADS IS THAT?
IT'S A RANDOMLY GENERATED NUMBER BETWEEN FIVE AND TWELVE.
RIGHT. OKAY.
LOTS OF HEADS. MAGIC SWORD. GOT IT.
BUT LUCAS IS WIELDING WINTER'S DARK BITE AND HE'LL PROBABLY GO FIRST IN THE INITIATIVE ORDER SO HE'S GONNA JUST MESS THAT THING UP.
AND THAT'S... BAD?
"YEAH, IT'S TERRIBLE!
"LUCAS THE LION GETS THE KILLING BLOW AND WILL JUST SITS THERE!"

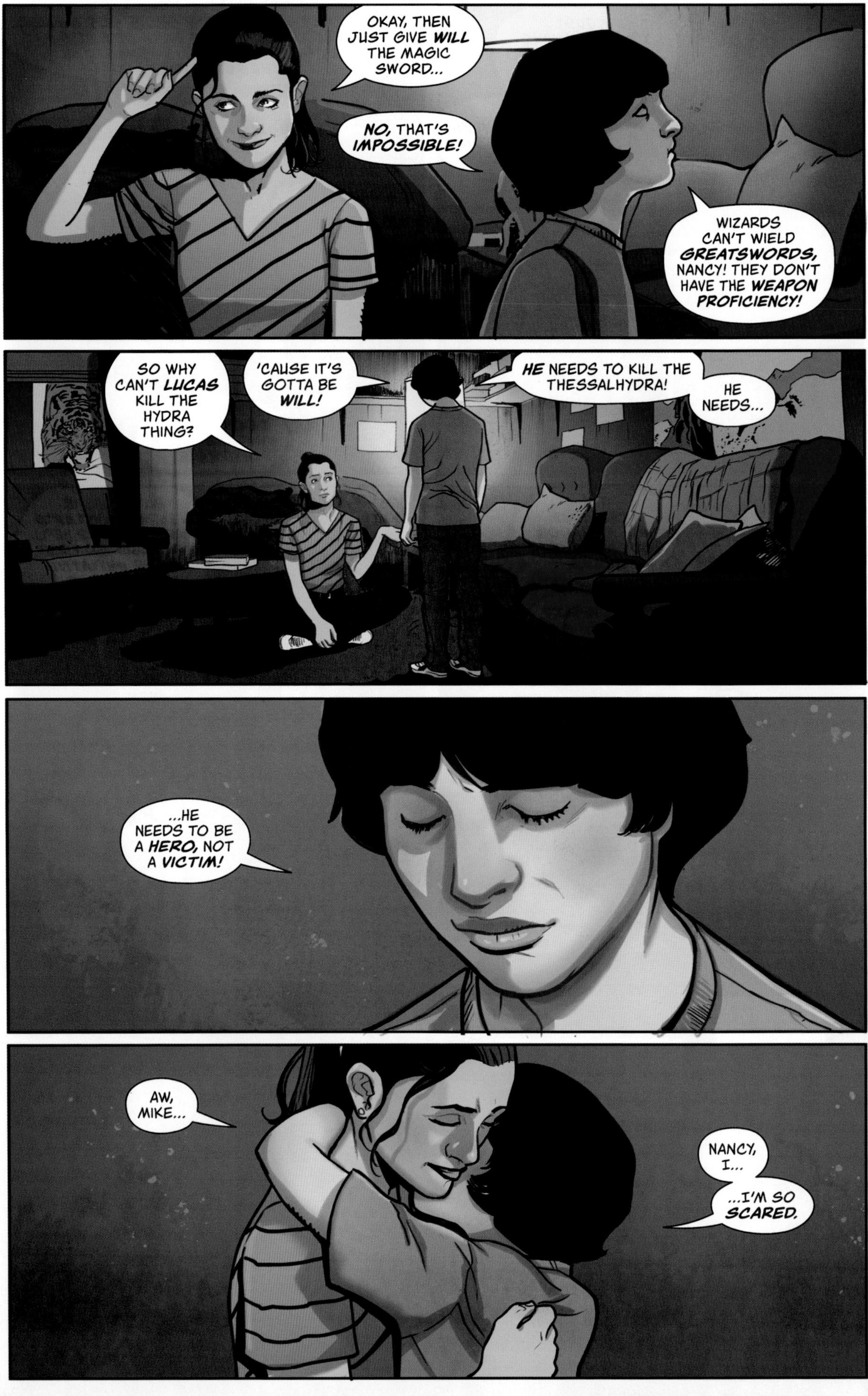
OKAY, THEN JUST GIVE WILL THE MAGIC SWORD...
NO, THAT'S IMPOSSIBLE!
WIZARDS CAN'T WIELD GREATSWORDS, NANCY! THEY DON'T HAVE THE WEAPON PROFICIENCY!
SO WHY CAN'T LUCAS KILL THE HYDRA THING?
'CAUSE IT'S GOTTA BE WILL!
HE NEEDS TO KILL THE THESSALHYDRA!
HE NEEDS...
...HE NEEDS TO BE A HERO, NOT A VICTIM!
AW, MIKE...
NANCY, I...
...I'M SO SCARED.

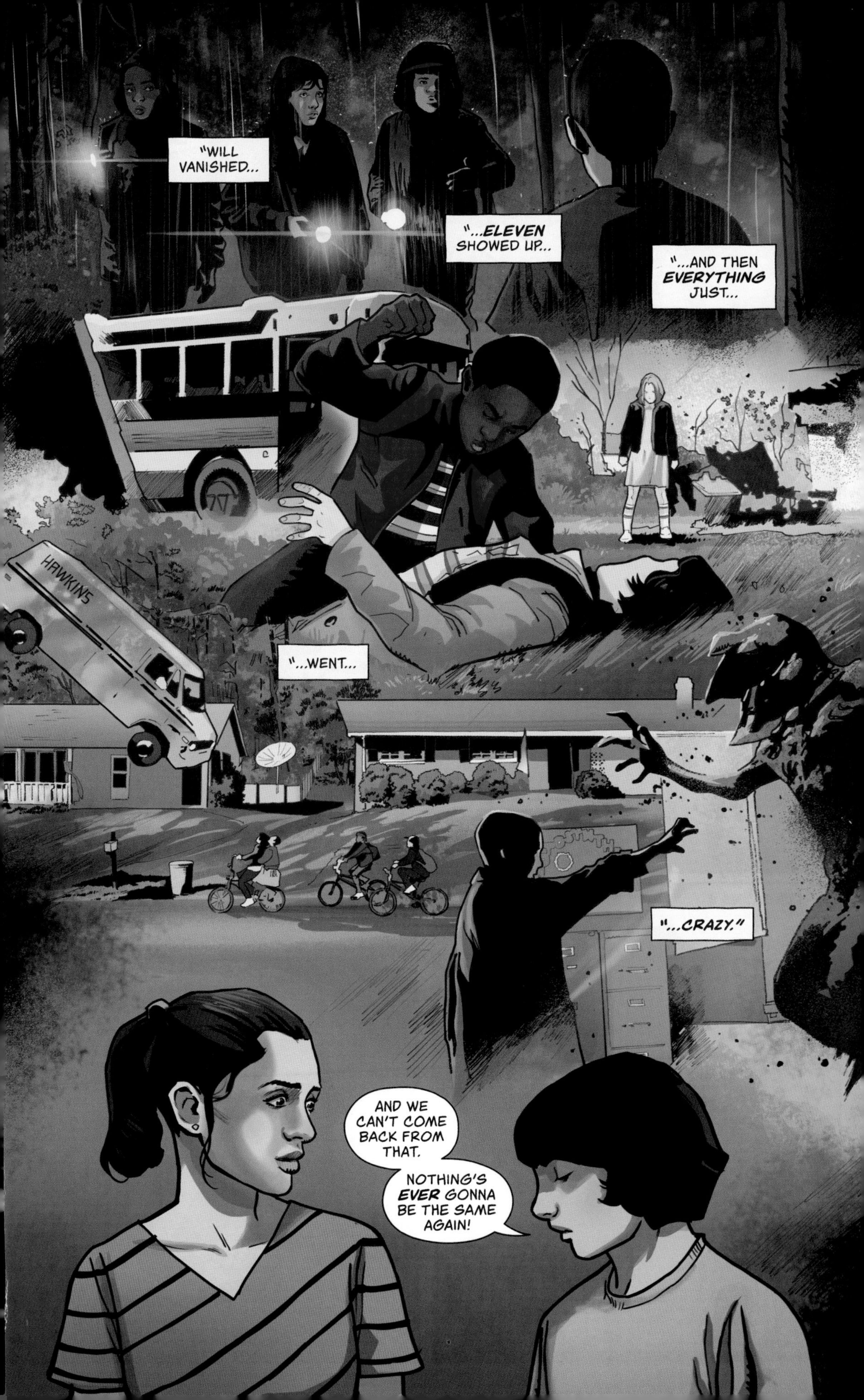
"WILL VANISHED...
"...ELEVEN SHOWED UP...
"...AND THEN EVERYTHING JUST...
HAWKINS
"...WENT...
"...CRAZY."
AND WE CAN'T COME BACK FROM THAT.
NOTHING'S EVER GONNA BE THE SAME AGAIN!

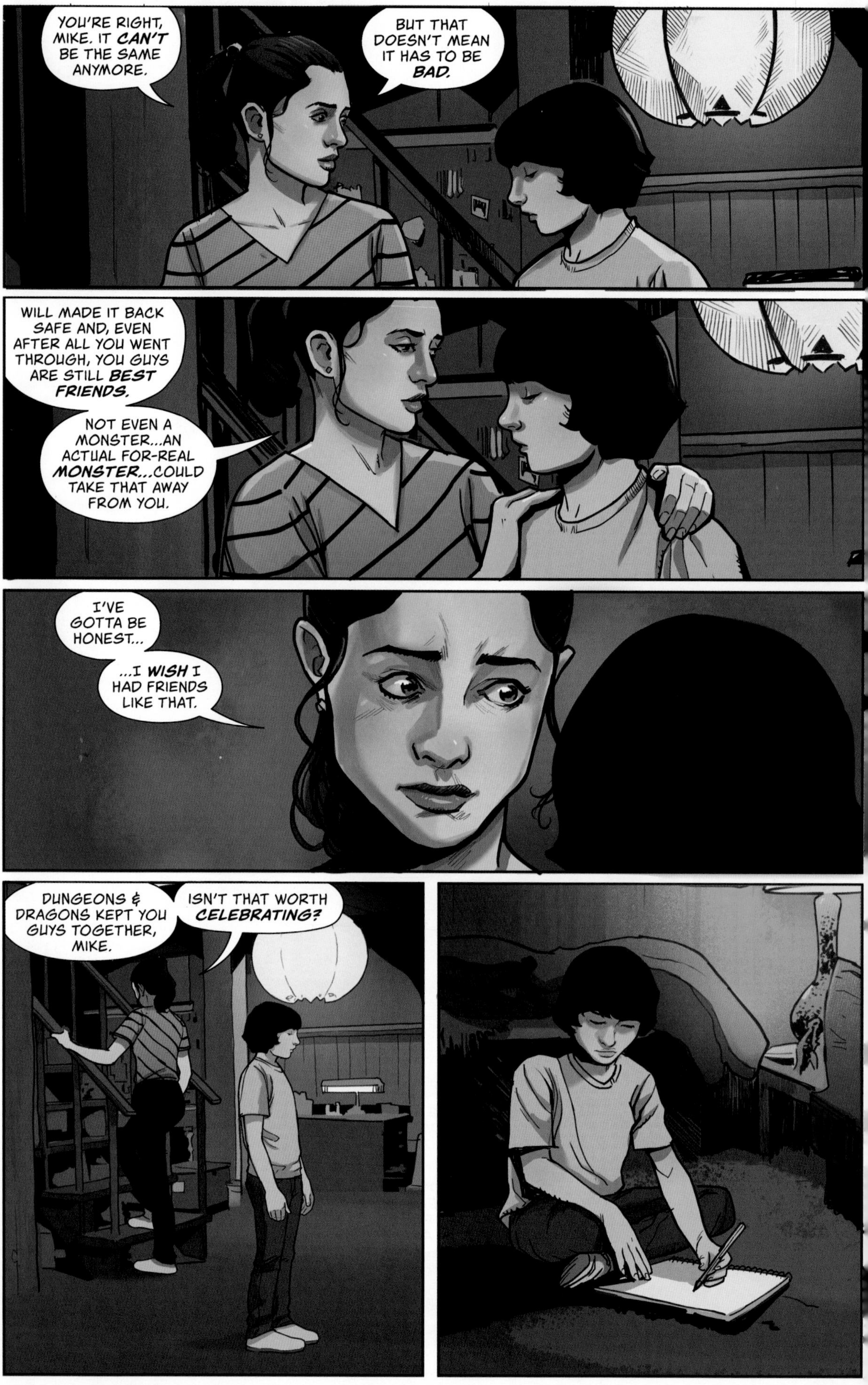
YOU'RE RIGHT, MIKE. IT *CAN'T* BE THE SAME ANYMORE.
BUT THAT DOESN'T MEAN IT HAS TO BE *BAD.*
WILL MADE IT BACK SAFE AND, EVEN AFTER ALL YOU WENT THROUGH, YOU GUYS ARE STILL *BEST FRIENDS.*
NOT EVEN A MONSTER...AN ACTUAL FOR-REAL *MONSTER...*COULD TAKE THAT AWAY FROM YOU.
I'VE GOTTA BE HONEST...
...I *WISH* I HAD FRIENDS LIKE THAT.
DUNGEONS & DRAGONS KEPT YOU GUYS TOGETHER, MIKE.
ISN'T THAT WORTH *CELEBRATING?*

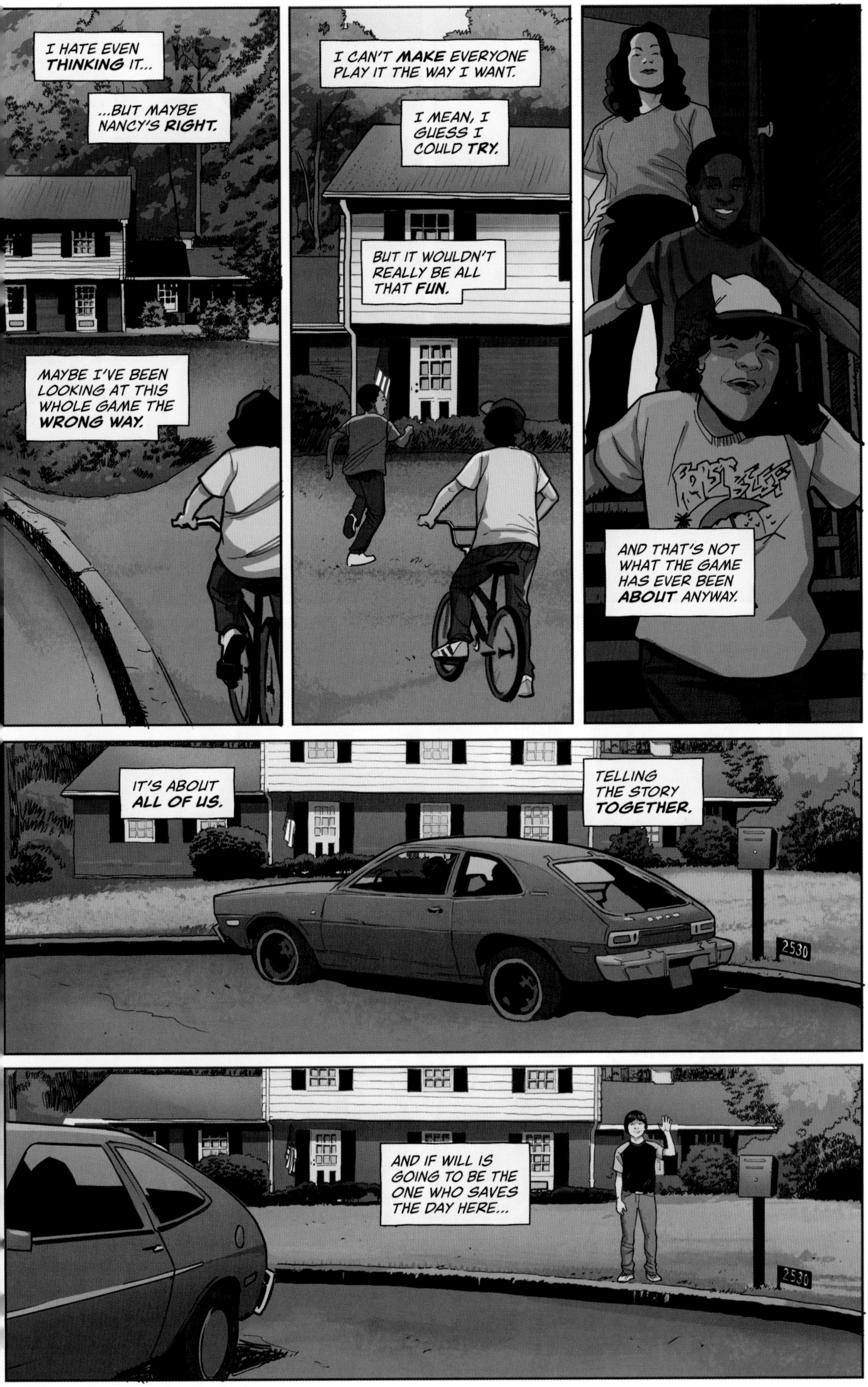
I HATE EVEN THINKING IT...
...BUT MAYBE NANCY'S RIGHT.
MAYBE I'VE BEEN LOOKING AT THIS WHOLE GAME THE WRONG WAY.
I CAN'T MAKE EVERYONE PLAY IT THE WAY I WANT.
I MEAN, I GUESS I COULD TRY.
BUT IT WOULDN'T REALLY BE ALL THAT FUN.
AND THAT'S NOT WHAT THE GAME HAS EVER BEEN ABOUT ANYWAY.
IT'S ABOUT ALL OF US.
TELLING THE STORY TOGETHER.
2530
AND IF WILL IS GOING TO BE THE ONE WHO SAVES THE DAY HERE...
2530

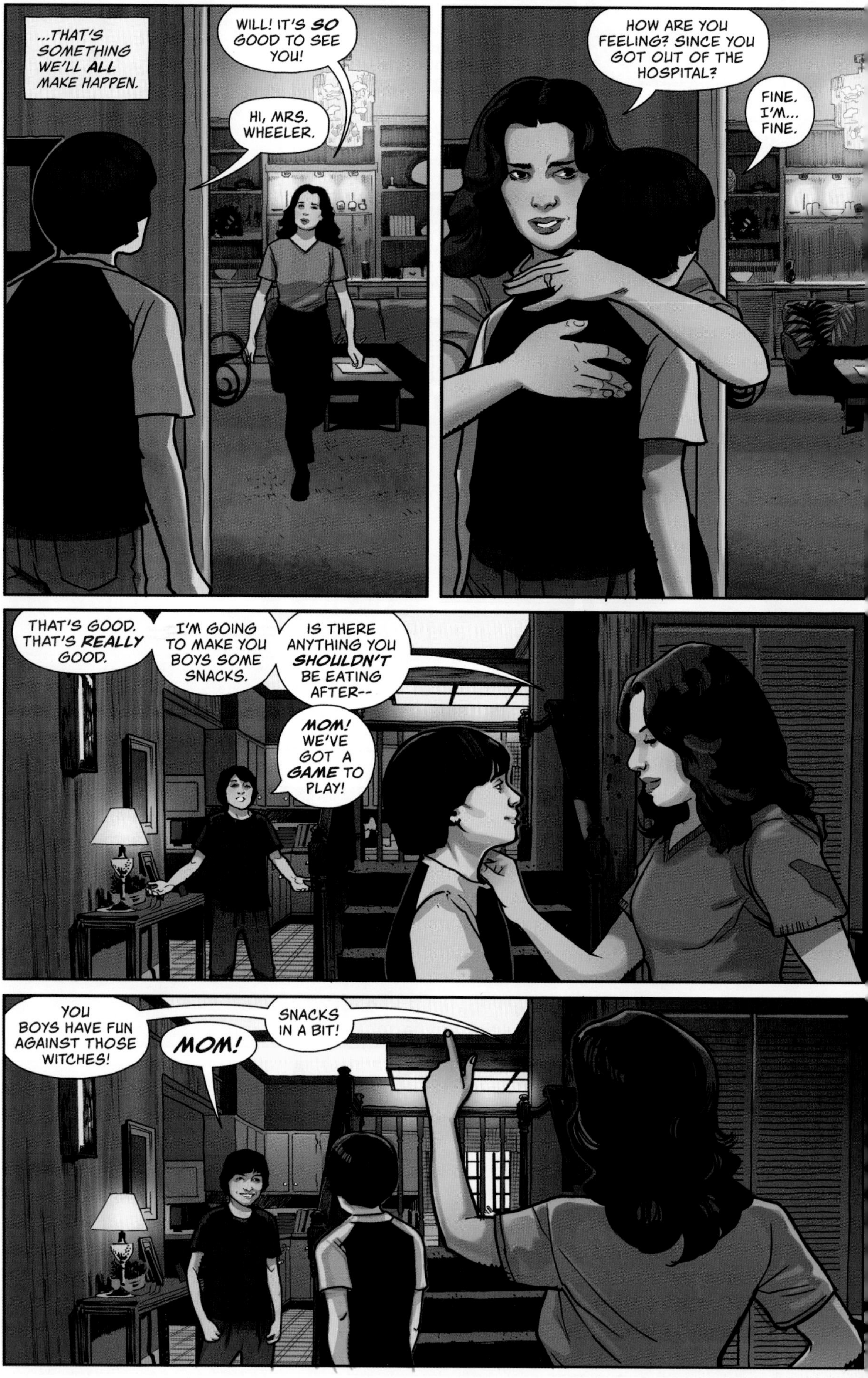
...THAT'S SOMETHING WE'LL ALL MAKE HAPPEN.
WILL! IT'S SO GOOD TO SEE YOU!
HI, MRS. WHEELER.
HOW ARE YOU FEELING? SINCE YOU GOT OUT OF THE HOSPITAL?
FINE. I'M... FINE.
THAT'S GOOD. THAT'S REALLY GOOD.
I'M GOING TO MAKE YOU BOYS SOME SNACKS.
IS THERE ANYTHING YOU SHOULDN'T BE EATING AFTER--
MOM! WE'VE GOT A GAME TO PLAY!
YOU BOYS HAVE FUN AGAINST THOSE WITCHES!
MOM!
SNACKS IN A BIT!

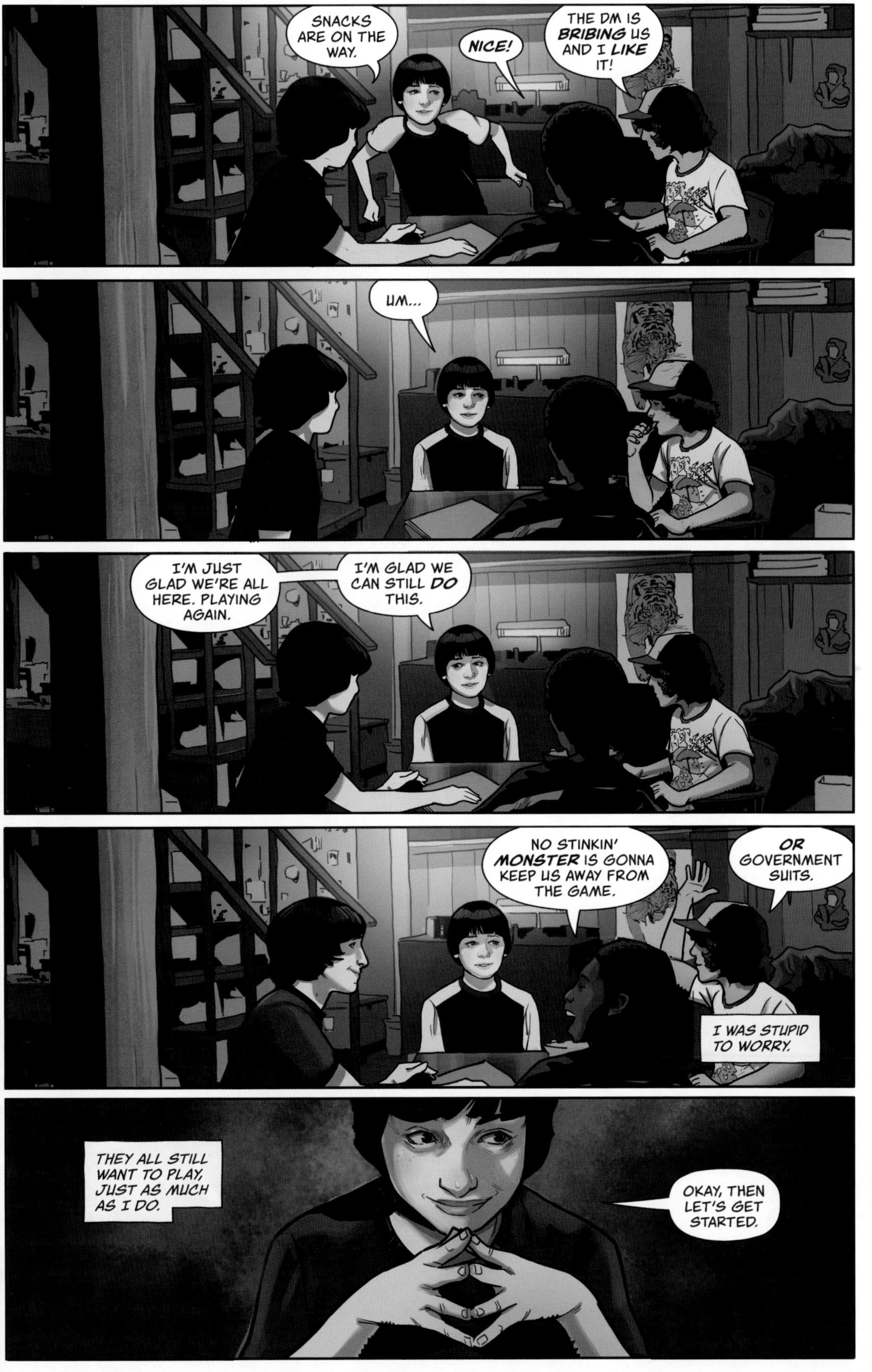
SNACKS ARE ON THE WAY.
NICE!
THE DM IS BRIBING US AND I LIKE IT!
UM...
I'M JUST GLAD WE'RE ALL HERE. PLAYING AGAIN.
I'M GLAD WE CAN STILL DO THIS.
NO STINKIN' MONSTER IS GONNA KEEP US AWAY FROM THE GAME.
OR GOVERNMENT SUITS.
I WAS STUPID TO WORRY.
THEY ALL STILL WANT TO PLAY, JUST AS MUCH AS I DO.
OKAY, THEN LET'S GET STARTED.

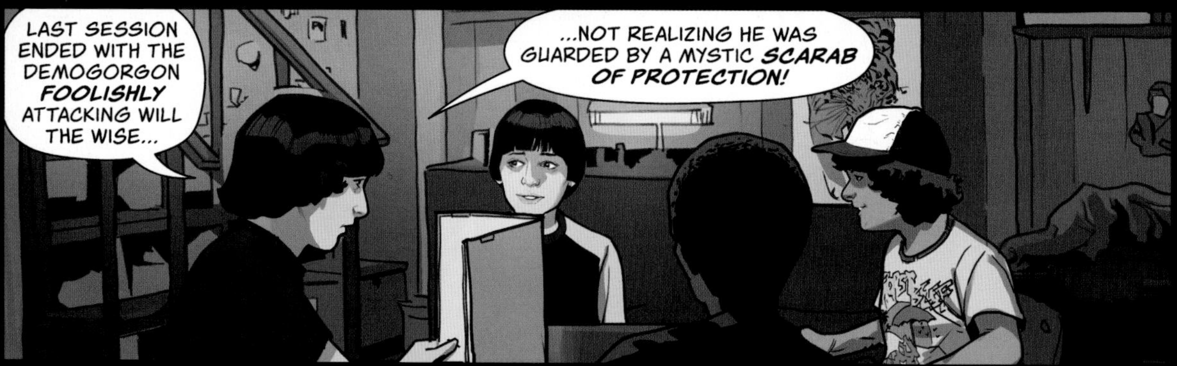
LAST SESSION ENDED WITH THE DEMOGORGON FOOLISHLY ATTACKING WILL THE WISE...
...NOT REALIZING HE WAS GUARDED BY A MYSTIC SCARAB OF PROTECTION!

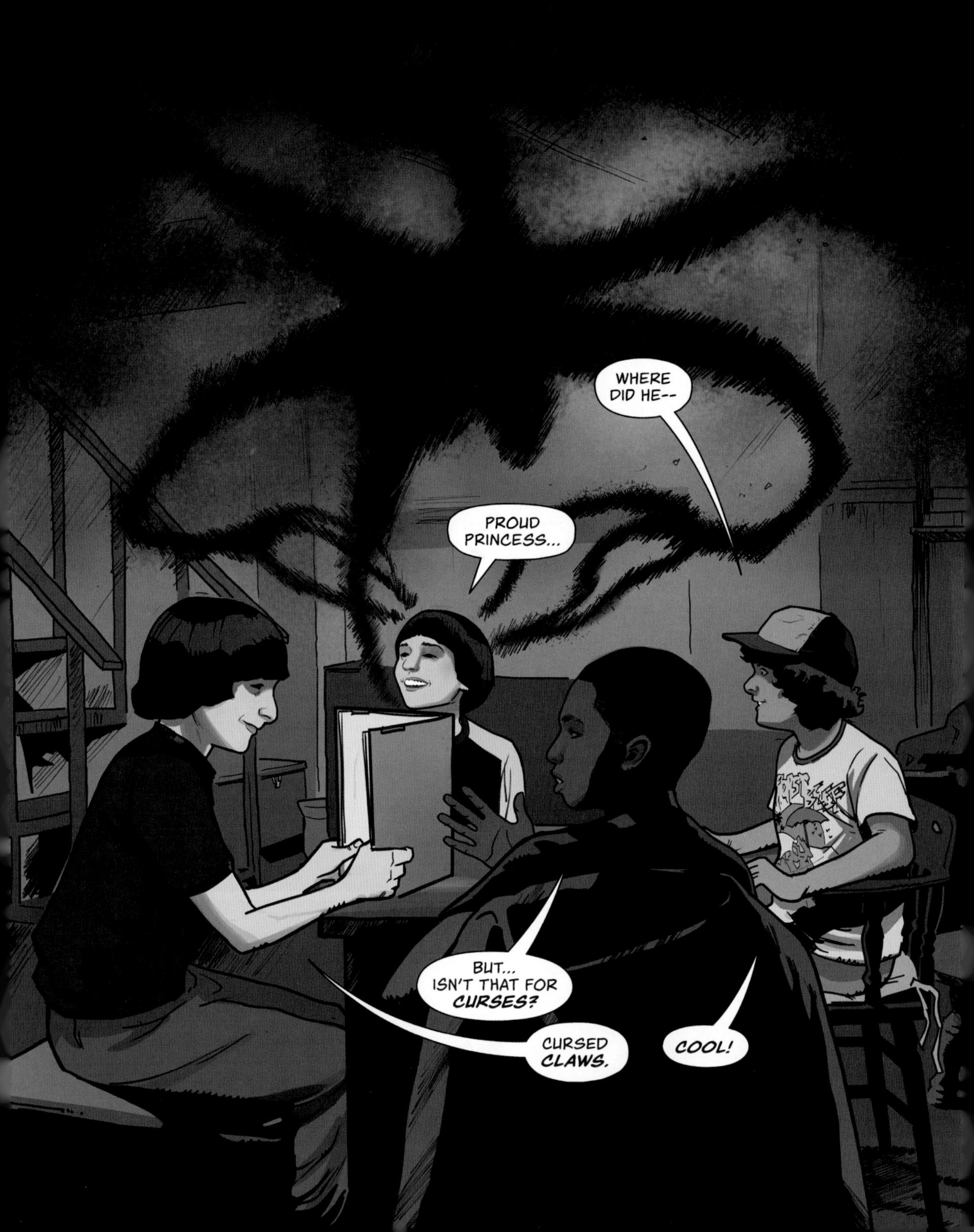
WHERE DID HE--
PROUD PRINCESS...
BUT... ISN'T THAT FOR CURSES?
CURSED CLAWS.
COOL!

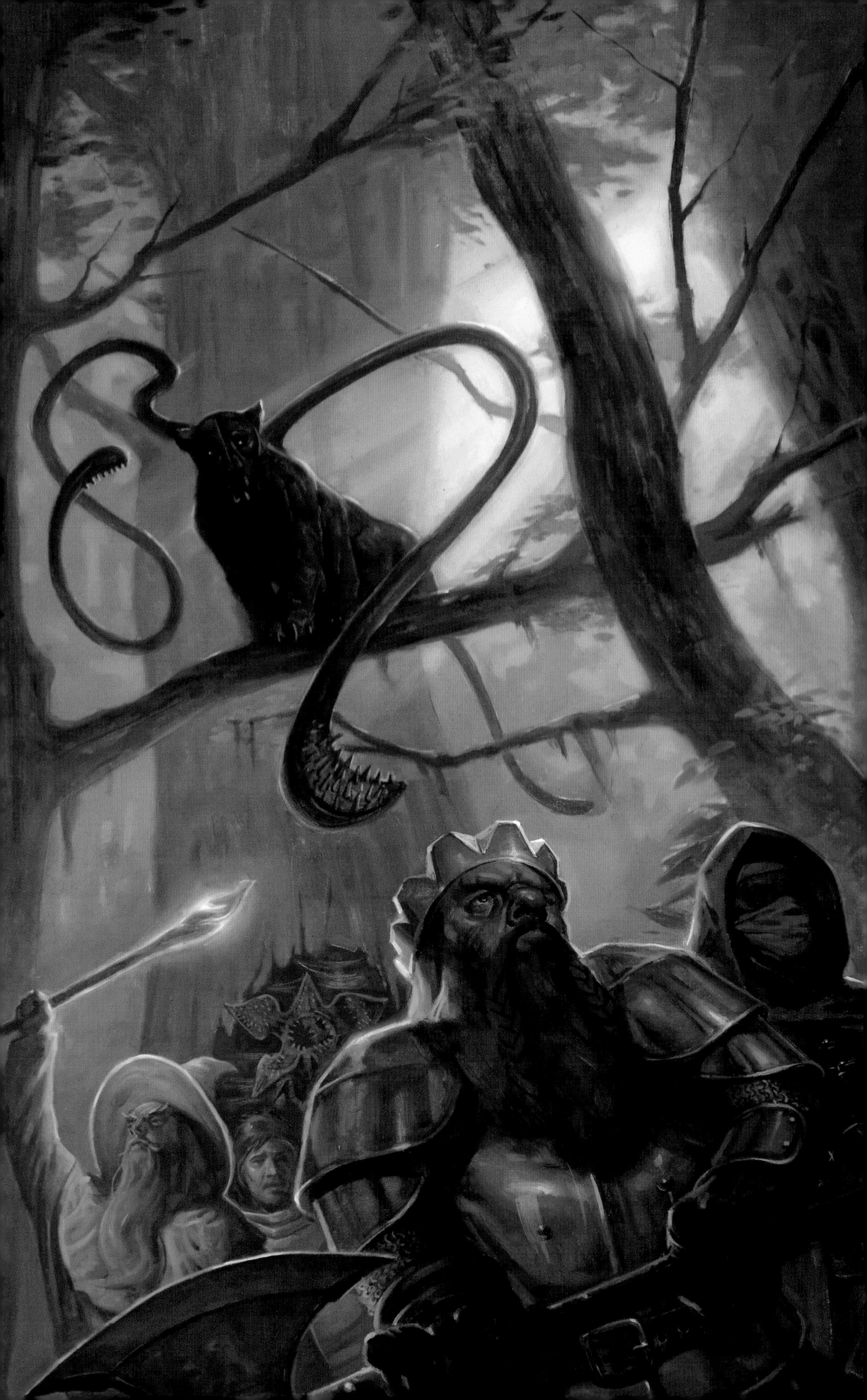

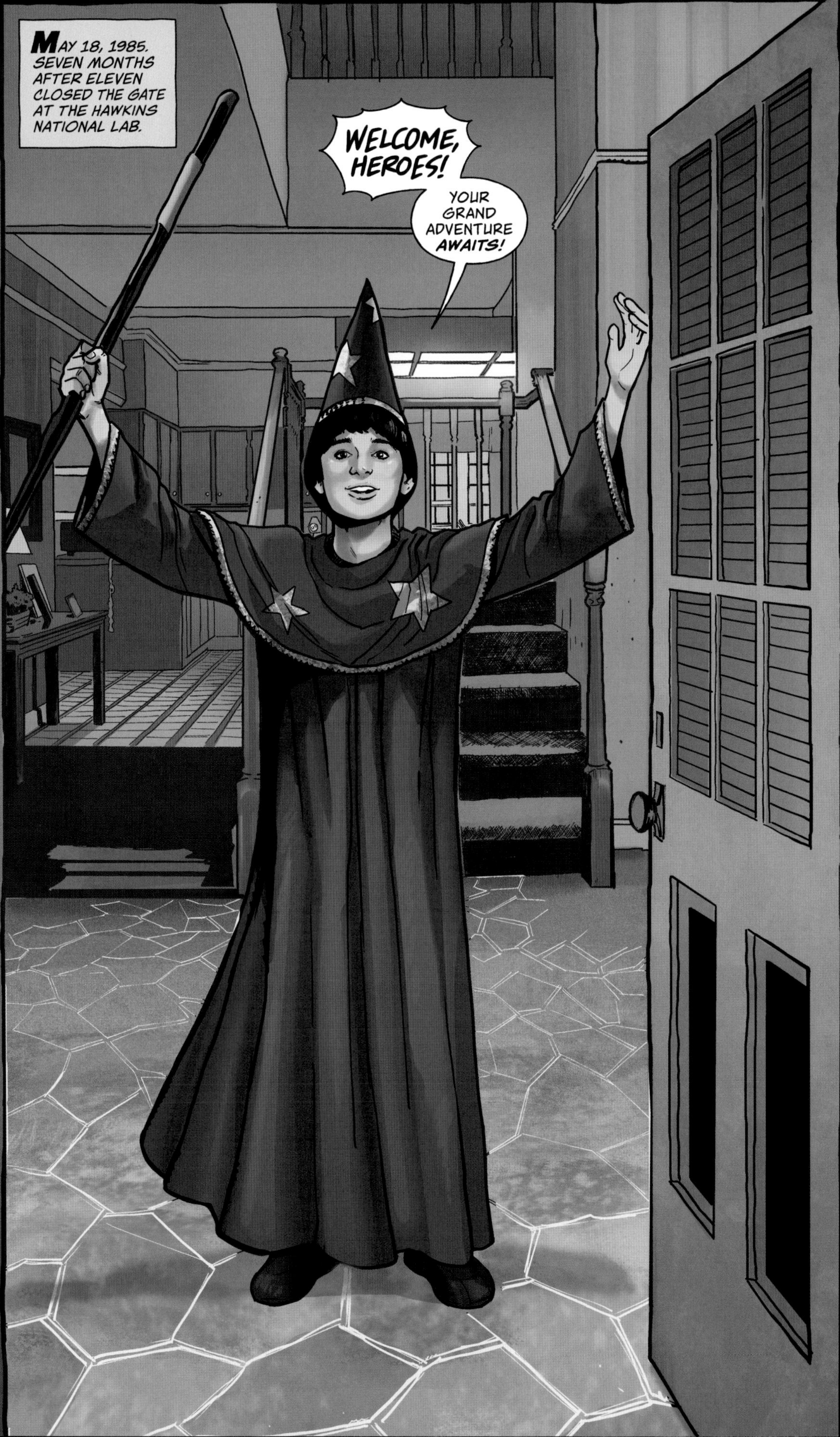
MAY 18, 1985. SEVEN MONTHS AFTER ELEVEN CLOSED THE GATE AT THE HAWKINS NATIONAL LAB.
WELCOME, HEROES!
YOUR GRAND ADVENTURE AWAITS!

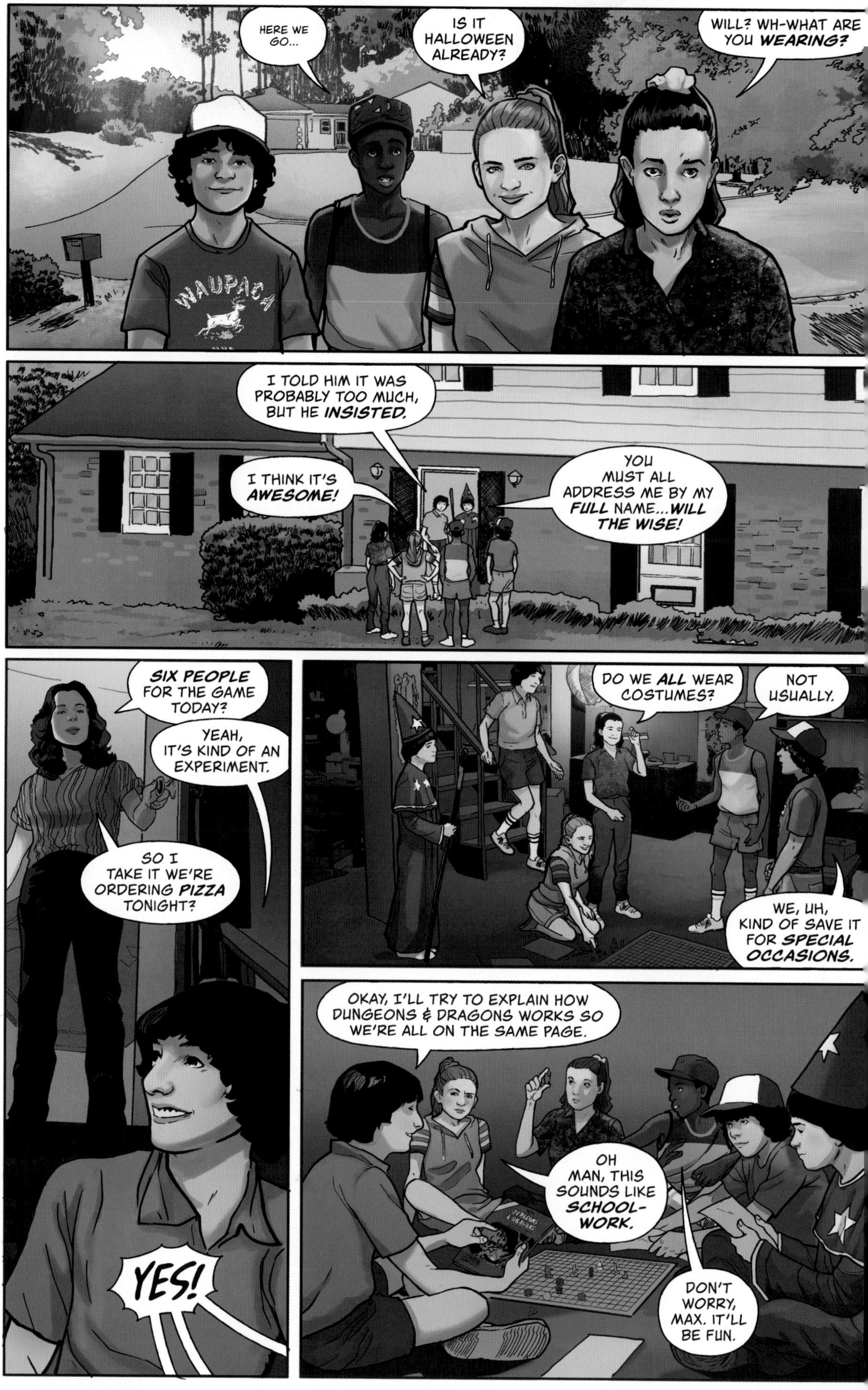

HERE WE GO...
IS IT HALLOWEEN ALREADY?
WILL? WH-WHAT ARE YOU *WEARING?*
WAUPACA
I TOLD HIM IT WAS PROBABLY TOO MUCH, BUT HE *INSISTED.*
I THINK IT'S *AWESOME!*
YOU MUST ALL ADDRESS ME BY MY *FULL* NAME...*WILL THE WISE!*
SIX PEOPLE FOR THE GAME TODAY?
YEAH, IT'S KIND OF AN EXPERIMENT.
SO I TAKE IT WE'RE ORDERING *PIZZA* TONIGHT?
YES!
DO WE *ALL* WEAR COSTUMES?
NOT USUALLY.
WE, UH, KIND OF SAVE IT FOR *SPECIAL OCCASIONS.*
OKAY, I'LL TRY TO EXPLAIN HOW DUNGEONS & DRAGONS WORKS SO WE'RE ALL ON THE SAME PAGE.
OH MAN, THIS SOUNDS LIKE *SCHOOL-WORK.*
DON'T WORRY, MAX. IT'LL BE FUN.

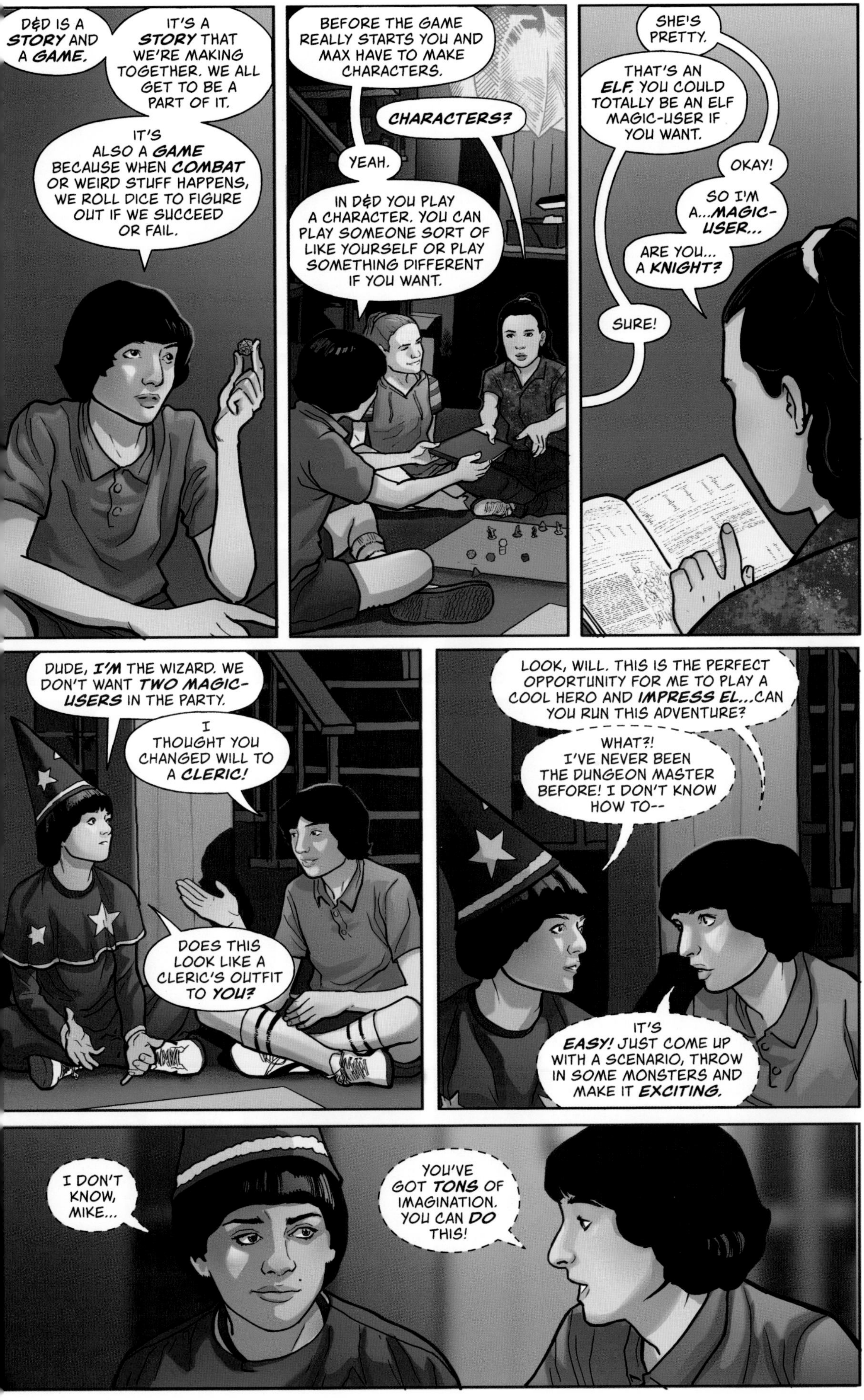
D&D IS A STORY AND A GAME.
IT'S A STORY THAT WE'RE MAKING TOGETHER. WE ALL GET TO BE A PART OF IT.
IT'S ALSO A GAME BECAUSE WHEN COMBAT OR WEIRD STUFF HAPPENS, WE ROLL DICE TO FIGURE OUT IF WE SUCCEED OR FAIL.
BEFORE THE GAME REALLY STARTS YOU AND MAX HAVE TO MAKE CHARACTERS.
CHARACTERS?
YEAH.
IN D&D YOU PLAY A CHARACTER. YOU CAN PLAY SOMEONE SORT OF LIKE YOURSELF OR PLAY SOMETHING DIFFERENT IF YOU WANT.
SHE'S PRETTY.
THAT'S AN ELF. YOU COULD TOTALLY BE AN ELF MAGIC-USER IF YOU WANT.
OKAY!
SO I'M A...MAGIC-USER...
ARE YOU... A KNIGHT?
SURE!
DUDE, I'M THE WIZARD. WE DON'T WANT TWO MAGIC-USERS IN THE PARTY.
I THOUGHT YOU CHANGED WILL TO A CLERIC!
DOES THIS LOOK LIKE A CLERIC'S OUTFIT TO YOU?
LOOK, WILL. THIS IS THE PERFECT OPPORTUNITY FOR ME TO PLAY A COOL HERO AND IMPRESS EL...CAN YOU RUN THIS ADVENTURE?
WHAT?! I'VE NEVER BEEN THE DUNGEON MASTER BEFORE! I DON'T KNOW HOW TO--
IT'S EASY! JUST COME UP WITH A SCENARIO, THROW IN SOME MONSTERS AND MAKE IT EXCITING.
I DON'T KNOW, MIKE...
YOU'VE GOT TONS OF IMAGINATION. YOU CAN DO THIS!

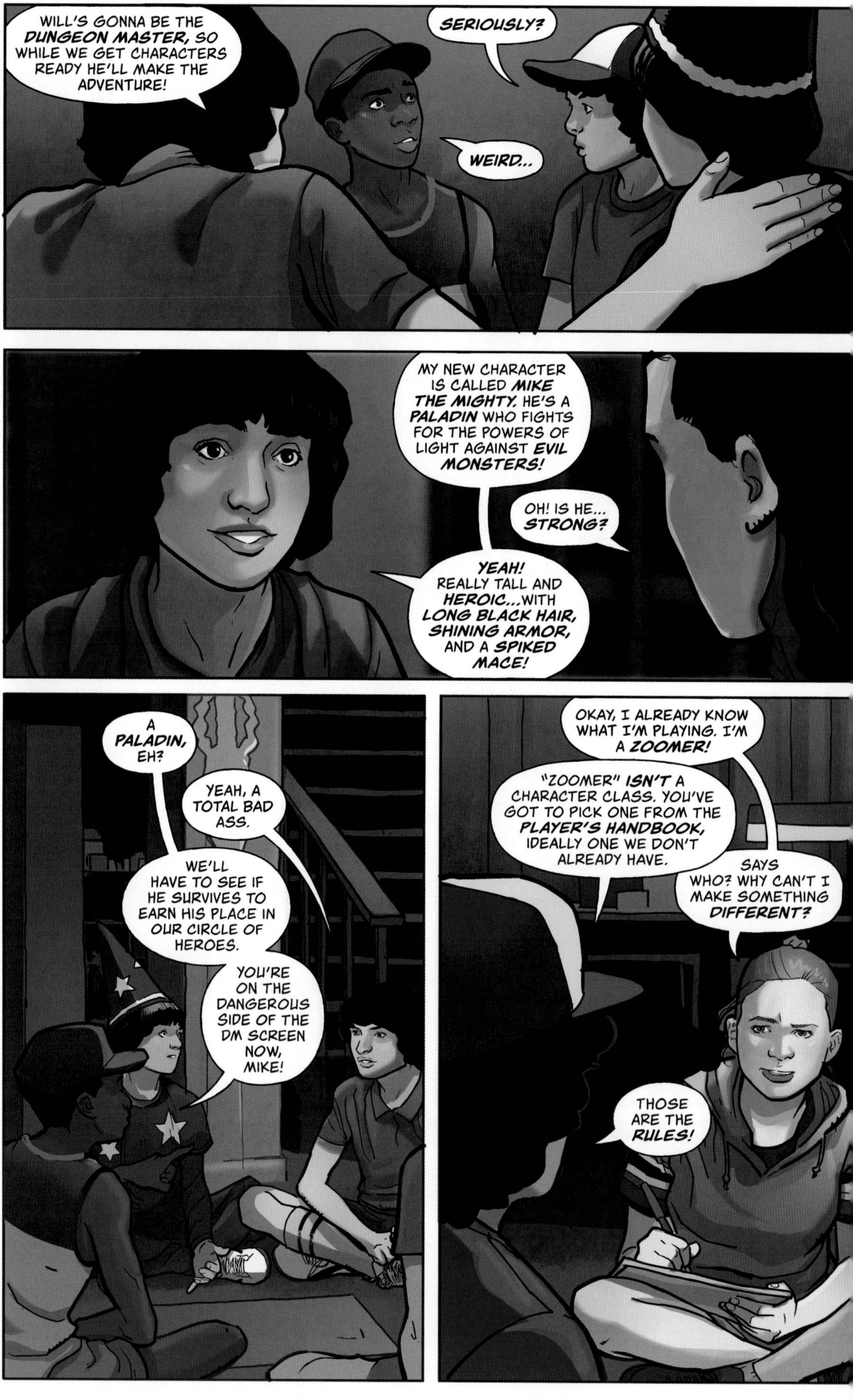

WILL'S GONNA BE THE DUNGEON MASTER, SO WHILE WE GET CHARACTERS READY HE'LL MAKE THE ADVENTURE!
SERIOUSLY?
WEIRD...
MY NEW CHARACTER IS CALLED MIKE THE MIGHTY. HE'S A PALADIN WHO FIGHTS FOR THE POWERS OF LIGHT AGAINST EVIL MONSTERS!
OH! IS HE... STRONG?
YEAH! REALLY TALL AND HEROIC...WITH LONG BLACK HAIR, SHINING ARMOR, AND A SPIKED MACE!
A PALADIN, EH?
YEAH, A TOTAL BAD ASS.
WE'LL HAVE TO SEE IF HE SURVIVES TO EARN HIS PLACE IN OUR CIRCLE OF HEROES.
YOU'RE ON THE DANGEROUS SIDE OF THE DM SCREEN NOW, MIKE!
OKAY, I ALREADY KNOW WHAT I'M PLAYING. I'M A ZOOMER!
"ZOOMER" ISN'T A CHARACTER CLASS. YOU'VE GOT TO PICK ONE FROM THE PLAYER'S HANDBOOK, IDEALLY ONE WE DON'T ALREADY HAVE.
SAYS WHO? WHY CAN'T I MAKE SOMETHING DIFFERENT?
THOSE ARE THE RULES!

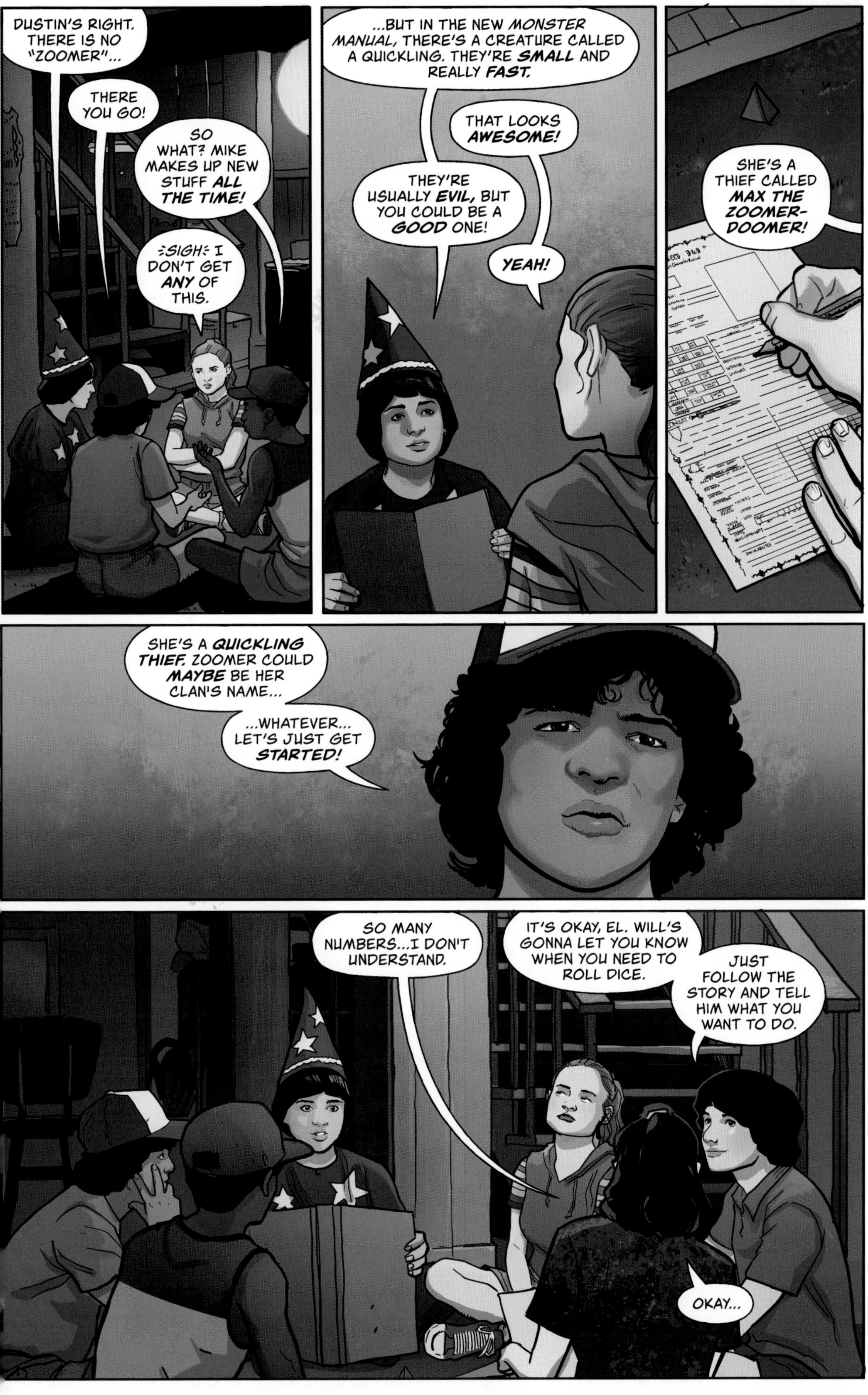
DUSTIN'S RIGHT. THERE IS NO "ZOOMER"...
THERE YOU GO!
SO WHAT? MIKE MAKES UP NEW STUFF ALL THE TIME!
=SIGH= I DON'T GET ANY OF THIS.
...BUT IN THE NEW MONSTER MANUAL, THERE'S A CREATURE CALLED A QUICKLING. THEY'RE SMALL AND REALLY FAST.
THAT LOOKS AWESOME!
THEY'RE USUALLY EVIL, BUT YOU COULD BE A GOOD ONE!
YEAH!
SHE'S A THIEF CALLED MAX THE ZOOMER-DOOMER!
SHE'S A QUICKLING THIEF. ZOOMER COULD MAYBE BE HER CLAN'S NAME...
...WHATEVER... LET'S JUST GET STARTED!
SO MANY NUMBERS...I DON'T UNDERSTAND.
IT'S OKAY, EL. WILL'S GONNA LET YOU KNOW WHEN YOU NEED TO ROLL DICE.
JUST FOLLOW THE STORY AND TELL HIM WHAT YOU WANT TO DO.
OKAY...

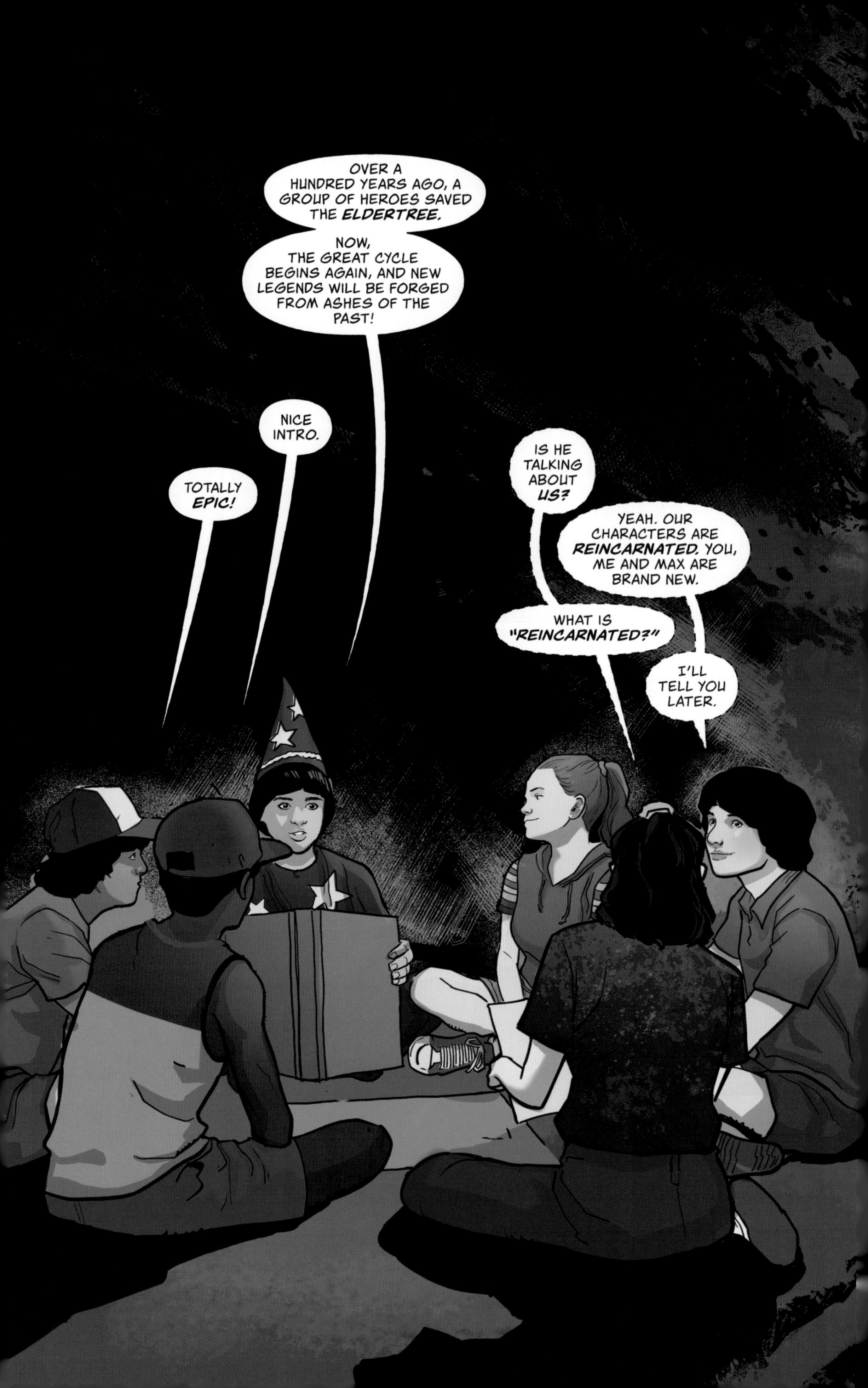
OVER A HUNDRED YEARS AGO, A GROUP OF HEROES SAVED THE ELDERTREE.
NOW, THE GREAT CYCLE BEGINS AGAIN, AND NEW LEGENDS WILL BE FORGED FROM ASHES OF THE PAST!
NICE INTRO.
TOTALLY EPIC!
IS HE TALKING ABOUT US?
YEAH. OUR CHARACTERS ARE REINCARNATED. YOU, ME AND MAX ARE BRAND NEW.
WHAT IS "REINCARNATED?"
I'LL TELL YOU LATER.

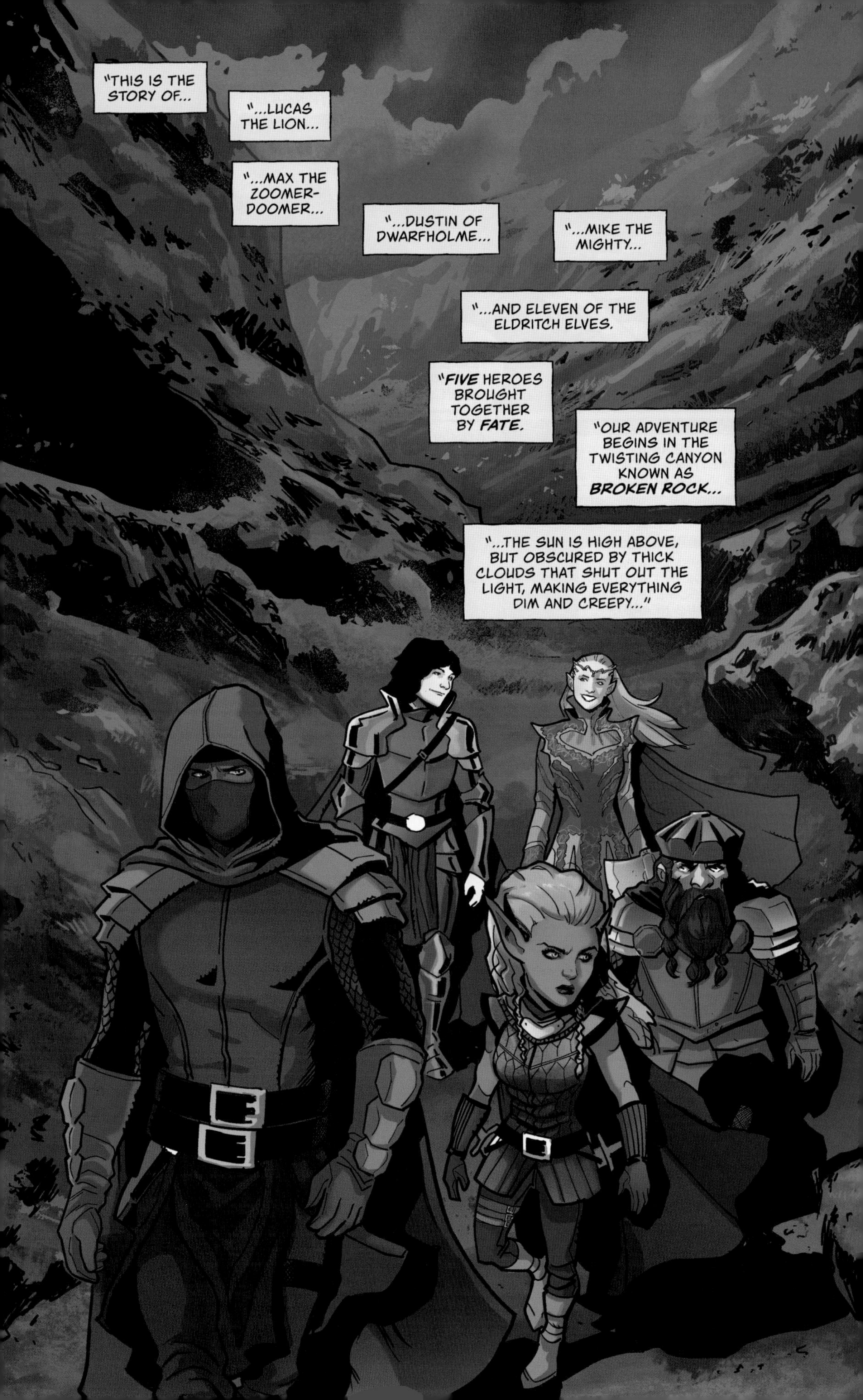
"THIS IS THE STORY OF...
"...LUCAS THE LION...
"...MAX THE ZOOMER-DOOMER...
"...DUSTIN OF DWARFHOLME...
"...MIKE THE MIGHTY...
"...AND ELEVEN OF THE ELDRITCH ELVES.
"FIVE HEROES BROUGHT TOGETHER BY FATE.
"OUR ADVENTURE BEGINS IN THE TWISTING CANYON KNOWN AS BROKEN ROCK...
"...THE SUN IS HIGH ABOVE, BUT OBSCURED BY THICK CLOUDS THAT SHUT OUT THE LIGHT, MAKING EVERYTHING DIM AND CREEPY..."

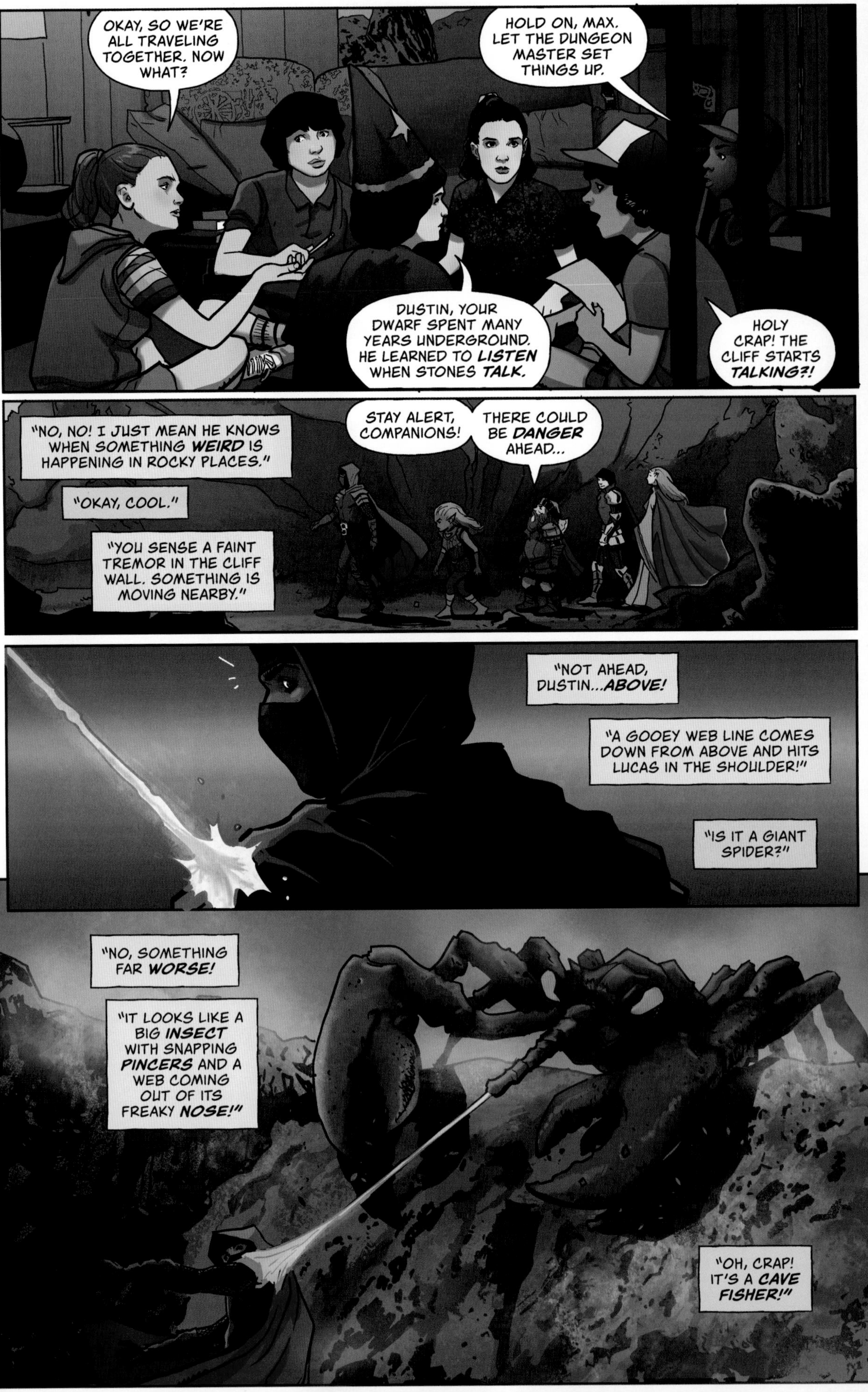
OKAY, SO WE'RE ALL TRAVELING TOGETHER. NOW WHAT?
HOLD ON, MAX. LET THE DUNGEON MASTER SET THINGS UP.
DUSTIN, YOUR DWARF SPENT MANY YEARS UNDERGROUND. HE LEARNED TO LISTEN WHEN STONES TALK.
HOLY CRAP! THE CLIFF STARTS TALKING?!
"NO, NO! I JUST MEAN HE KNOWS WHEN SOMETHING WEIRD IS HAPPENING IN ROCKY PLACES."
"OKAY, COOL."
"YOU SENSE A FAINT TREMOR IN THE CLIFF WALL. SOMETHING IS MOVING NEARBY."
STAY ALERT, COMPANIONS!
THERE COULD BE DANGER AHEAD...
"NOT AHEAD, DUSTIN...ABOVE!
"A GOOEY WEB LINE COMES DOWN FROM ABOVE AND HITS LUCAS IN THE SHOULDER!"
"IS IT A GIANT SPIDER?"
"NO, SOMETHING FAR WORSE!
"IT LOOKS LIKE A BIG INSECT WITH SNAPPING PINCERS AND A WEB COMING OUT OF ITS FREAKY NOSE!"
"OH, CRAP! IT'S A CAVE FISHER!"

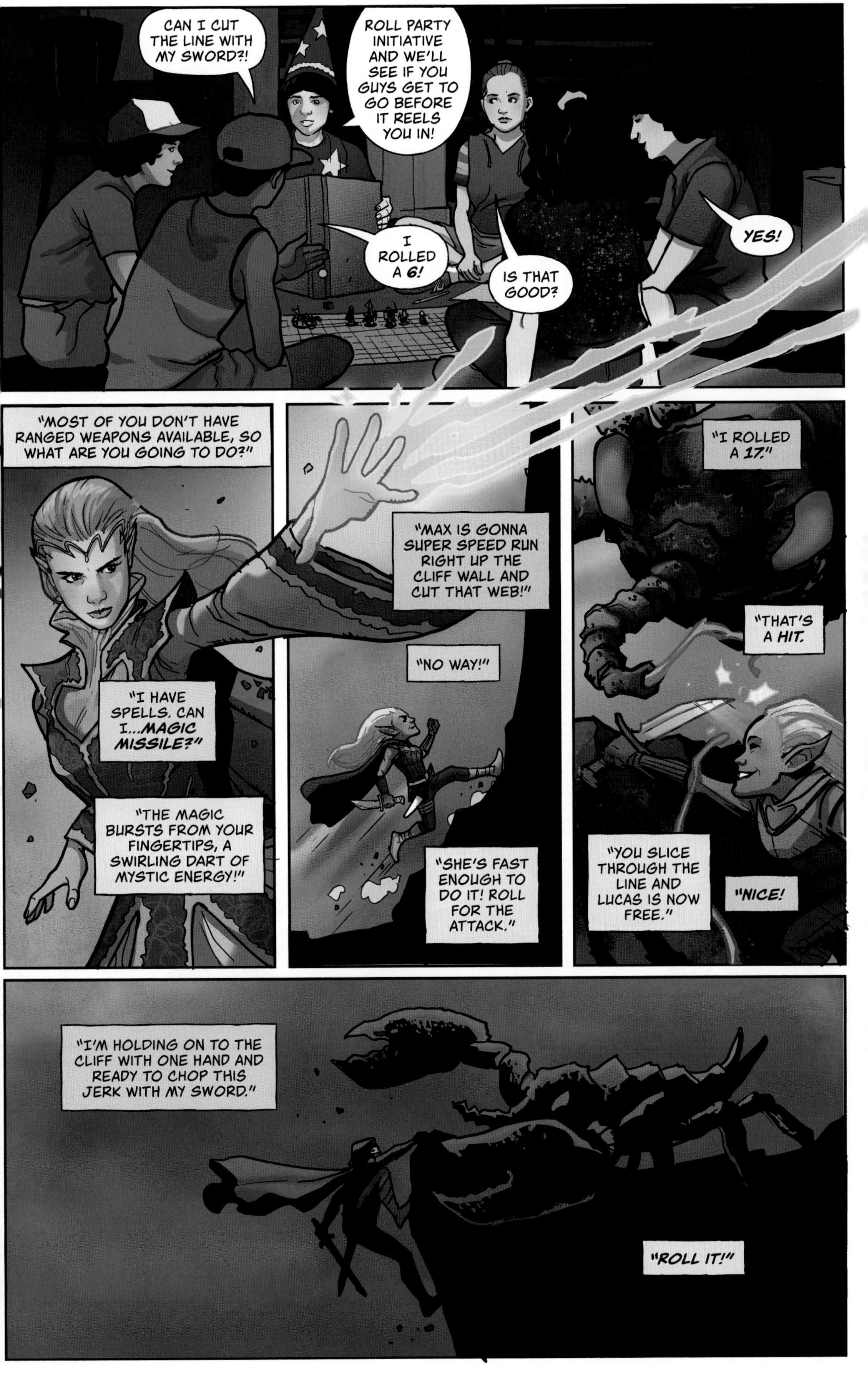
CAN I CUT THE LINE WITH MY SWORD?!
ROLL PARTY INITIATIVE AND WE'LL SEE IF YOU GUYS GET TO GO BEFORE IT REELS YOU IN!
I ROLLED A 6!
IS THAT GOOD?
YES!
"MOST OF YOU DON'T HAVE RANGED WEAPONS AVAILABLE, SO WHAT ARE YOU GOING TO DO?"
"I HAVE SPELLS. CAN I...MAGIC MISSILE?"
"THE MAGIC BURSTS FROM YOUR FINGERTIPS, A SWIRLING DART OF MYSTIC ENERGY!"
"MAX IS GONNA SUPER SPEED RUN RIGHT UP THE CLIFF WALL AND CUT THAT WEB!"
"NO WAY!"
"SHE'S FAST ENOUGH TO DO IT! ROLL FOR THE ATTACK."
"I ROLLED A 17."
"THAT'S A HIT.
"YOU SLICE THROUGH THE LINE AND LUCAS IS NOW FREE."
"NICE!
"I'M HOLDING ON TO THE CLIFF WITH ONE HAND AND READY TO CHOP THIS JERK WITH MY SWORD."
"ROLL IT!"

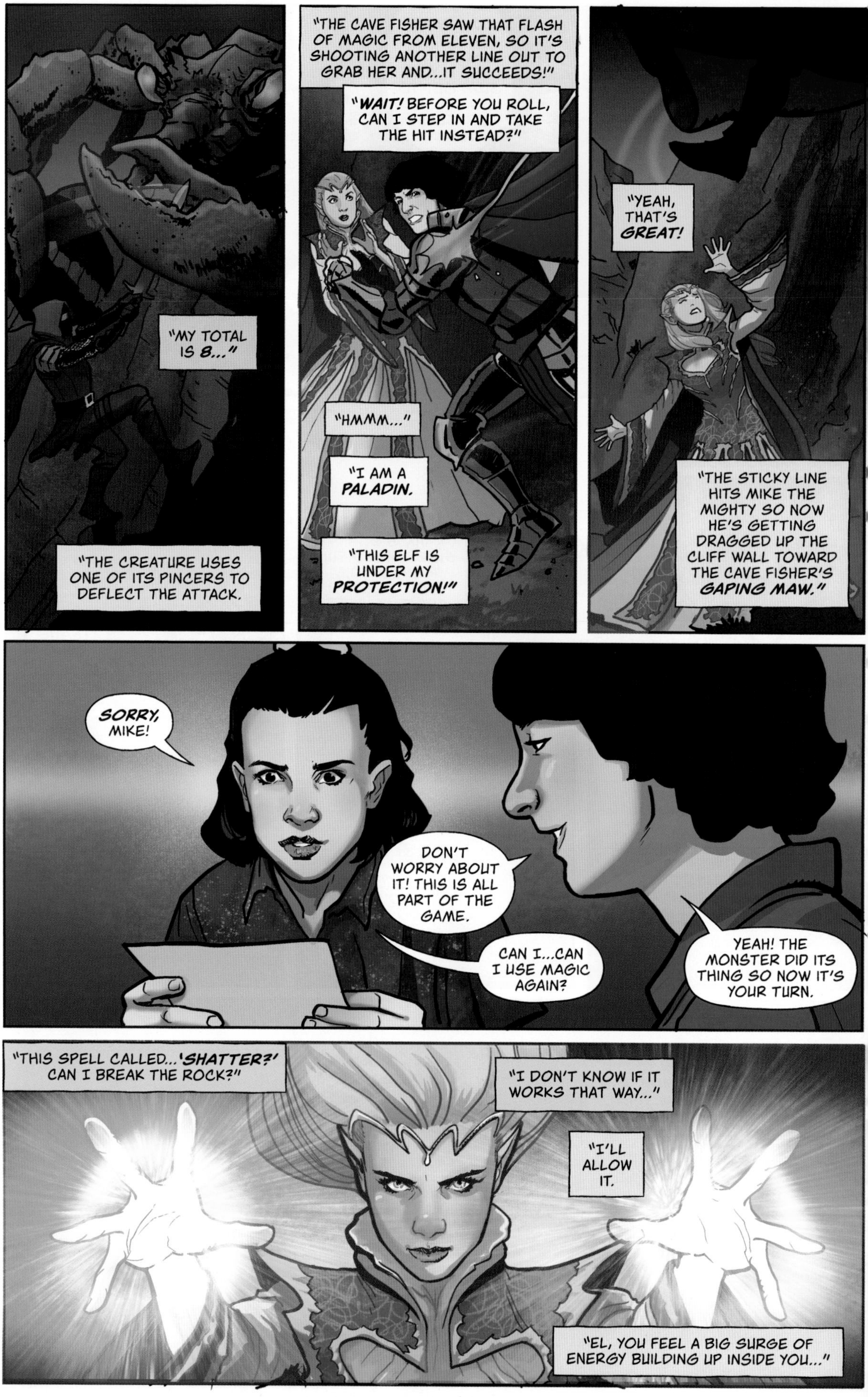
"MY TOTAL IS 8..."
"THE CREATURE USES ONE OF ITS PINCERS TO DEFLECT THE ATTACK.
"THE CAVE FISHER SAW THAT FLASH OF MAGIC FROM ELEVEN, SO IT'S SHOOTING ANOTHER LINE OUT TO GRAB HER AND...IT SUCCEEDS!"
"WAIT! BEFORE YOU ROLL, CAN I STEP IN AND TAKE THE HIT INSTEAD?"
"HMMM..."
"I AM A PALADIN.
"THIS ELF IS UNDER MY PROTECTION!"
"YEAH, THAT'S GREAT!
"THE STICKY LINE HITS MIKE THE MIGHTY SO NOW HE'S GETTING DRAGGED UP THE CLIFF WALL TOWARD THE CAVE FISHER'S GAPING MAW."
SORRY, MIKE!
DON'T WORRY ABOUT IT! THIS IS ALL PART OF THE GAME.
CAN I...CAN I USE MAGIC AGAIN?
YEAH! THE MONSTER DID ITS THING SO NOW IT'S YOUR TURN.
"THIS SPELL CALLED...'SHATTER?' CAN I BREAK THE ROCK?"
"I DON'T KNOW IF IT WORKS THAT WAY..."
"I'LL ALLOW IT.
"EL, YOU FEEL A BIG SURGE OF ENERGY BUILDING UP INSIDE YOU..."

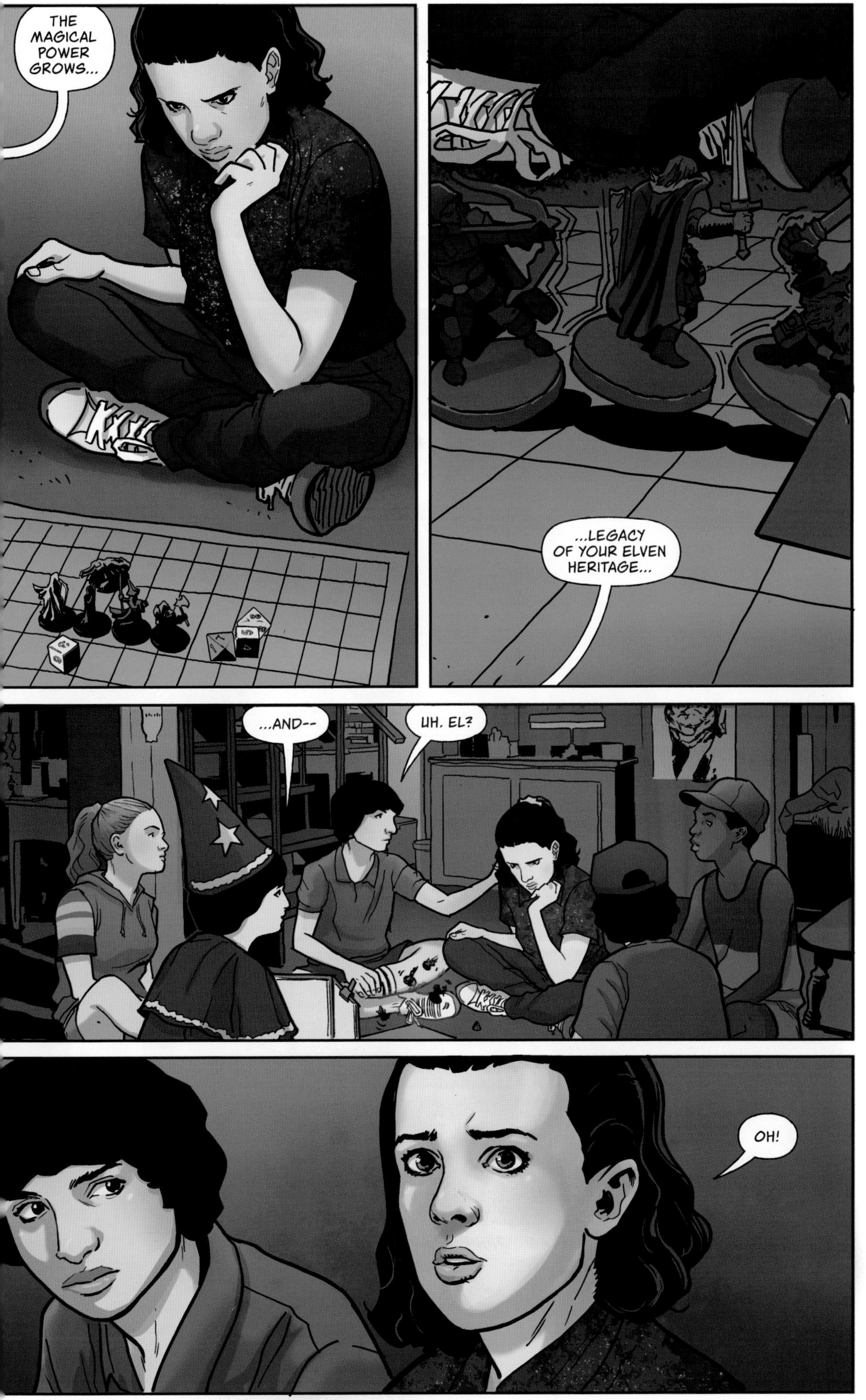
THE MAGICAL POWER GROWS...
...LEGACY OF YOUR ELVEN HERITAGE...
...AND--
UH. EL?
OH!

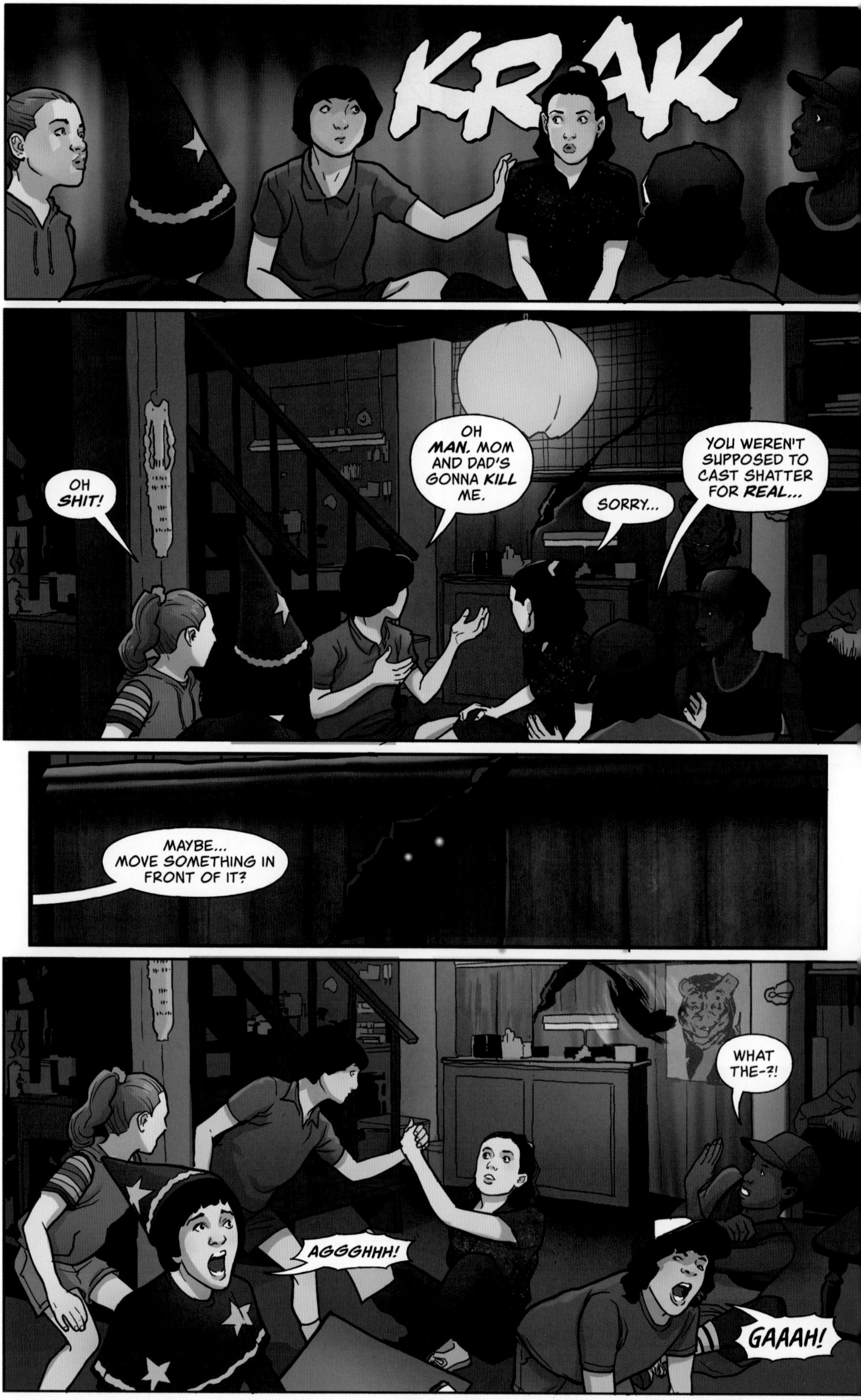
KRAK
OH SHIT!
OH MAN. MOM AND DAD'S GONNA KILL ME.
SORRY...
YOU WEREN'T SUPPOSED TO CAST SHATTER FOR REAL...
MAYBE... MOVE SOMETHING IN FRONT OF IT?
WHAT THE-?!
AGGGHHH!
GAAAH!

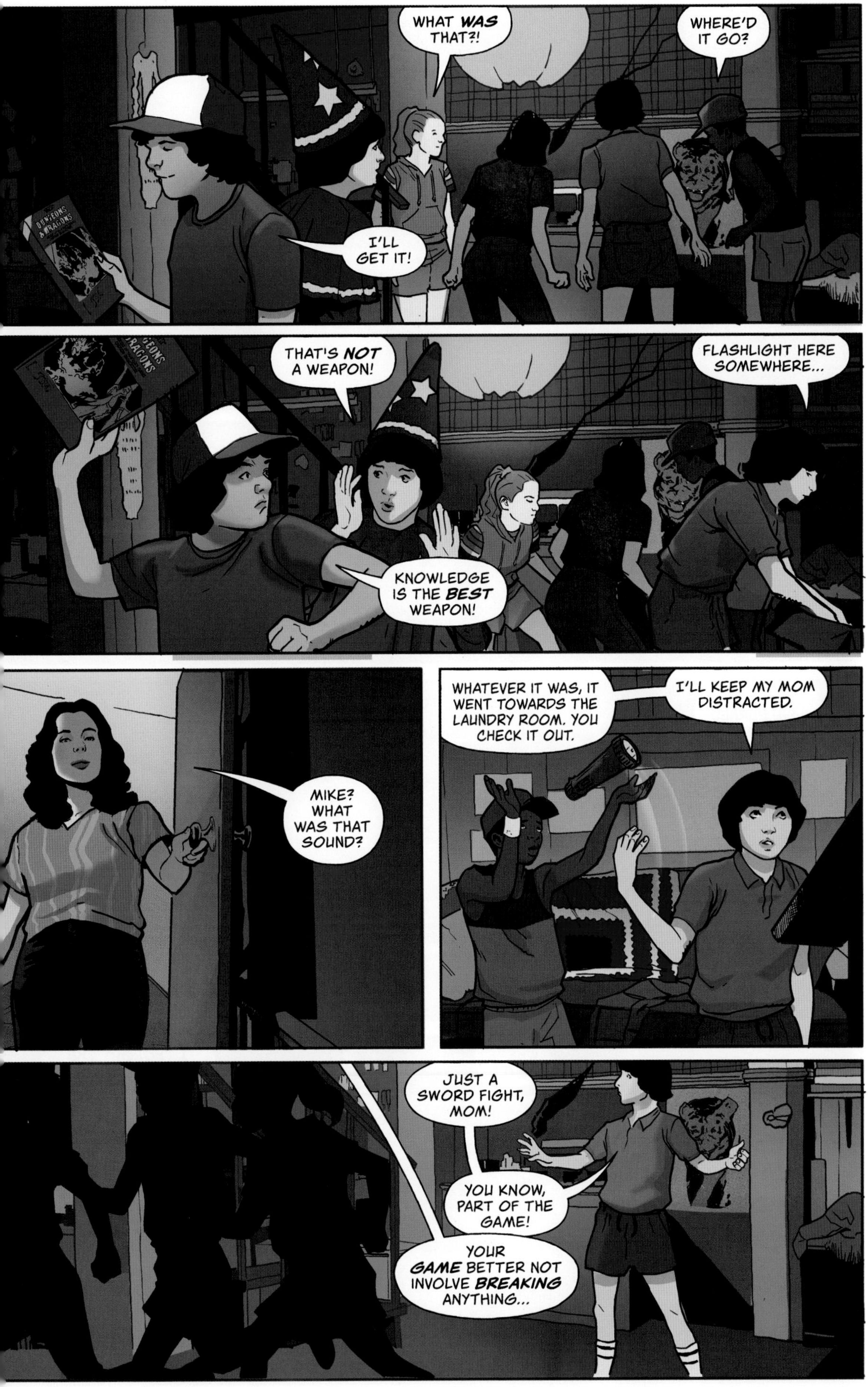

WHAT **WAS** THAT?!
WHERE'D IT GO?
I'LL GET IT!
THAT'S **NOT** A WEAPON!
FLASHLIGHT HERE SOMEWHERE...
KNOWLEDGE IS THE **BEST** WEAPON!
MIKE? WHAT WAS THAT SOUND?
WHATEVER IT WAS, IT WENT TOWARDS THE LAUNDRY ROOM. YOU CHECK IT OUT.
I'LL KEEP MY MOM DISTRACTED.
JUST A SWORD FIGHT, MOM!
YOU KNOW, PART OF THE GAME!
YOUR **GAME** BETTER NOT INVOLVE **BREAKING** ANYTHING...

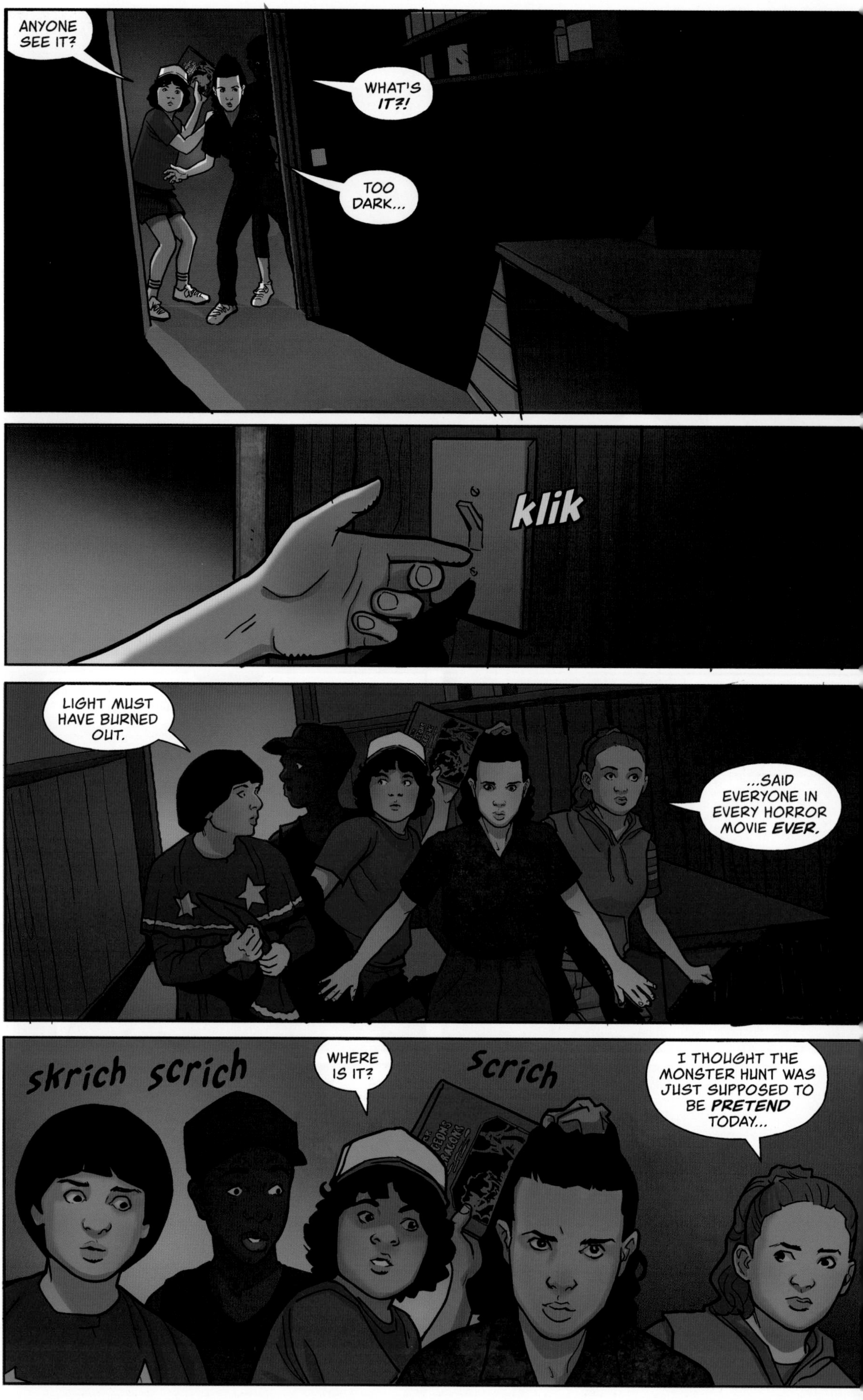

ANYONE SEE IT?
WHAT'S IT?!
TOO DARK...
klik
LIGHT MUST HAVE BURNED OUT.
...SAID EVERYONE IN EVERY HORROR MOVIE EVER.
skrich scrich
WHERE IS IT?
scrich
I THOUGHT THE MONSTER HUNT WAS JUST SUPPOSED TO BE PRETEND TODAY...

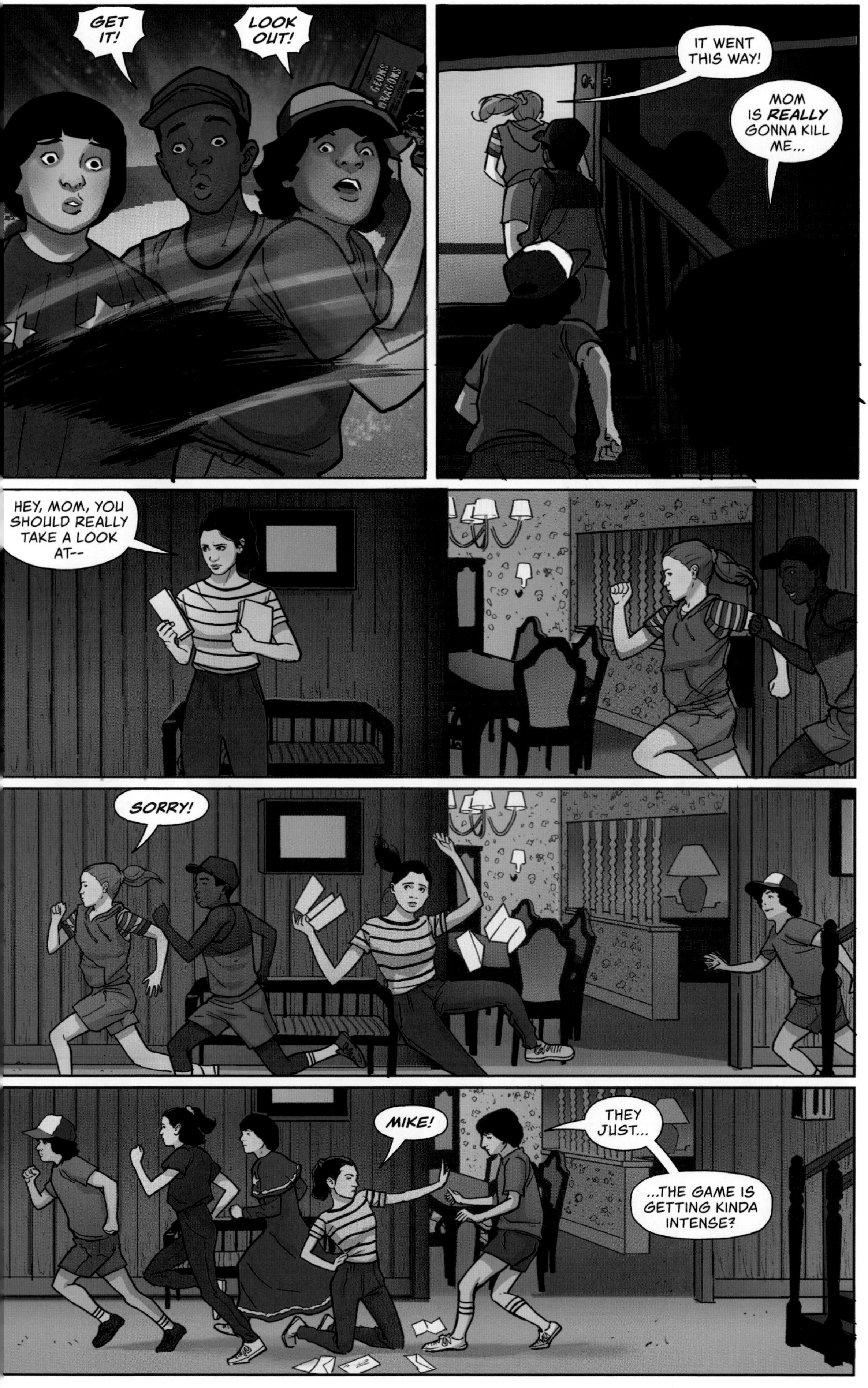
GET IT!
LOOK OUT!
IT WENT THIS WAY!
MOM IS **REALLY** GONNA KILL ME...
HEY, MOM, YOU SHOULD REALLY TAKE A LOOK AT--
SORRY!
MIKE!
THEY JUST...
...THE GAME IS GETTING KINDA INTENSE?

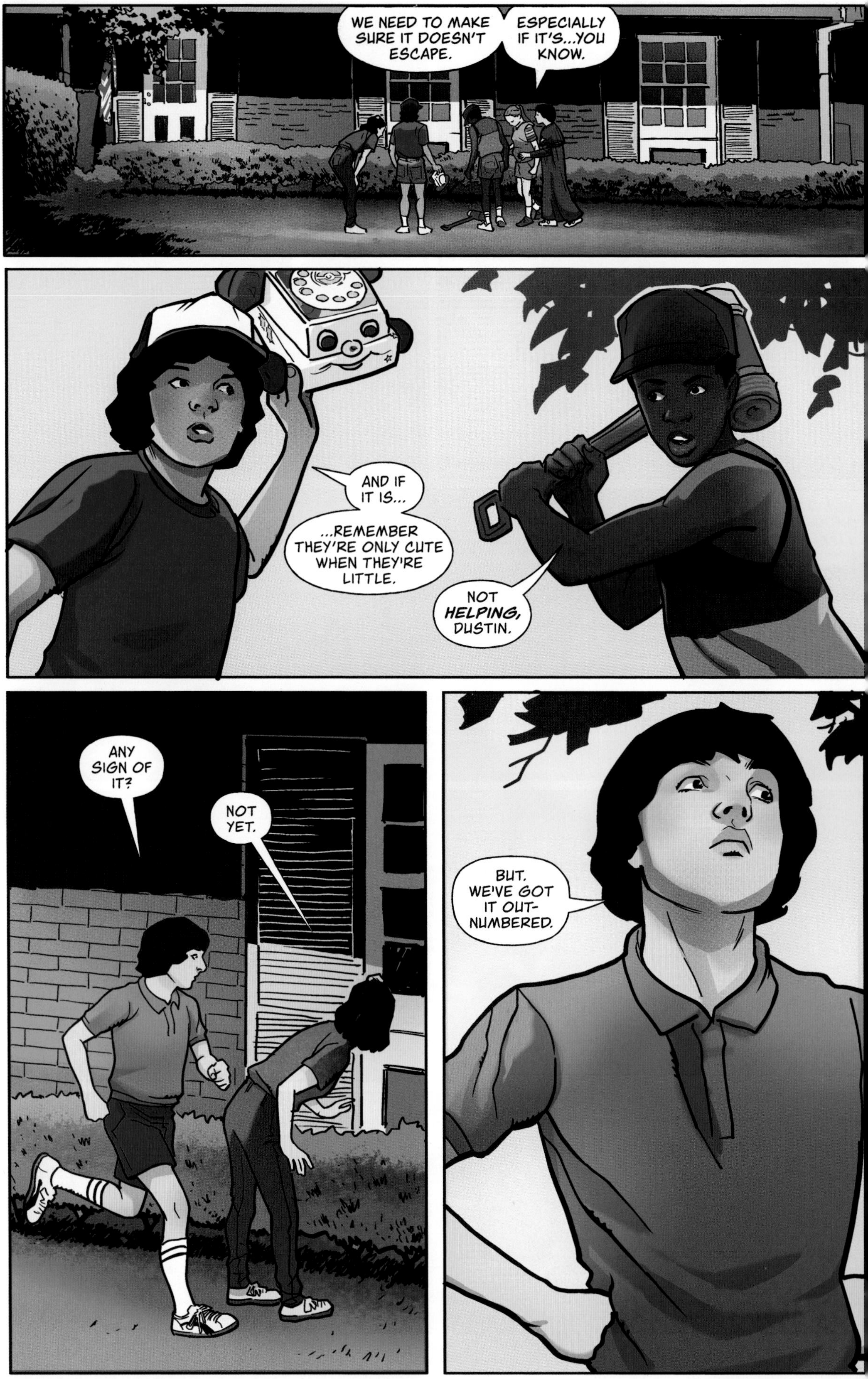
WE NEED TO MAKE SURE IT DOESN'T ESCAPE.
ESPECIALLY IF IT'S...YOU KNOW.
AND IF IT IS...
...REMEMBER THEY'RE ONLY CUTE WHEN THEY'RE LITTLE.
NOT HELPING, DUSTIN.
ANY SIGN OF IT?
NOT YET.
BUT. WE'VE GOT IT OUT-NUMBERED.

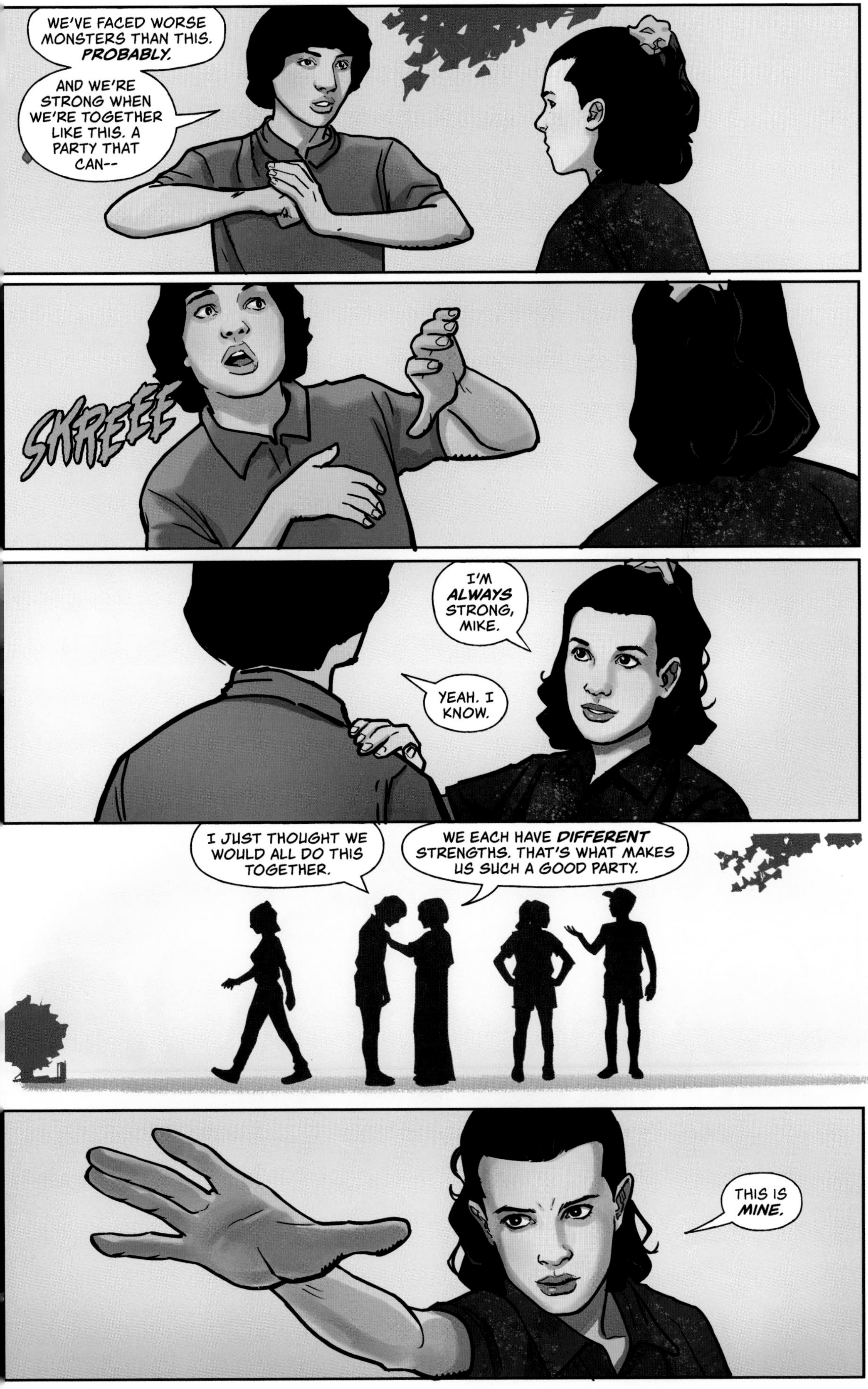
WE'VE FACED WORSE MONSTERS THAN THIS. PROBABLY.
AND WE'RE STRONG WHEN WE'RE TOGETHER LIKE THIS. A PARTY THAT CAN--
SKREEE
I'M ALWAYS STRONG, MIKE.
YEAH. I KNOW.
I JUST THOUGHT WE WOULD ALL DO THIS TOGETHER.
WE EACH HAVE DIFFERENT STRENGTHS. THAT'S WHAT MAKES US SUCH A GOOD PARTY.
THIS IS MINE.

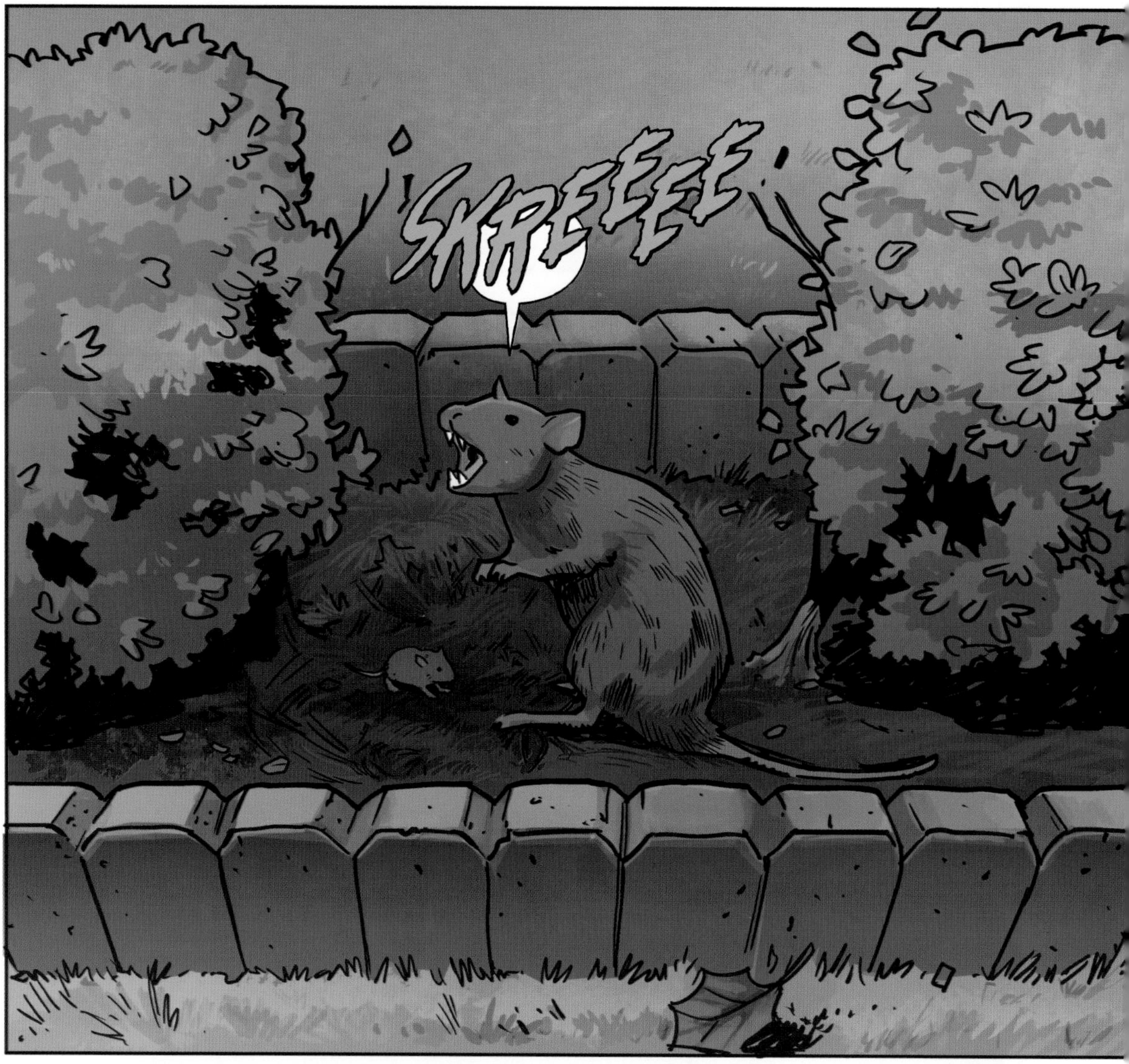
SKREEEE

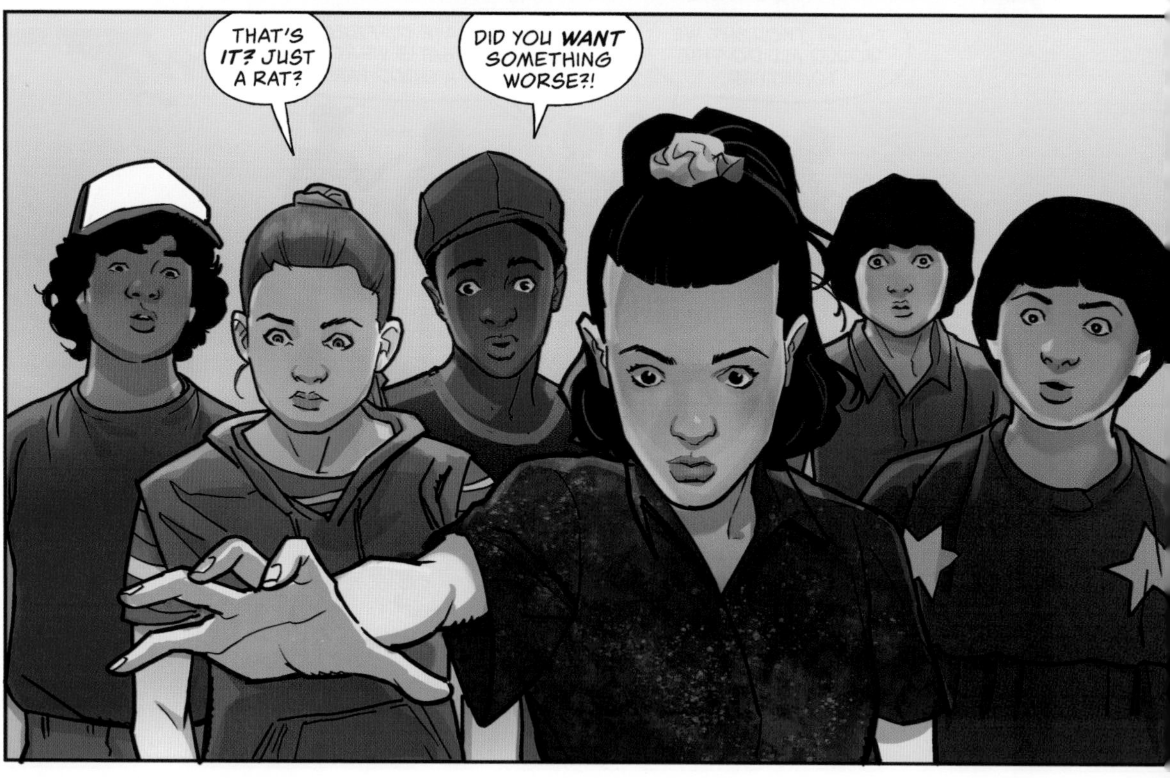
THAT'S IT? JUST A RAT?
DID YOU WANT SOMETHING WORSE?!

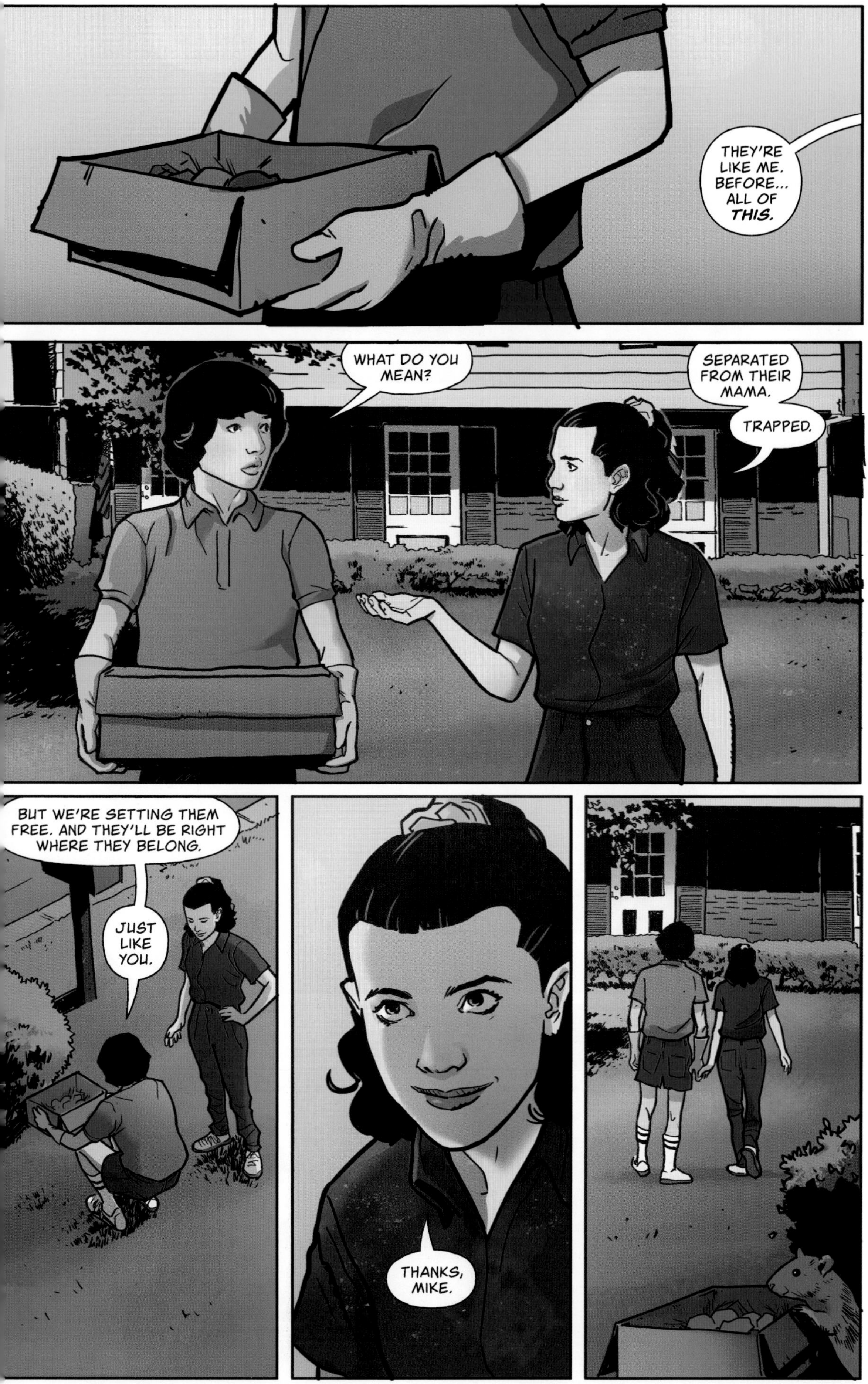
THEY'RE LIKE ME. BEFORE... ALL OF THIS.
WHAT DO YOU MEAN?
SEPARATED FROM THEIR MAMA.
TRAPPED.
BUT WE'RE SETTING THEM FREE. AND THEY'LL BE RIGHT WHERE THEY BELONG.
JUST LIKE YOU.
THANKS, MIKE.

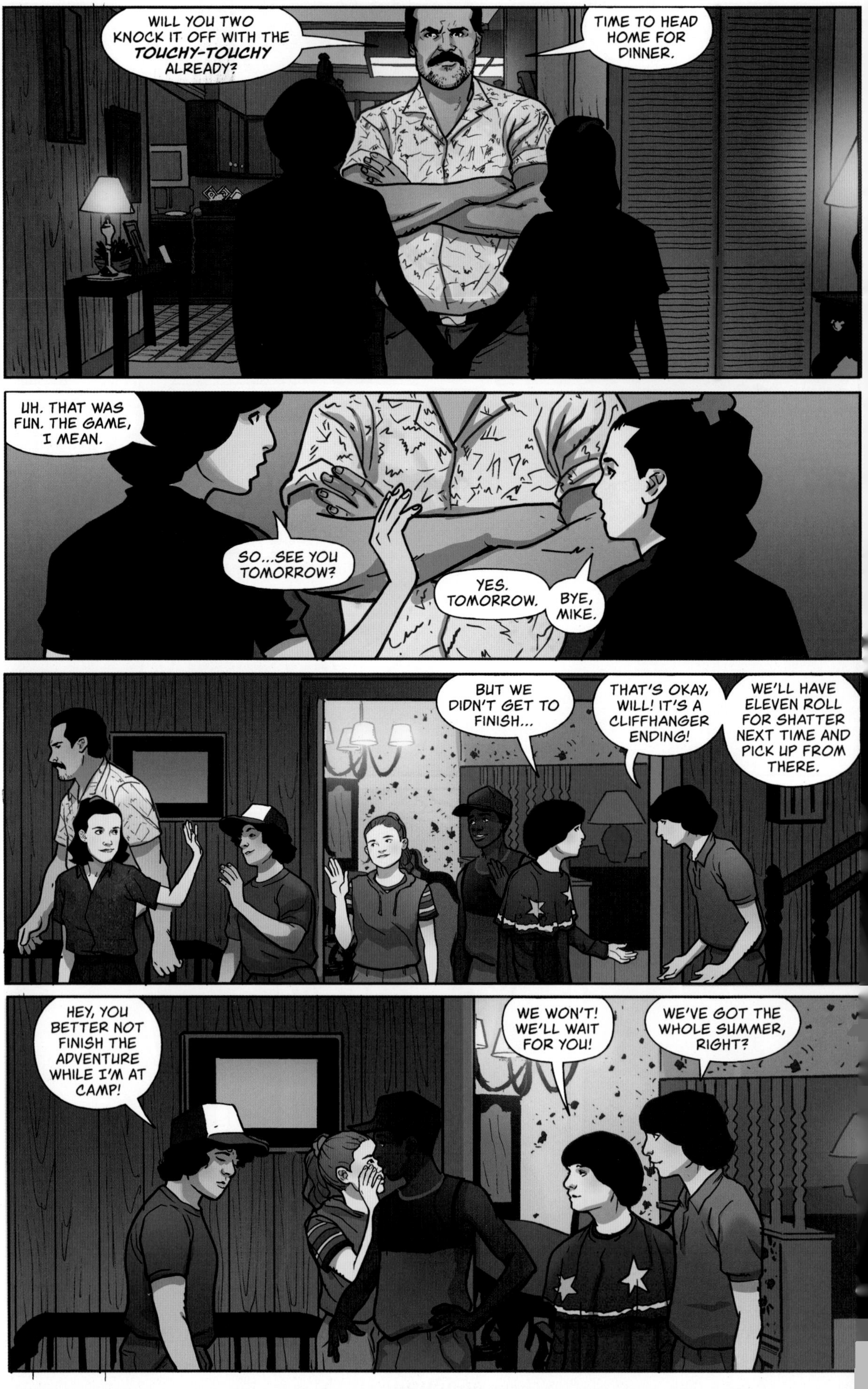
WILL YOU TWO KNOCK IT OFF WITH THE TOUCHY-TOUCHY ALREADY?
TIME TO HEAD HOME FOR DINNER.
UH. THAT WAS FUN. THE GAME, I MEAN.
SO...SEE YOU TOMORROW?
YES. TOMORROW.
BYE, MIKE.
BUT WE DIDN'T GET TO FINISH...
THAT'S OKAY, WILL! IT'S A CLIFFHANGER ENDING!
WE'LL HAVE ELEVEN ROLL FOR SHATTER NEXT TIME AND PICK UP FROM THERE.
HEY, YOU BETTER NOT FINISH THE ADVENTURE WHILE I'M AT CAMP!
WE WON'T! WE'LL WAIT FOR YOU!
WE'VE GOT THE WHOLE SUMMER, RIGHT?

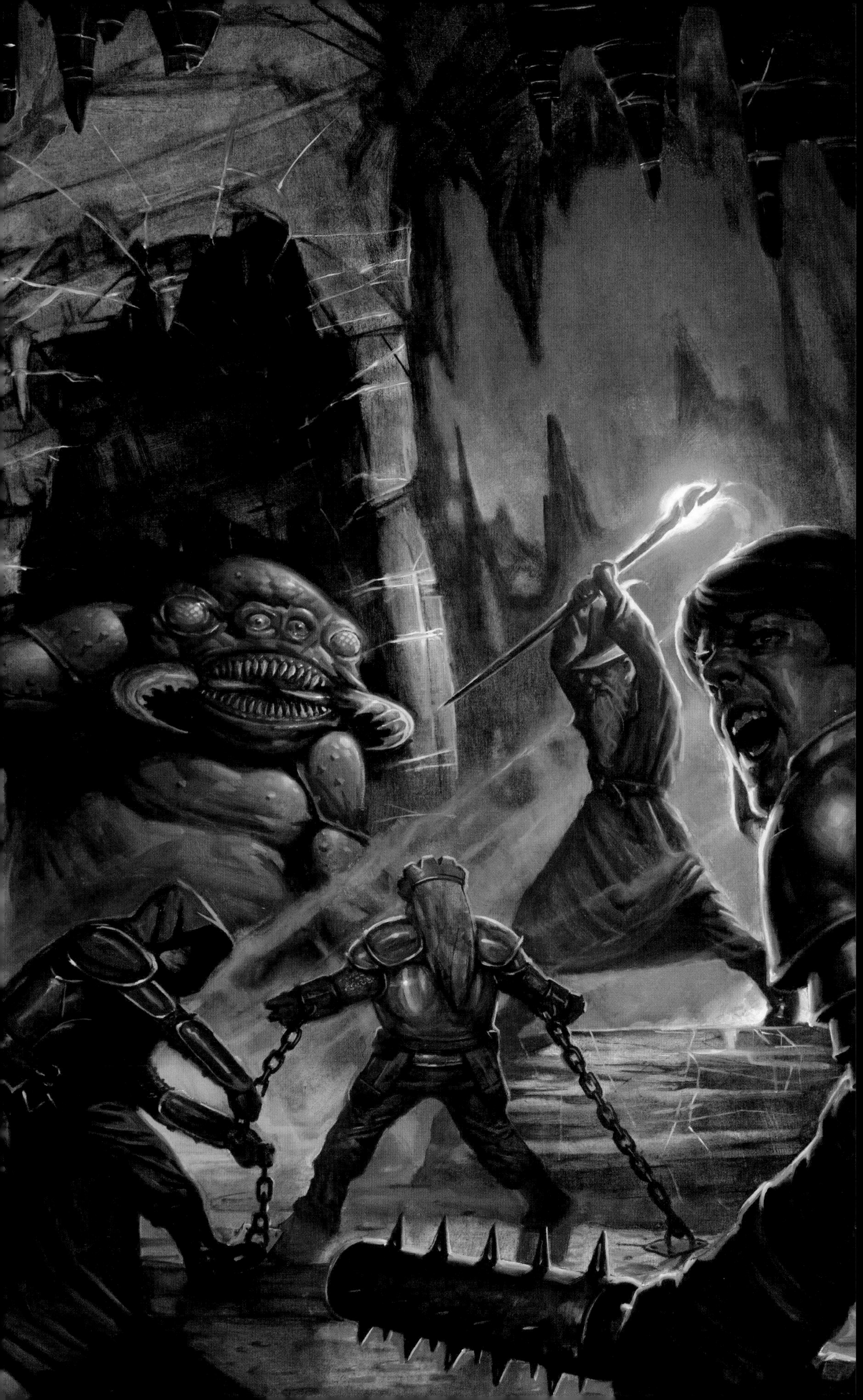

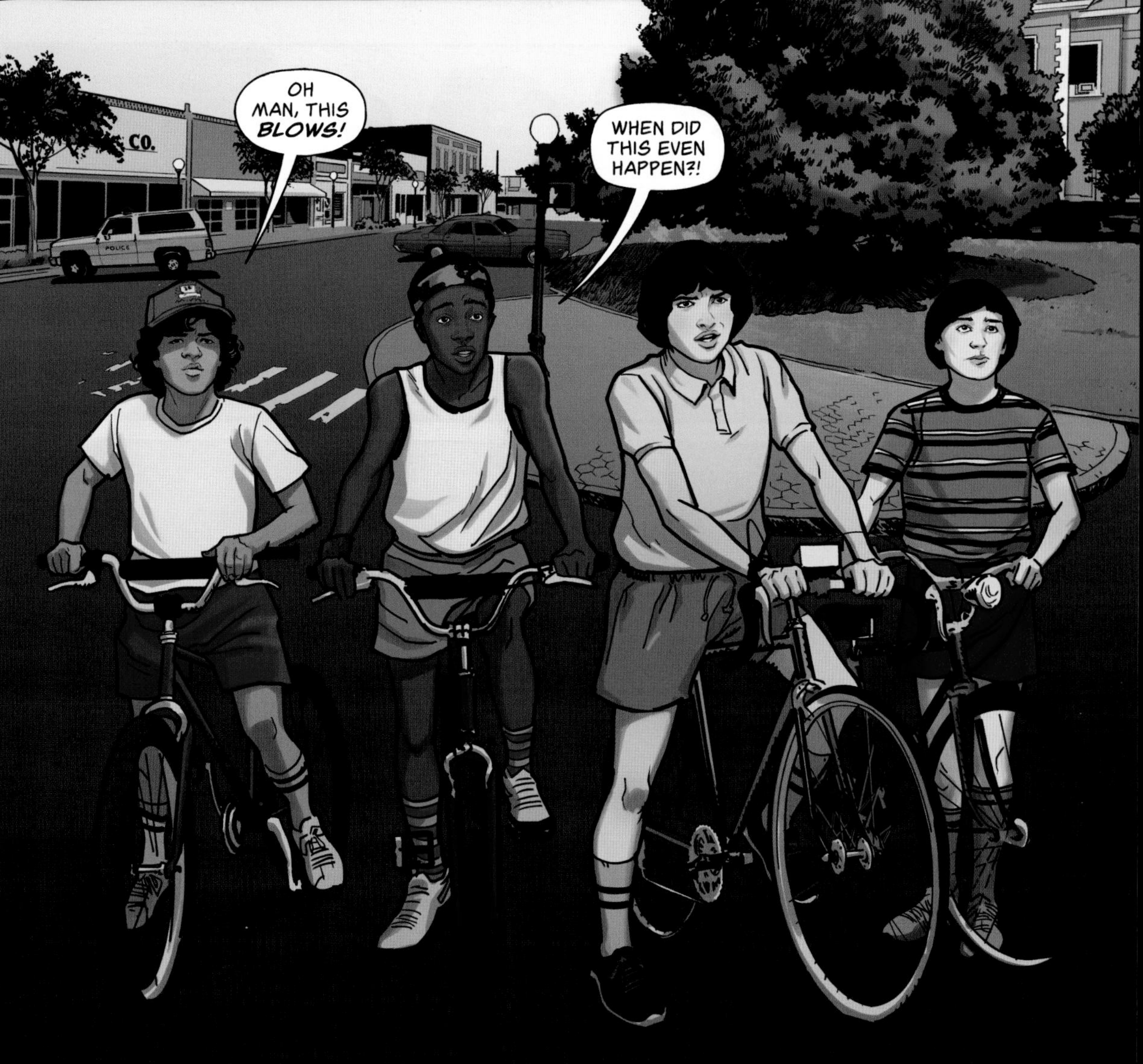
CO.
OH MAN, THIS BLOWS!
WHEN DID THIS EVEN HAPPEN?!
POLICE

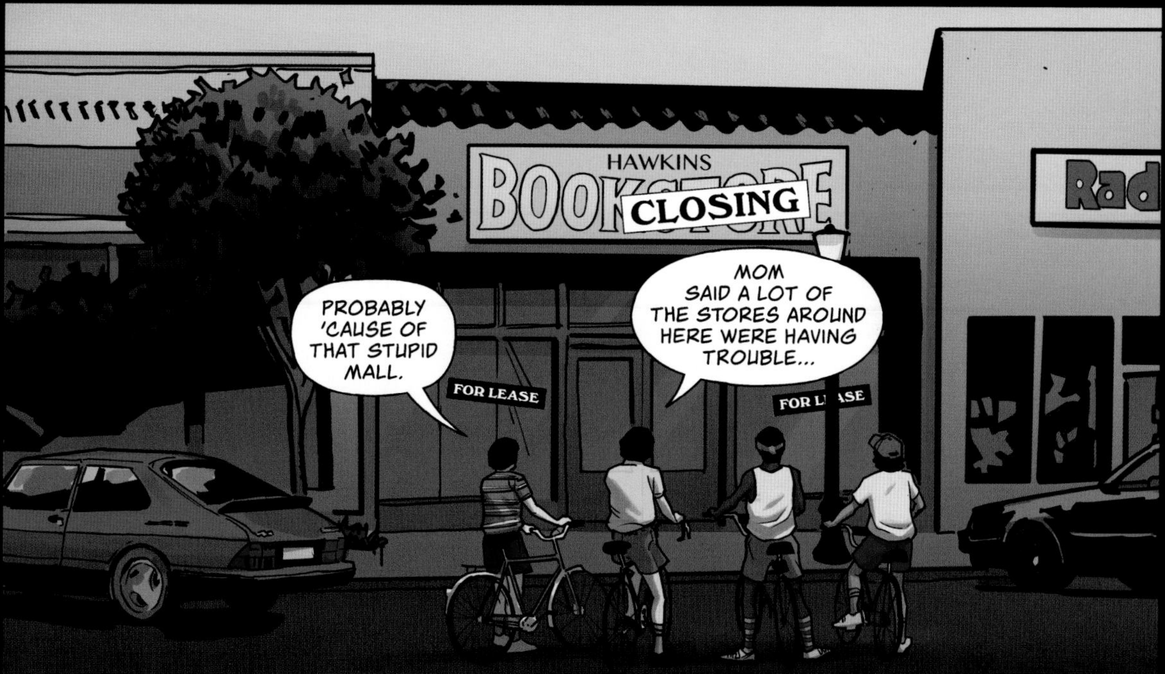
HAWKINS BOOKSTORE
CLOSING
Rad
PROBABLY 'CAUSE OF THAT STUPID MALL.
MOM SAID A LOT OF THE STORES AROUND HERE WERE HAVING TROUBLE...
FOR LEASE
FOR LEASE

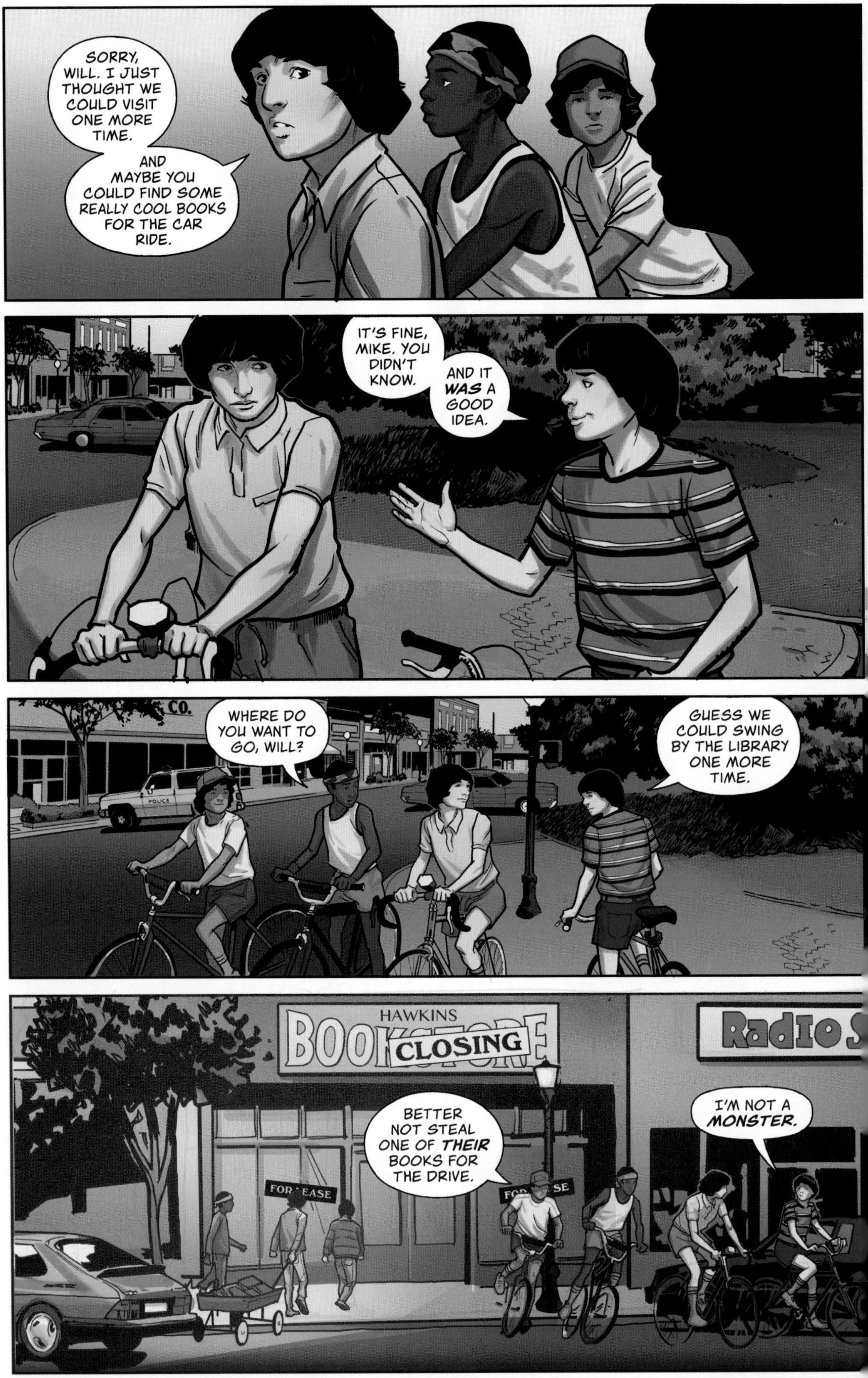
SORRY, WILL. I JUST THOUGHT WE COULD VISIT ONE MORE TIME.
AND MAYBE YOU COULD FIND SOME REALLY COOL BOOKS FOR THE CAR RIDE.
IT'S FINE, MIKE. YOU DIDN'T KNOW.
AND IT WAS A GOOD IDEA.
CO.
WHERE DO YOU WANT TO GO, WILL?
POLICE
GUESS WE COULD SWING BY THE LIBRARY ONE MORE TIME.
HAWKINS
CLOSING
BETTER NOT STEAL ONE OF THEIR BOOKS FOR THE DRIVE.
I'M NOT A MONSTER.

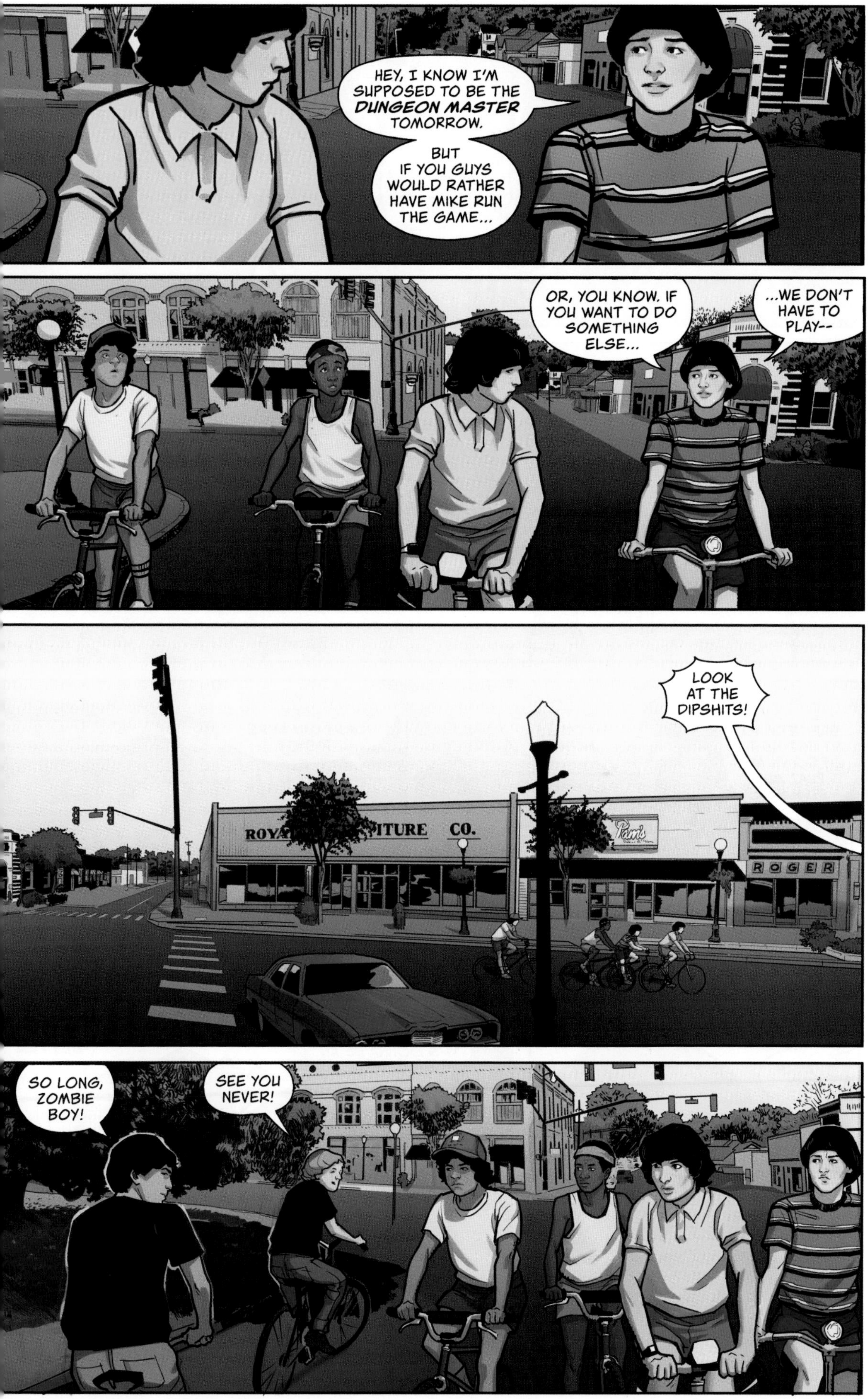
HEY, I KNOW I'M SUPPOSED TO BE THE *DUNGEON MASTER* TOMORROW.
BUT IF YOU GUYS WOULD RATHER HAVE MIKE RUN THE GAME...
OR, YOU KNOW. IF YOU WANT TO DO SOMETHING ELSE...
...WE DON'T HAVE TO PLAY--
LOOK AT THE DIPSHITS!
ROYA ... ITURE CO.
Pam's
ROGER
SO LONG, ZOMBIE BOY!
SEE YOU NEVER!

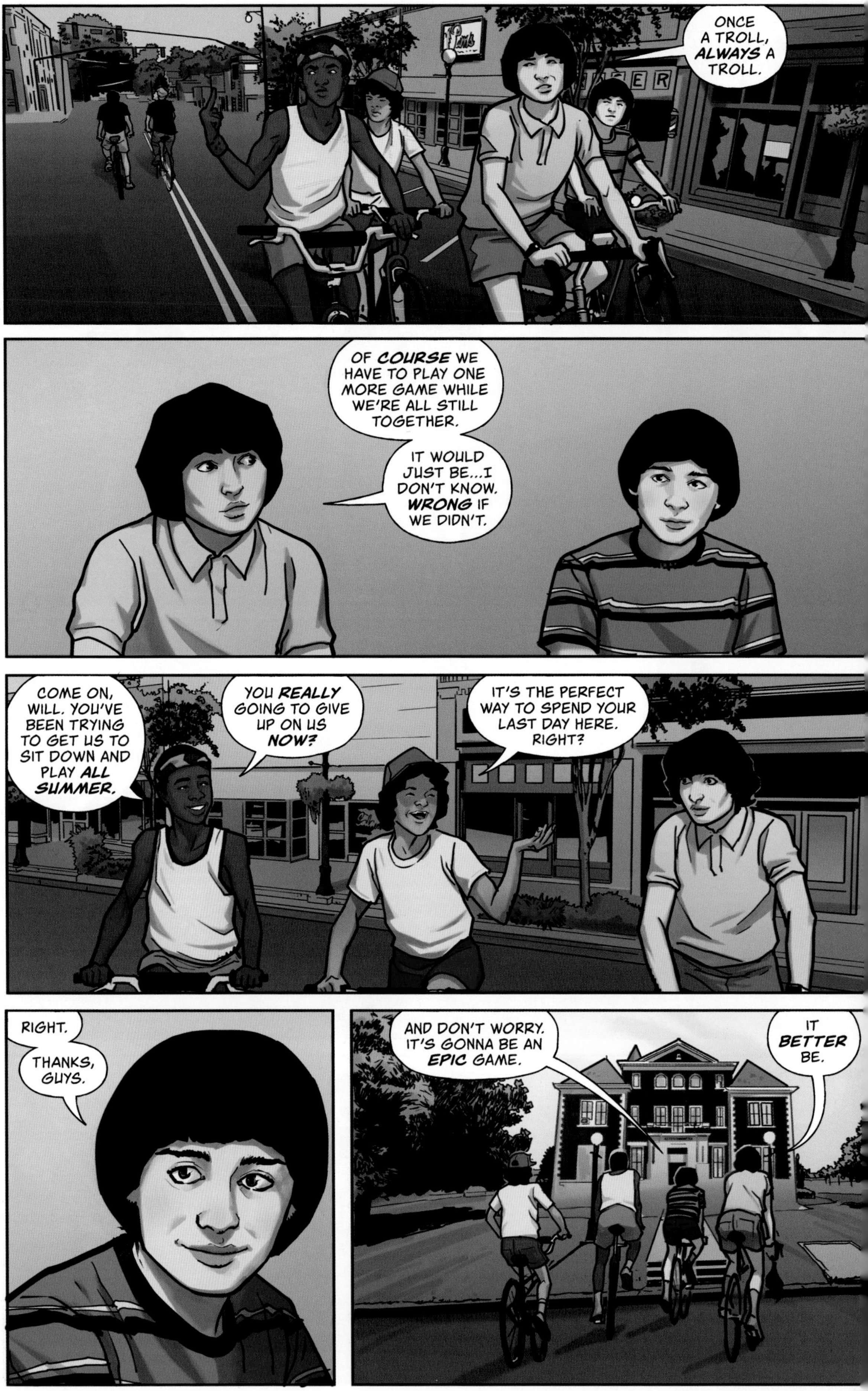
ONCE A TROLL, ALWAYS A TROLL.
OF COURSE WE HAVE TO PLAY ONE MORE GAME WHILE WE'RE ALL STILL TOGETHER.
IT WOULD JUST BE...I DON'T KNOW. WRONG IF WE DIDN'T.
COME ON, WILL. YOU'VE BEEN TRYING TO GET US TO SIT DOWN AND PLAY ALL SUMMER.
YOU REALLY GOING TO GIVE UP ON US NOW?
IT'S THE PERFECT WAY TO SPEND YOUR LAST DAY HERE. RIGHT?
RIGHT.
THANKS, GUYS.
AND DON'T WORRY. IT'S GONNA BE AN EPIC GAME.
IT BETTER BE.

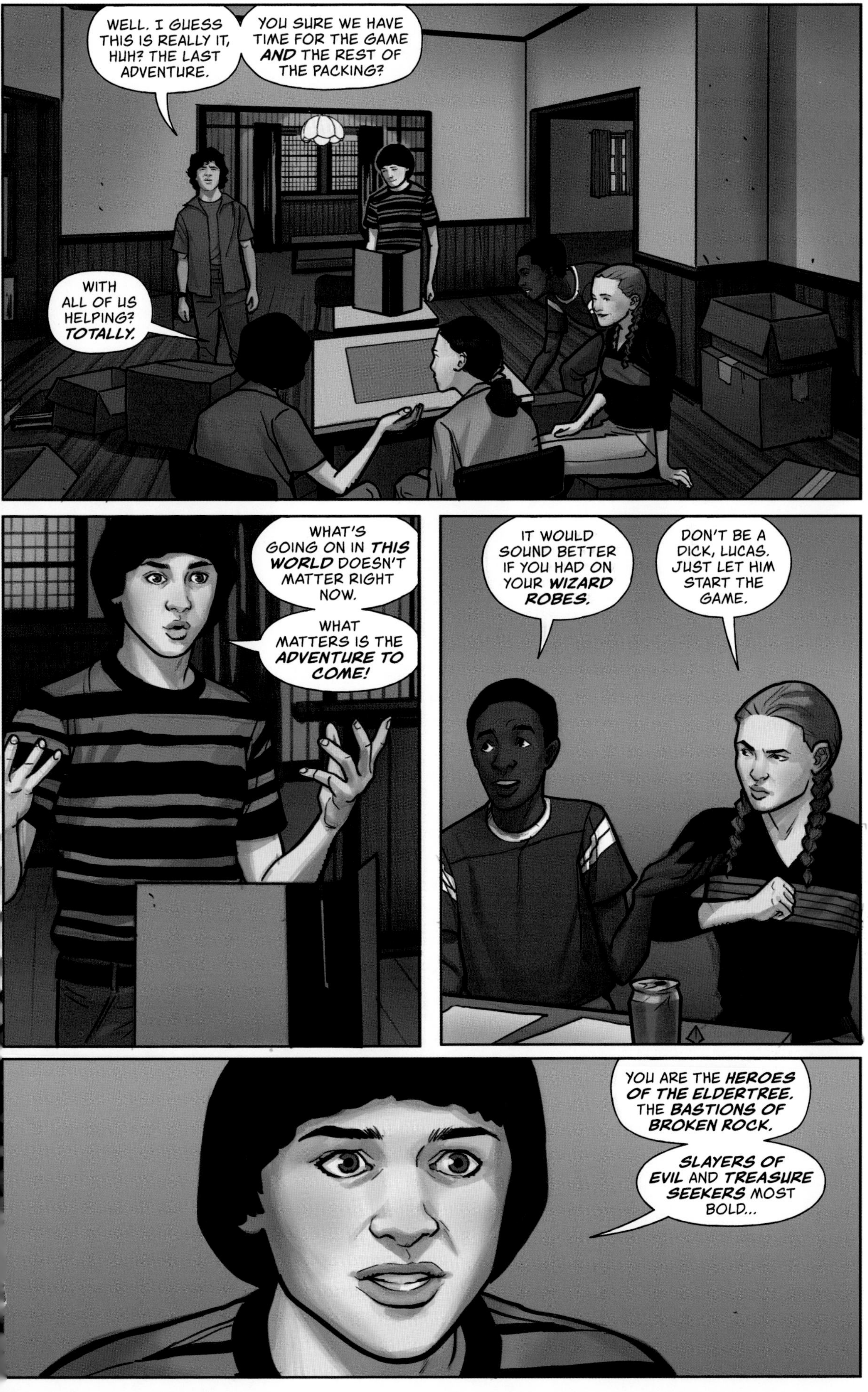
WELL. I GUESS THIS IS REALLY IT, HUH? THE LAST ADVENTURE.
YOU SURE WE HAVE TIME FOR THE GAME **AND** THE REST OF THE PACKING?
WITH ALL OF US HELPING? ***TOTALLY.***
WHAT'S GOING ON IN **THIS WORLD** DOESN'T MATTER RIGHT NOW.
WHAT MATTERS IS THE ***ADVENTURE TO COME!***
IT WOULD SOUND BETTER IF YOU HAD ON YOUR ***WIZARD ROBES.***
DON'T BE A DICK, LUCAS. JUST LET HIM START THE GAME.
YOU ARE THE ***HEROES OF THE ELDERTREE.*** THE ***BASTIONS OF BROKEN ROCK.***
SLAYERS OF EVIL AND ***TREASURE SEEKERS*** MOST BOLD...

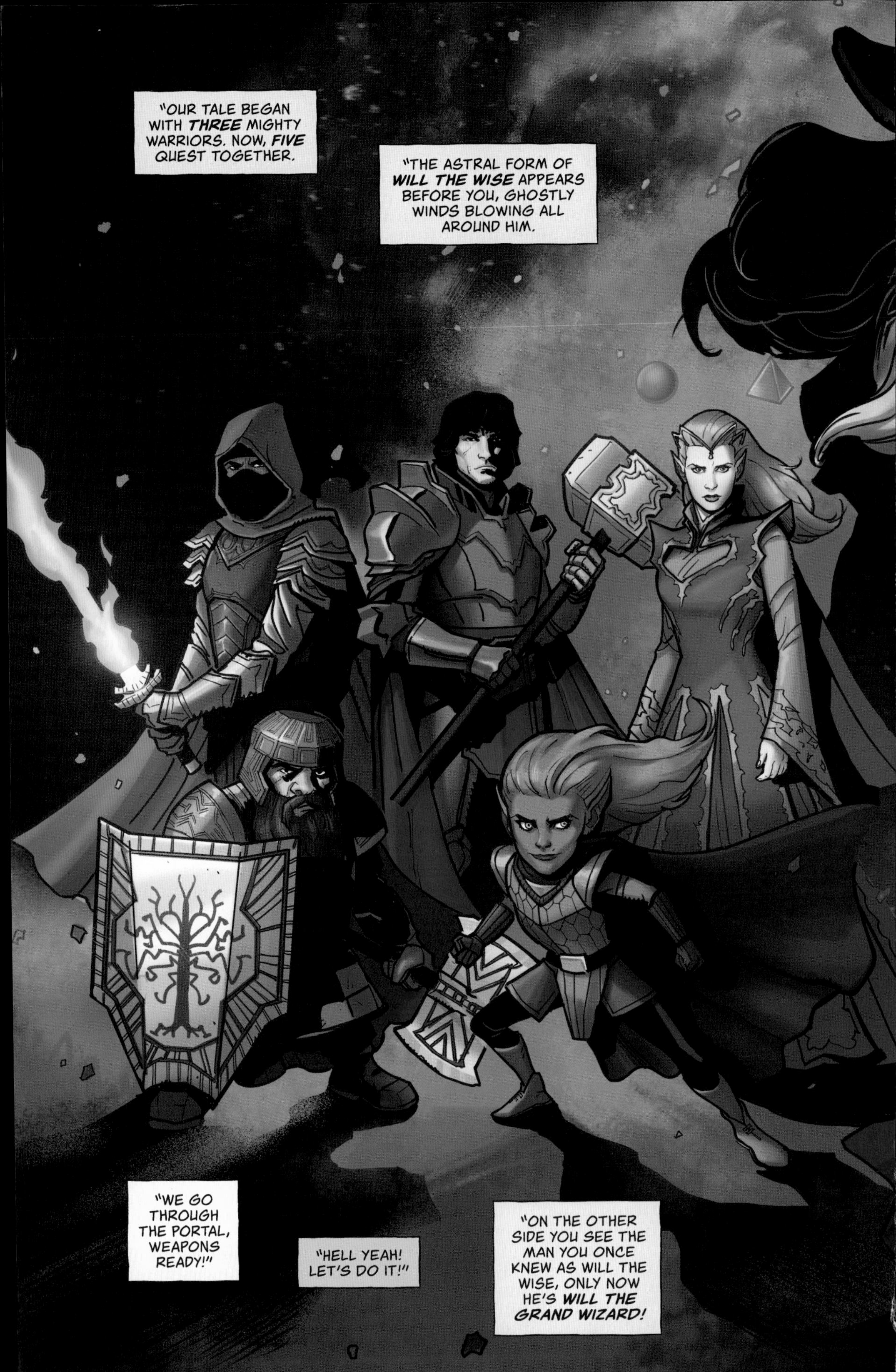
"OUR TALE BEGAN WITH ***THREE*** MIGHTY WARRIORS. NOW, ***FIVE*** QUEST TOGETHER.
"THE ASTRAL FORM OF ***WILL THE WISE*** APPEARS BEFORE YOU, GHOSTLY WINDS BLOWING ALL AROUND HIM.
"WE GO THROUGH THE PORTAL, WEAPONS READY!"
"HELL YEAH! LET'S DO IT!"
"ON THE OTHER SIDE YOU SEE THE MAN YOU ONCE KNEW AS WILL THE WISE, ONLY NOW HE'S ***WILL THE GRAND WIZARD!***

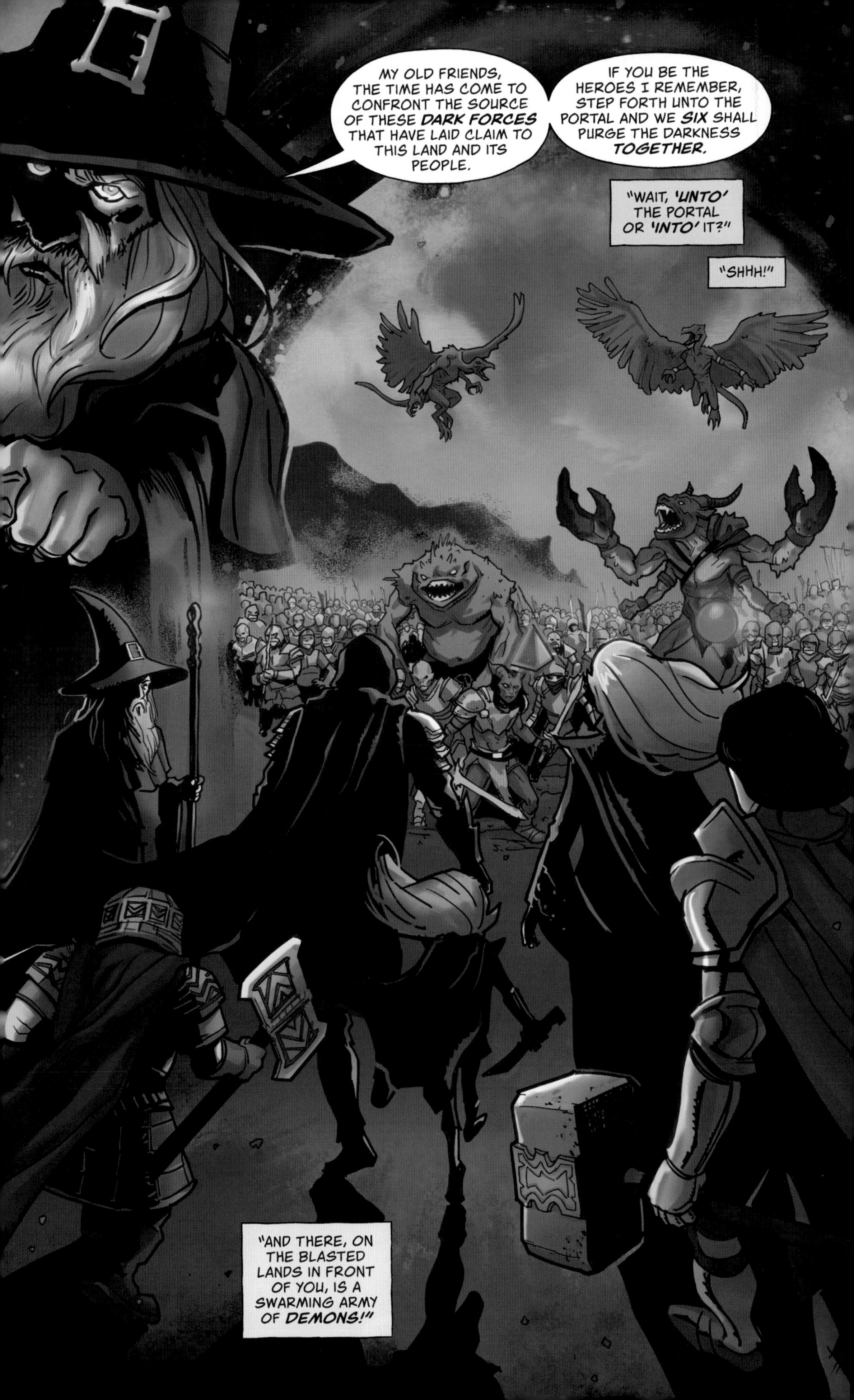
MY OLD FRIENDS, THE TIME HAS COME TO CONFRONT THE SOURCE OF THESE **DARK FORCES** THAT HAVE LAID CLAIM TO THIS LAND AND ITS PEOPLE.
IF YOU BE THE HEROES I REMEMBER, STEP FORTH UNTO THE PORTAL AND WE **SIX** SHALL PURGE THE DARKNESS **TOGETHER.**
"WAIT, **'UNTO'** THE PORTAL OR **'INTO'** IT?"
"SHHH!"
"AND THERE, ON THE BLASTED LANDS IN FRONT OF YOU, IS A SWARMING ARMY OF **DEMONS!**"

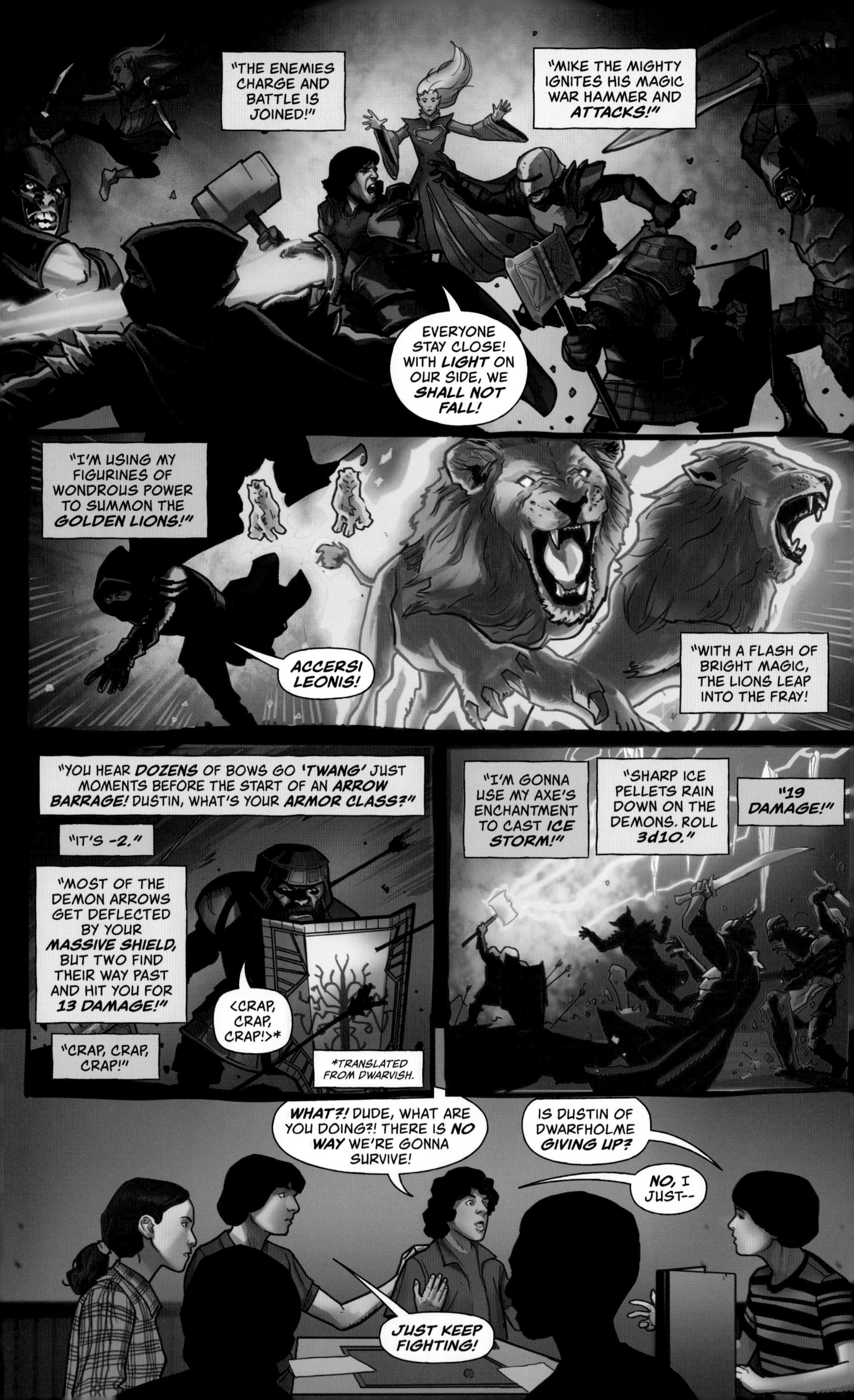

"THE ENEMIES CHARGE AND BATTLE IS JOINED!"
"MIKE THE MIGHTY IGNITES HIS MAGIC WAR HAMMER AND ATTACKS!"
EVERYONE STAY CLOSE! WITH LIGHT ON OUR SIDE, WE SHALL NOT FALL!
"I'M USING MY FIGURINES OF WONDROUS POWER TO SUMMON THE GOLDEN LIONS!"
ACCERSI LEONIS!
"WITH A FLASH OF BRIGHT MAGIC, THE LIONS LEAP INTO THE FRAY!
"YOU HEAR DOZENS OF BOWS GO 'TWANG' JUST MOMENTS BEFORE THE START OF AN ARROW BARRAGE! DUSTIN, WHAT'S YOUR ARMOR CLASS?"
"IT'S -2."
"MOST OF THE DEMON ARROWS GET DEFLECTED BY YOUR MASSIVE SHIELD, BUT TWO FIND THEIR WAY PAST AND HIT YOU FOR 13 DAMAGE!"
<CRAP, CRAP, CRAP!>*
"CRAP, CRAP, CRAP!"
*TRANSLATED FROM DWARVISH.
"I'M GONNA USE MY AXE'S ENCHANTMENT TO CAST ICE STORM!"
"SHARP ICE PELLETS RAIN DOWN ON THE DEMONS. ROLL 3d10."
"19 DAMAGE!"
WHAT?! DUDE, WHAT ARE YOU DOING?! THERE IS NO WAY WE'RE GONNA SURVIVE!
IS DUSTIN OF DWARFHOLME GIVING UP?
NO, I JUST--
JUST KEEP FIGHTING!

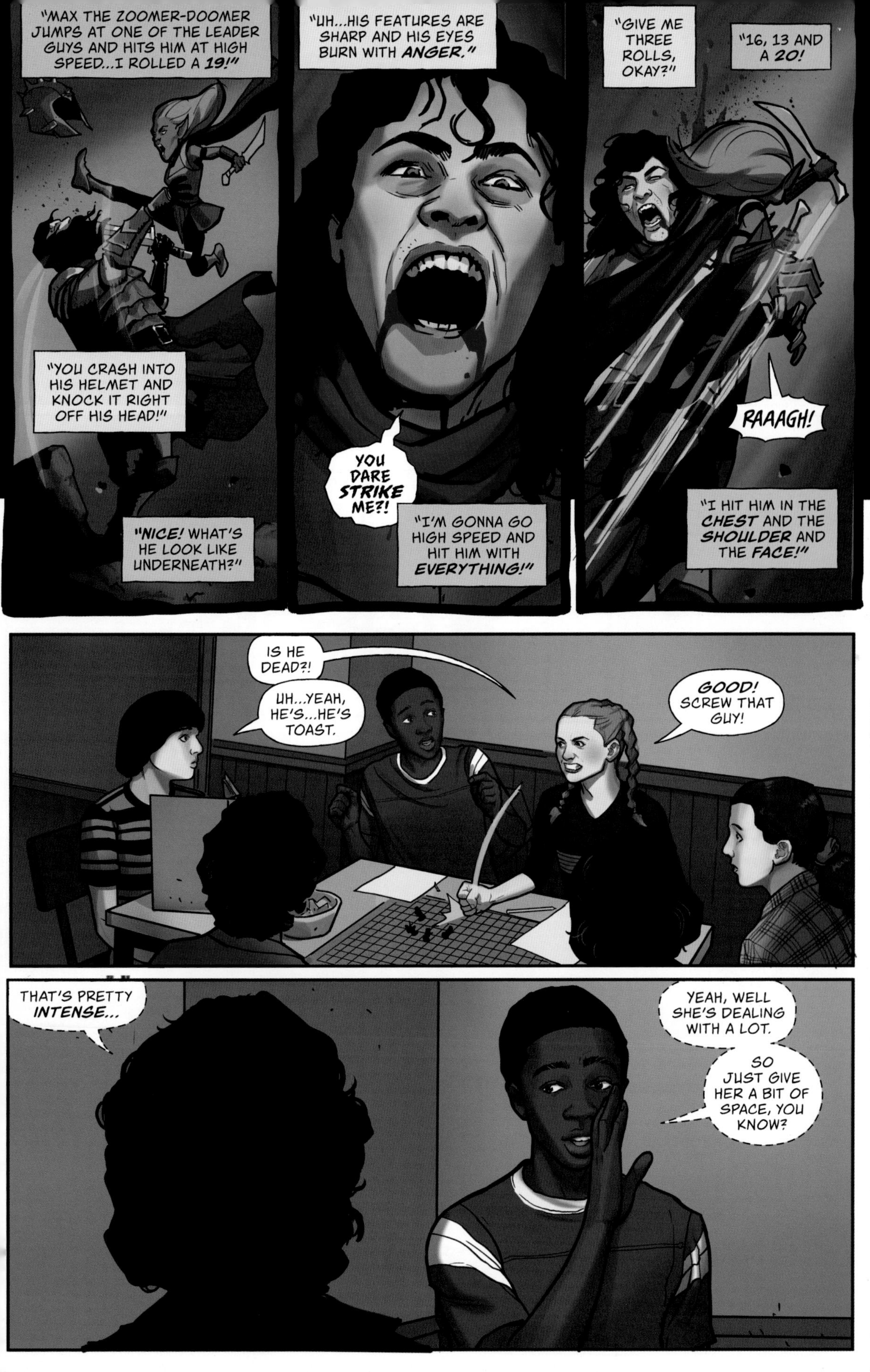
"MAX THE ZOOMER-DOOMER JUMPS AT ONE OF THE LEADER GUYS AND HITS HIM AT HIGH SPEED...I ROLLED A 19!"
"YOU CRASH INTO HIS HELMET AND KNOCK IT RIGHT OFF HIS HEAD!"
"NICE! WHAT'S HE LOOK LIKE UNDERNEATH?"
"UH...HIS FEATURES ARE SHARP AND HIS EYES BURN WITH ANGER."
YOU DARE STRIKE ME?!
"I'M GONNA GO HIGH SPEED AND HIT HIM WITH EVERYTHING!"
"GIVE ME THREE ROLLS, OKAY?"
"16, 13 AND A 20!
RAAAGH!
"I HIT HIM IN THE CHEST AND THE SHOULDER AND THE FACE!"
IS HE DEAD?!
UH...YEAH, HE'S...HE'S TOAST.
GOOD! SCREW THAT GUY!
THAT'S PRETTY INTENSE...
YEAH, WELL SHE'S DEALING WITH A LOT.
SO JUST GIVE HER A BIT OF SPACE, YOU KNOW?

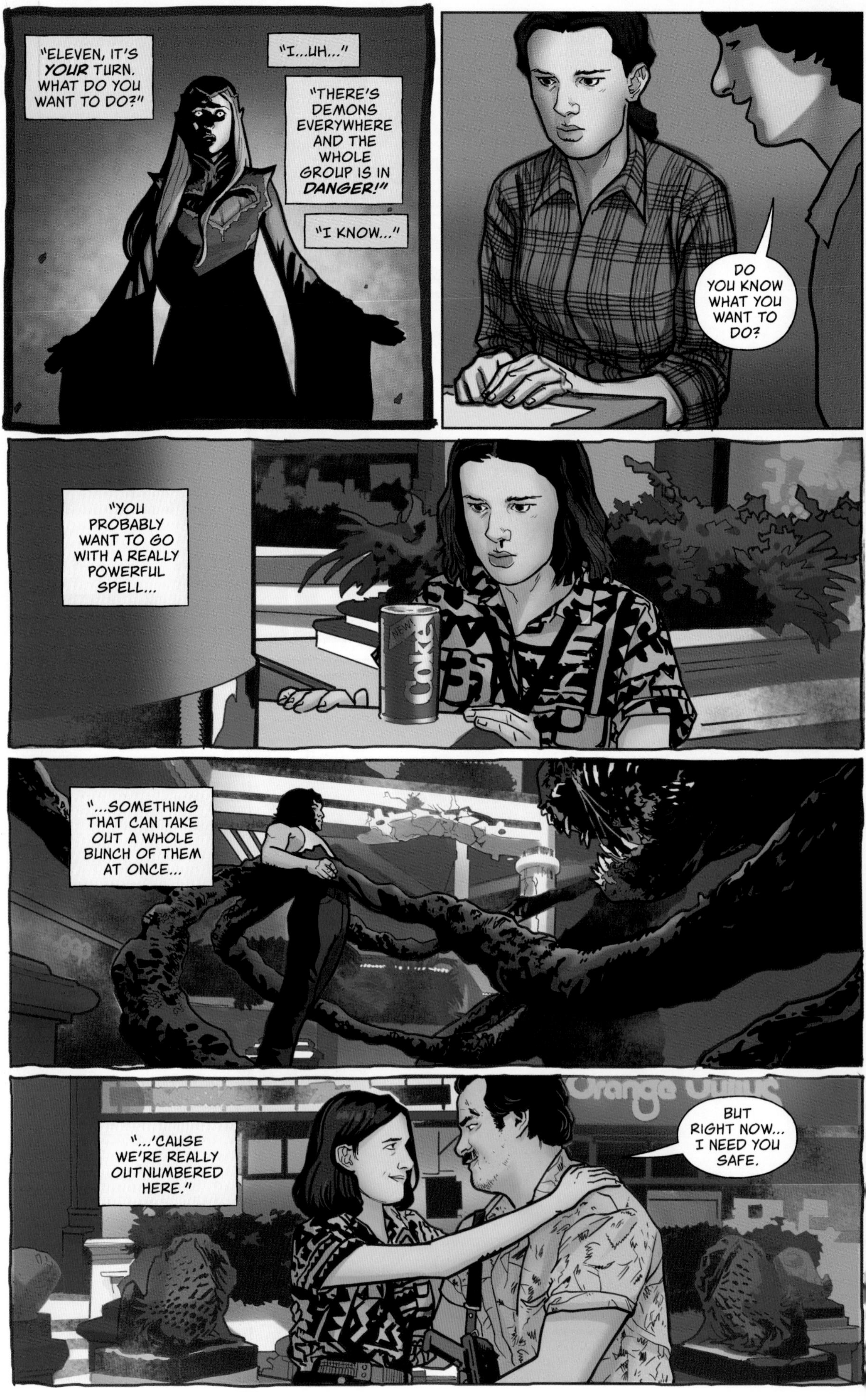
"ELEVEN, IT'S *YOUR* TURN. WHAT DO YOU WANT TO DO?"
"I...UH..."
"THERE'S DEMONS EVERYWHERE AND THE WHOLE GROUP IS IN *DANGER!*"
"I KNOW..."
DO YOU KNOW WHAT YOU WANT TO DO?
"YOU PROBABLY WANT TO GO WITH A REALLY POWERFUL SPELL...
NEW! Coke
"...SOMETHING THAT CAN TAKE OUT A WHOLE BUNCH OF THEM AT ONCE...
"...'CAUSE WE'RE REALLY OUTNUMBERED HERE."
BUT RIGHT NOW... I NEED YOU SAFE.

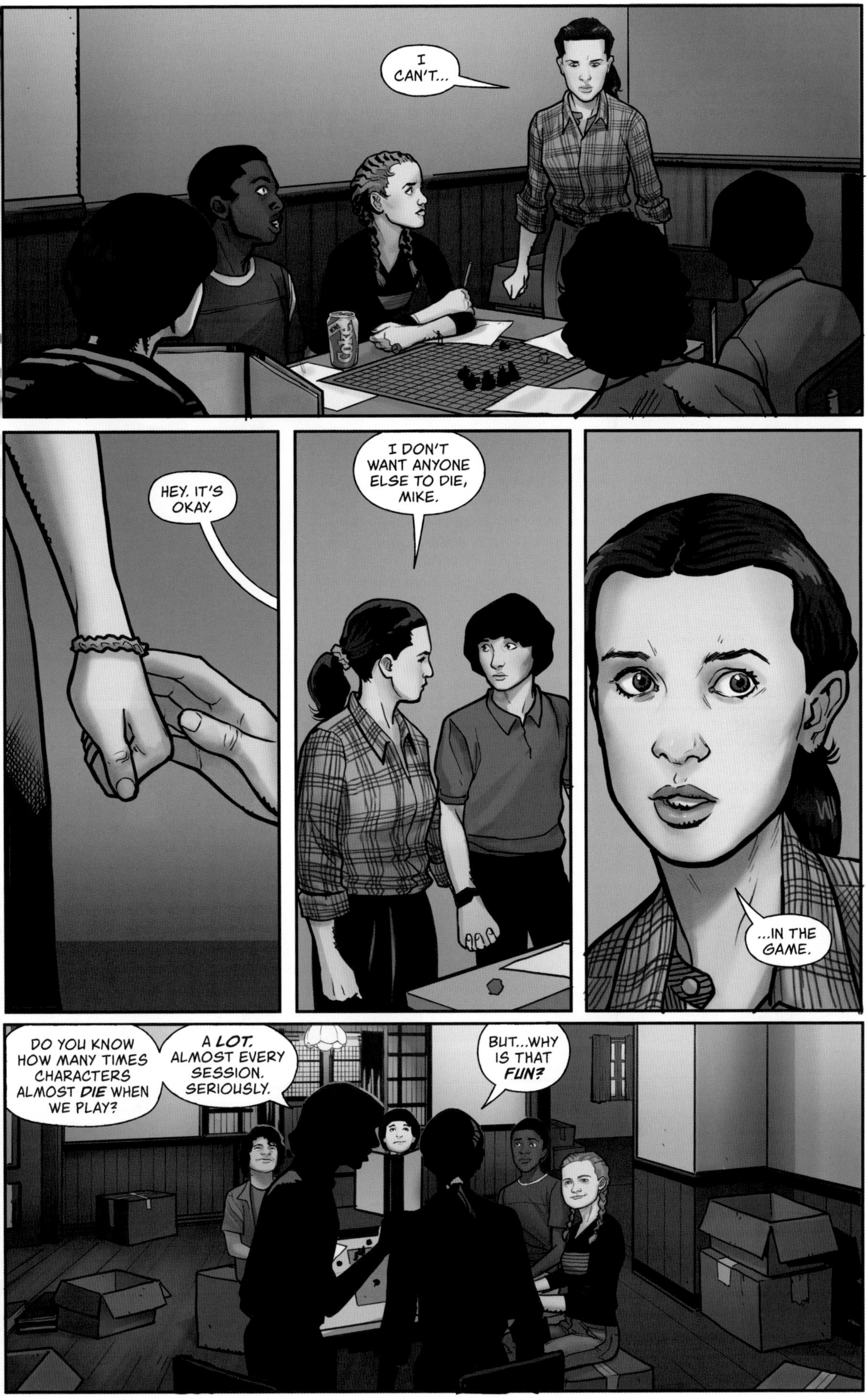
I CAN'T...
HEY. IT'S OKAY.
I DON'T WANT ANYONE ELSE TO DIE, MIKE.
...IN THE GAME.
DO YOU KNOW HOW MANY TIMES CHARACTERS ALMOST DIE WHEN WE PLAY?
A LOT. ALMOST EVERY SESSION. SERIOUSLY.
BUT...WHY IS THAT FUN?

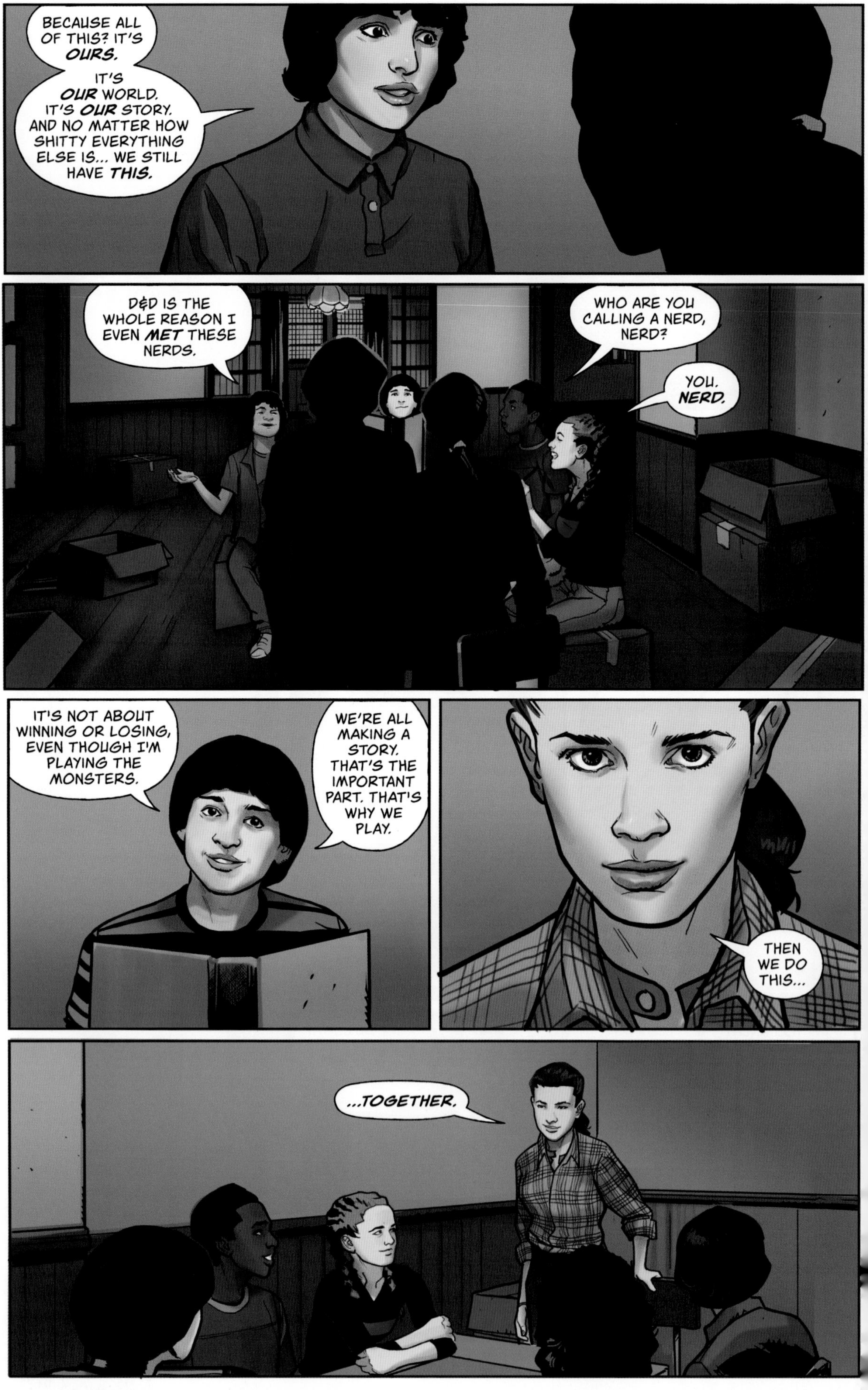
BECAUSE ALL OF THIS? IT'S *OURS.*
IT'S *OUR* WORLD. IT'S *OUR* STORY. AND NO MATTER HOW SHITTY EVERYTHING ELSE IS... WE STILL HAVE *THIS.*
D&D IS THE WHOLE REASON I EVEN *MET* THESE NERDS.
WHO ARE YOU CALLING A NERD, NERD?
YOU. *NERD.*
IT'S NOT ABOUT WINNING OR LOSING, EVEN THOUGH I'M PLAYING THE MONSTERS.
WE'RE ALL MAKING A STORY. THAT'S THE IMPORTANT PART. THAT'S WHY WE PLAY.
THEN WE DO THIS...
...TOGETHER.

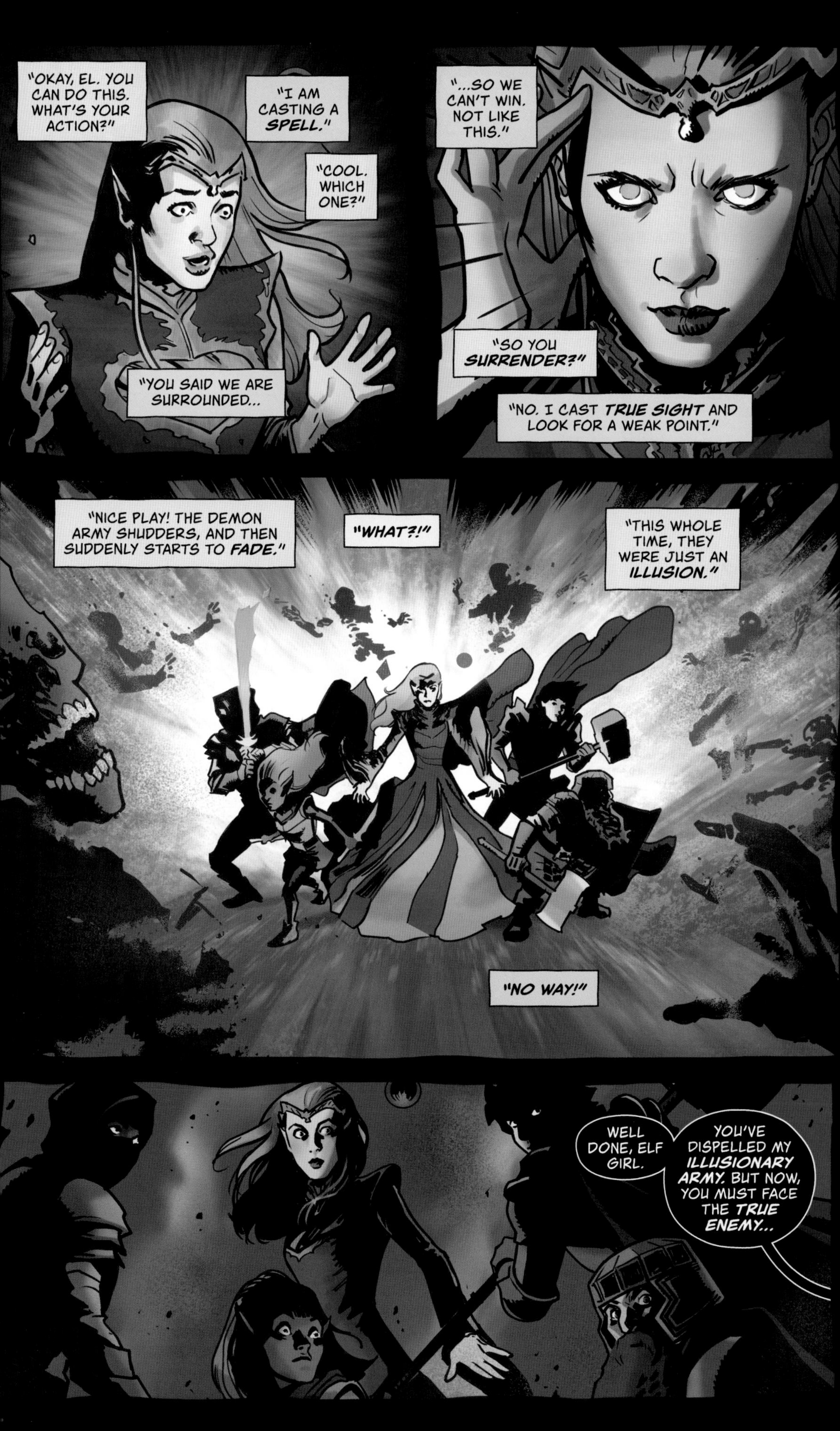
"OKAY, EL. YOU CAN DO THIS. WHAT'S YOUR ACTION?"
"I AM CASTING A *SPELL.*"
"COOL. WHICH ONE?"
"YOU SAID WE ARE SURROUNDED...
"...SO WE CAN'T WIN. NOT LIKE THIS."
"SO YOU *SURRENDER?*"
"NO. I CAST *TRUE SIGHT* AND LOOK FOR A WEAK POINT."
"NICE PLAY! THE DEMON ARMY SHUDDERS, AND THEN SUDDENLY STARTS TO *FADE.*"
"WHAT?!"
"THIS WHOLE TIME, THEY WERE JUST AN *ILLUSION.*"
"NO WAY!"
WELL DONE, ELF GIRL.
YOU'VE DISPELLED MY *ILLUSIONARY ARMY.* BUT NOW, YOU MUST FACE THE *TRUE ENEMY...*

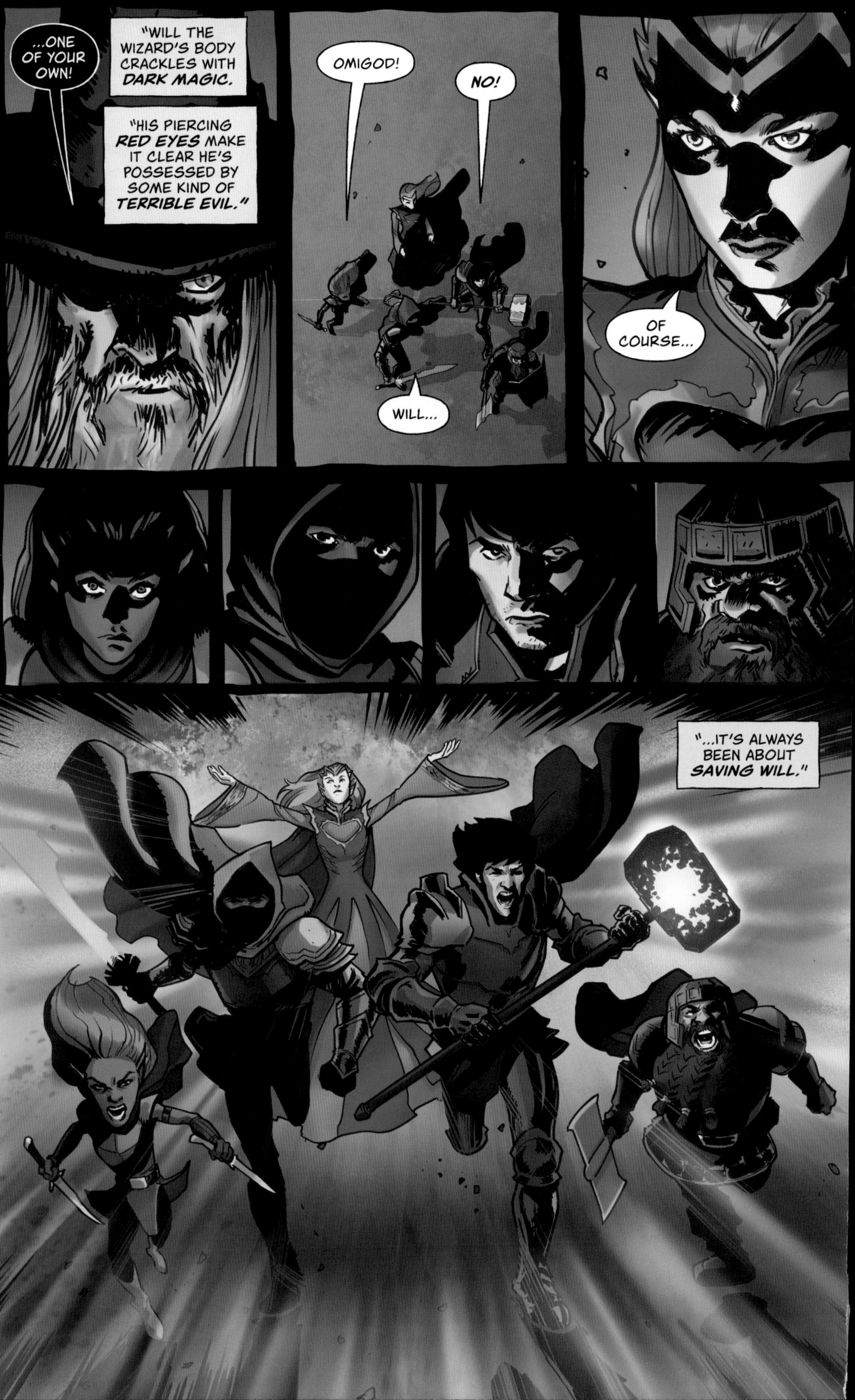
...ONE OF YOUR OWN!
"WILL THE WIZARD'S BODY CRACKLES WITH **DARK MAGIC.**
"HIS PIERCING **RED EYES** MAKE IT CLEAR HE'S POSSESSED BY SOME KIND OF **TERRIBLE EVIL.**"
OMIGOD!
NO!
WILL...
OF COURSE...
"...IT'S ALWAYS BEEN ABOUT **SAVING WILL.**"

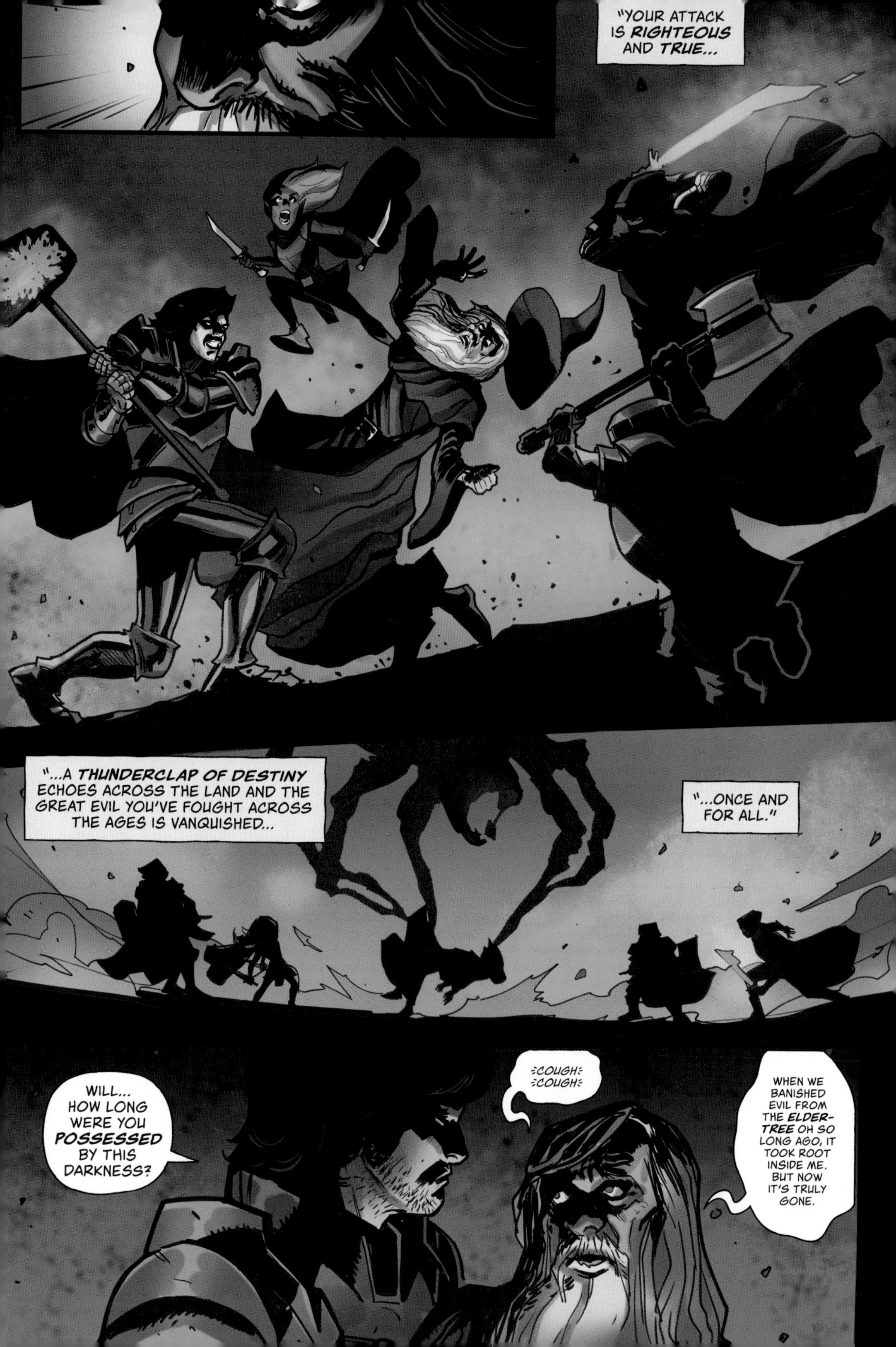
"YOUR ATTACK IS RIGHTEOUS AND TRUE...
"...A THUNDERCLAP OF DESTINY ECHOES ACROSS THE LAND AND THE GREAT EVIL YOU'VE FOUGHT ACROSS THE AGES IS VANQUISHED...
"...ONCE AND FOR ALL."
WILL... HOW LONG WERE YOU POSSESSED BY THIS DARKNESS?
COUGH COUGH
WHEN WE BANISHED EVIL FROM THE ELDER-TREE OH SO LONG AGO, IT TOOK ROOT INSIDE ME. BUT NOW IT'S TRULY GONE.

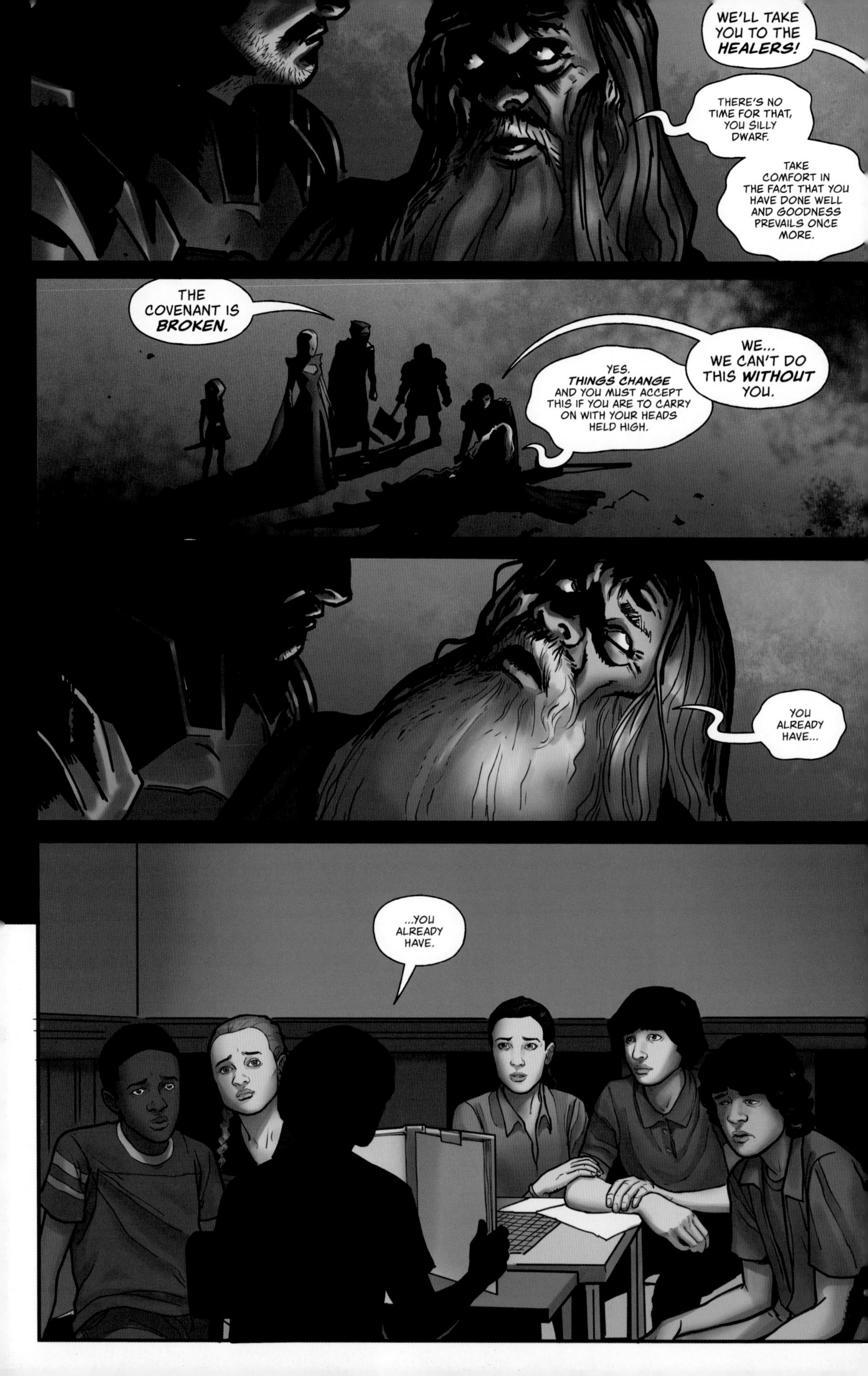
WE'LL TAKE YOU TO THE HEALERS!
THERE'S NO TIME FOR THAT, YOU SILLY DWARF.
TAKE COMFORT IN THE FACT THAT YOU HAVE DONE WELL AND GOODNESS PREVAILS ONCE MORE.
THE COVENANT IS BROKEN.
YES. THINGS CHANGE AND YOU MUST ACCEPT THIS IF YOU ARE TO CARRY ON WITH YOUR HEADS HELD HIGH.
WE... WE CAN'T DO THIS WITHOUT YOU.
YOU ALREADY HAVE...
...YOU ALREADY HAVE.

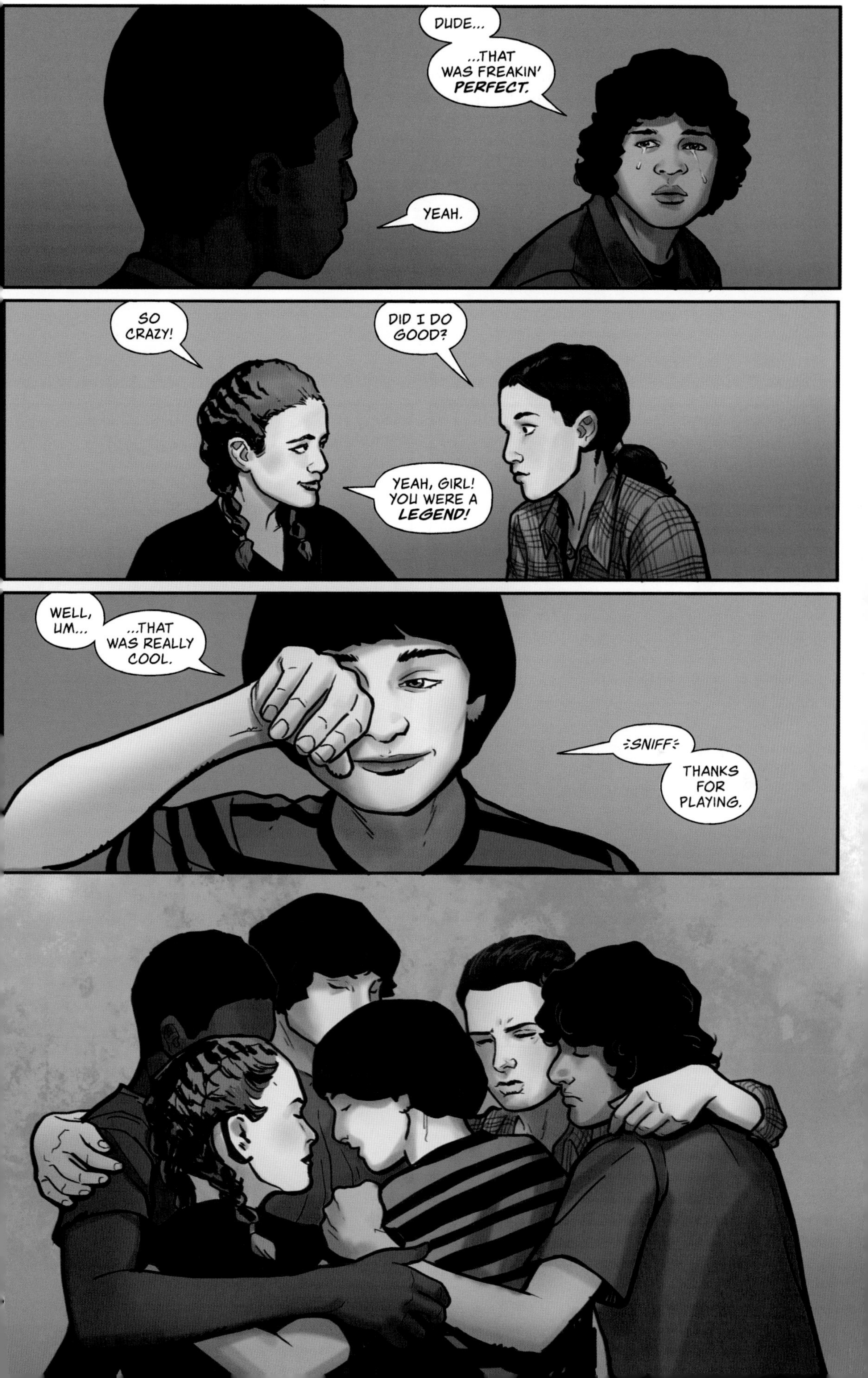
DUDE...
...THAT WAS FREAKIN' PERFECT.
YEAH.
SO CRAZY!
DID I DO GOOD?
YEAH, GIRL! YOU WERE A LEGEND!
WELL, UM...
...THAT WAS REALLY COOL.
SNIFF
THANKS FOR PLAYING.

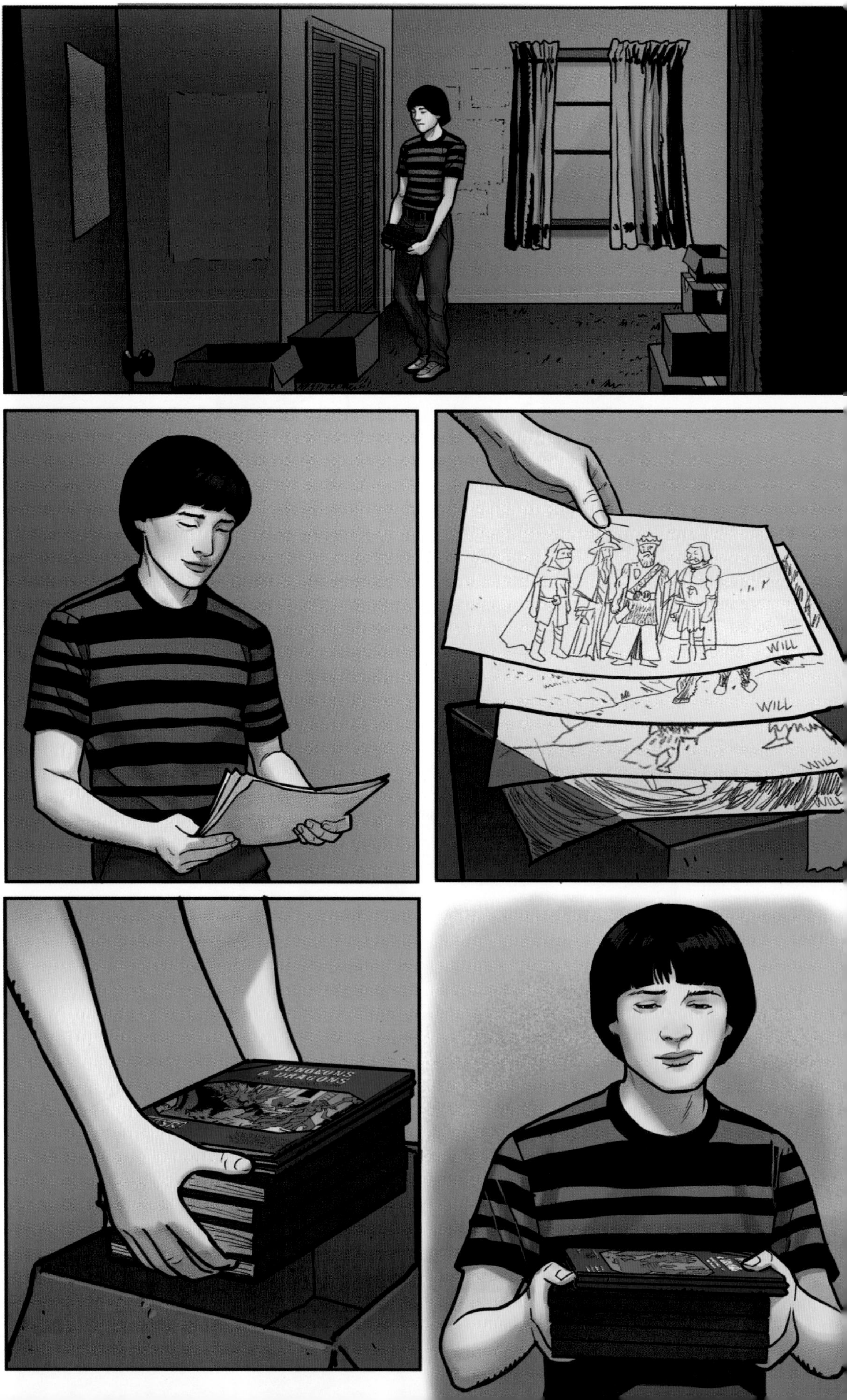
WILL
WILL
WILL
WILL
DUNGEONS & DRAGONS

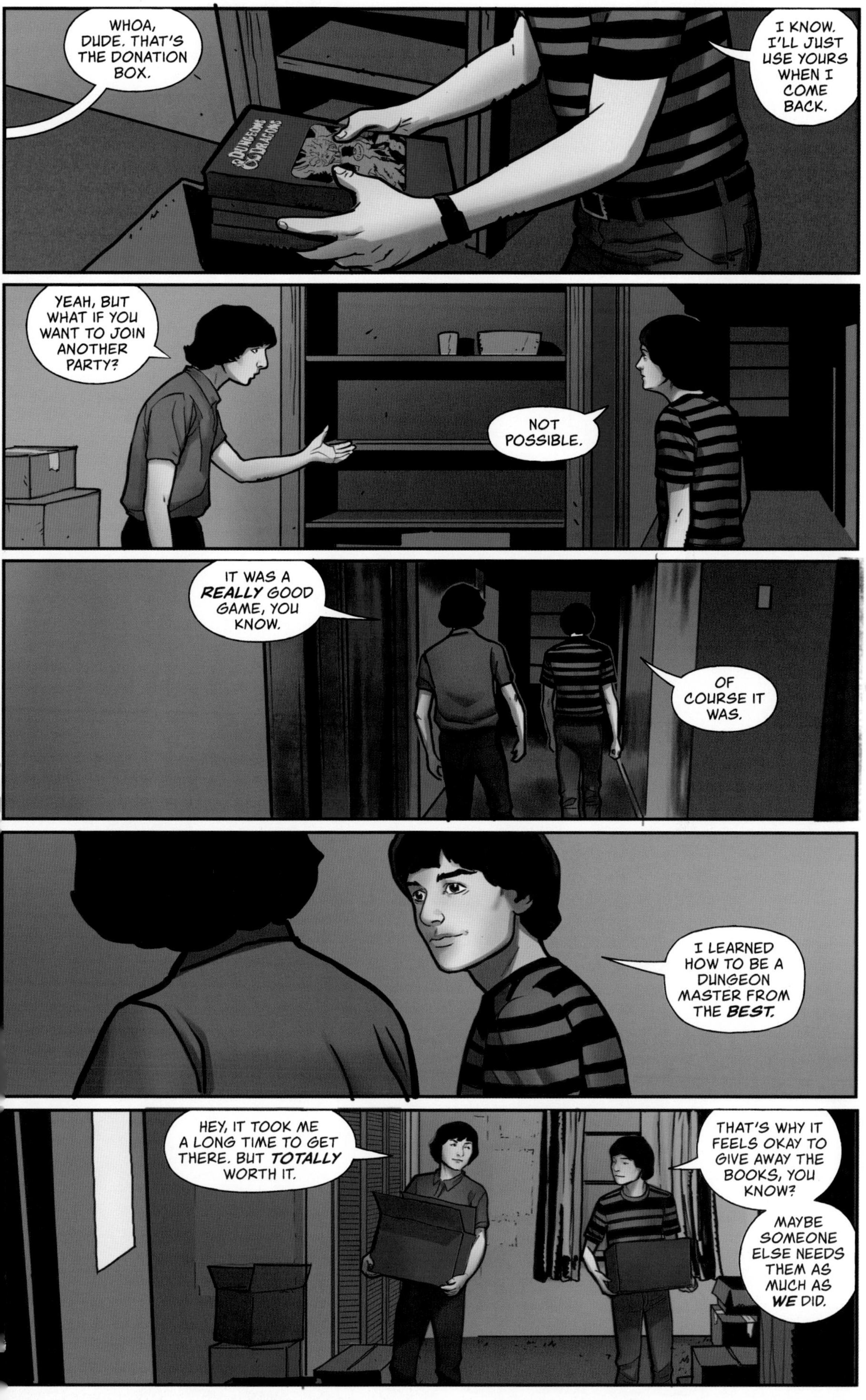
WHOA, DUDE. THAT'S THE DONATION BOX.
I KNOW. I'LL JUST USE YOURS WHEN I COME BACK.
DUNGEONS & DRAGONS
YEAH, BUT WHAT IF YOU WANT TO JOIN ANOTHER PARTY?
NOT POSSIBLE.
IT WAS A REALLY GOOD GAME, YOU KNOW.
OF COURSE IT WAS.
I LEARNED HOW TO BE A DUNGEON MASTER FROM THE BEST.
HEY, IT TOOK ME A LONG TIME TO GET THERE. BUT TOTALLY WORTH IT.
THAT'S WHY IT FEELS OKAY TO GIVE AWAY THE BOOKS, YOU KNOW?
MAYBE SOMEONE ELSE NEEDS THEM AS MUCH AS WE DID.

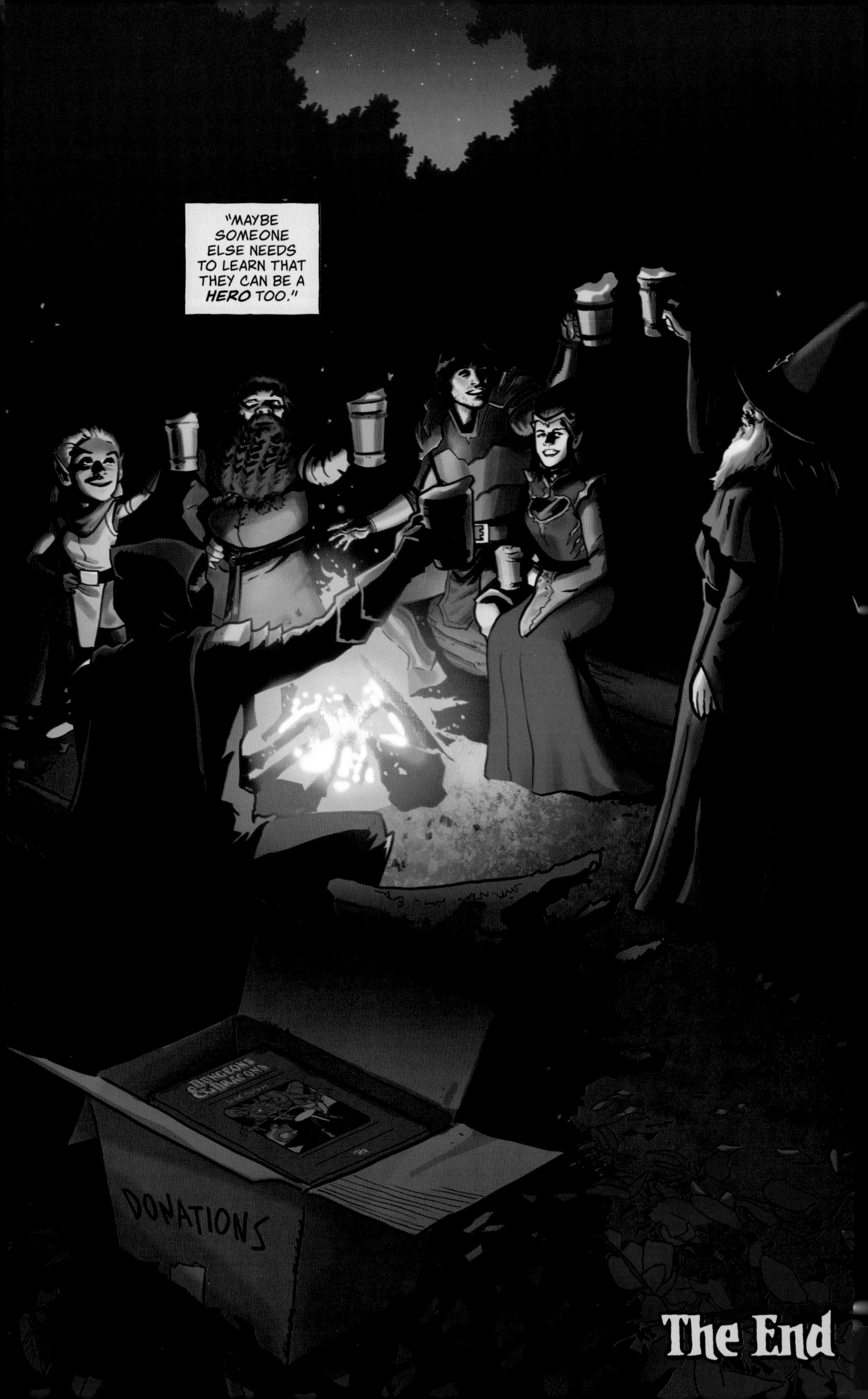
"MAYBE SOMEONE ELSE NEEDS TO LEARN THAT THEY CAN BE A HERO TOO."
DUNGEONS & DRAGONS
DONATIONS
The End

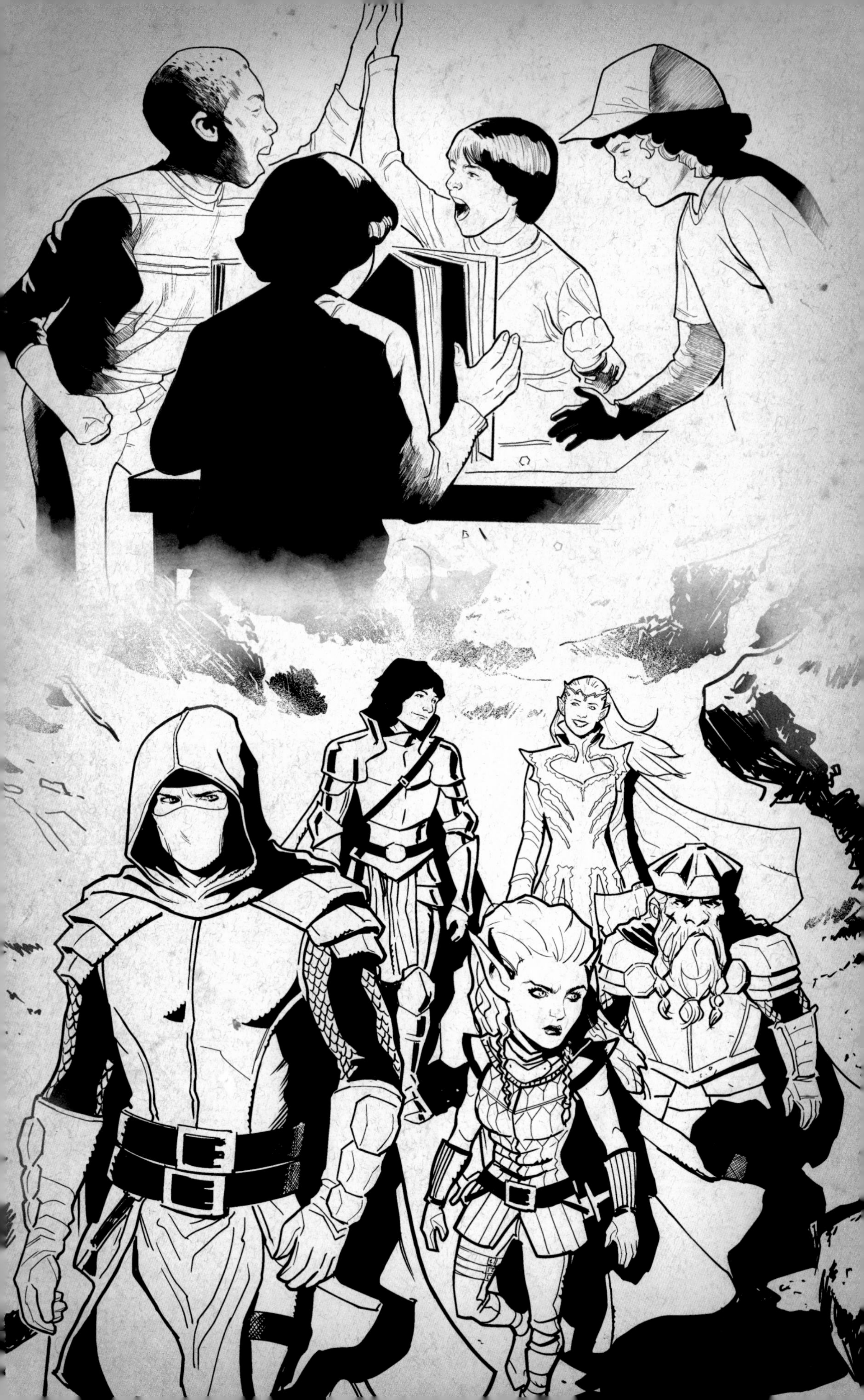

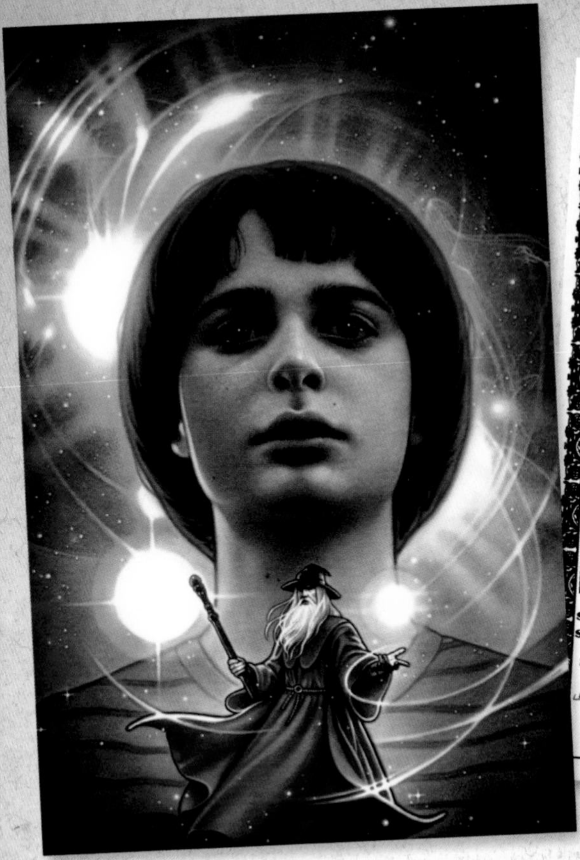

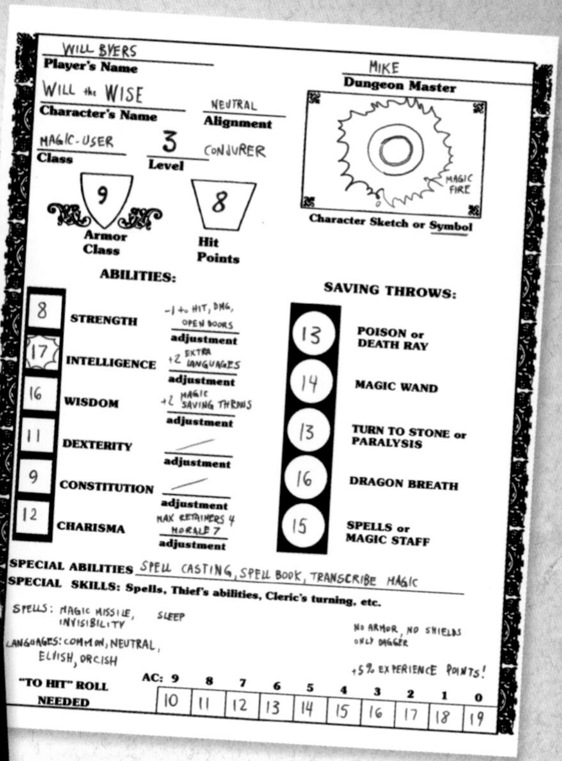

WILL BYERS
Player's Name

MIKE
Dungeon Master

WILL the WISE
Character's Name

NEUTRAL
Alignment

MAGIC-USER
Class

3
Level

CONJURER

MAGIC FIRE

Character Sketch or Symbol

9
Armor Class

8
Hit Points

ABILITIES:

8	STRENGTH	-1 to HIT, DMG, OPEN DOORS adjustment
17	INTELLIGENCE	+2 EXTRA LANGUAGES adjustment
16	WISDOM	+2 MAGIC SAVING THROWS adjustment
11	DEXTERITY	adjustment
9	CONSTITUTION	adjustment
12	CHARISMA	MAX RETAINERS 4 MORALE 7 adjustment

SAVING THROWS:

13	POISON or DEATH RAY
14	MAGIC WAND
13	TURN TO STONE or PARALYSIS
16	DRAGON BREATH
15	SPELLS or MAGIC STAFF

SPECIAL ABILITIES SPELL CASTING, SPELL BOOK, TRANSCRIBE MAGIC
SPECIAL SKILLS: Spells, Thief's abilities, Cleric's turning, etc.

SPELLS: MAGIC MISSILE, INVISIBILITY, SLEEP
LANGUAGES: COMMON, NEUTRAL, ELVISH, ORCISH
NO ARMOR, NO SHIELDS ONLY DAGGER
+5% EXPERIENCE POINTS!

"TO HIT" ROLL NEEDED										
AC:	9	8	7	6	5	4	3	2	1	0
	10	11	12	13	14	15	16	17	18	19

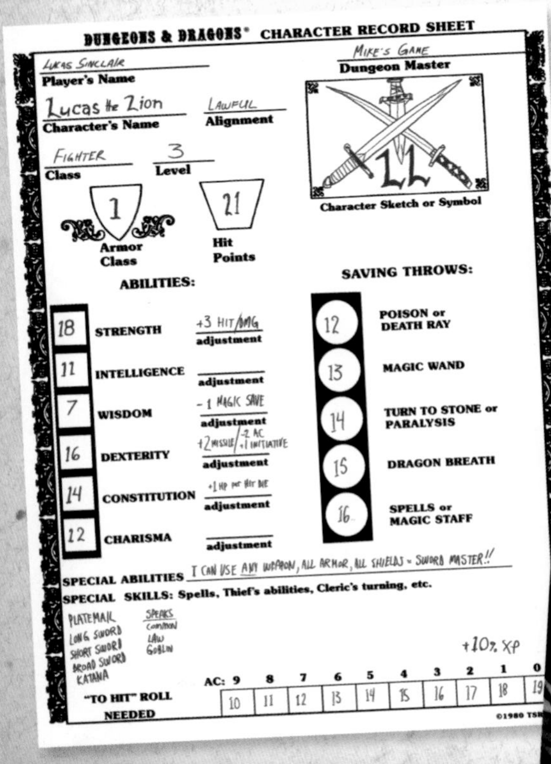

DUNGEONS & DRAGONS® CHARACTER RECORD SHEET

Lucas Sinclair
Player's Name

Mike's Game
Dungeon Master

Lucas the Lion
Character's Name

LAWFUL
Alignment

FIGHTER
Class

3
Level

1
Armor Class

21
Hit Points

LL

Character Sketch or Symbol

ABILITIES:

18	STRENGTH	+3 HIT/DMG adjustment
11	INTELLIGENCE	adjustment
7	WISDOM	-1 MAGIC SAVE adjustment
16	DEXTERITY	+2 MISSILE / -2 AC +1 INITIATIVE adjustment
14	CONSTITUTION	+1 HP per HIT DIE adjustment
12	CHARISMA	adjustment

SAVING THROWS:

12	POISON or DEATH RAY
13	MAGIC WAND
14	TURN TO STONE or PARALYSIS
15	DRAGON BREATH
16	SPELLS or MAGIC STAFF

SPECIAL ABILITIES I CAN USE ANY WEAPON, ALL ARMOR, ALL SHIELDS = SWORD MASTER!!
SPECIAL SKILLS: Spells, Thief's abilities, Cleric's turning, etc.

PLATEMAIL
LONG SWORD
SHORT SWORD
BROAD SWORD
KATANA

SPEAKS
COMMON
LAW
GOBLIN

+10% XP

"TO HIT" ROLL NEEDED										
AC:	9	8	7	6	5	4	3	2	1	0
	10	11	12	13	14	15	16	17	18	19

©1980 TSR

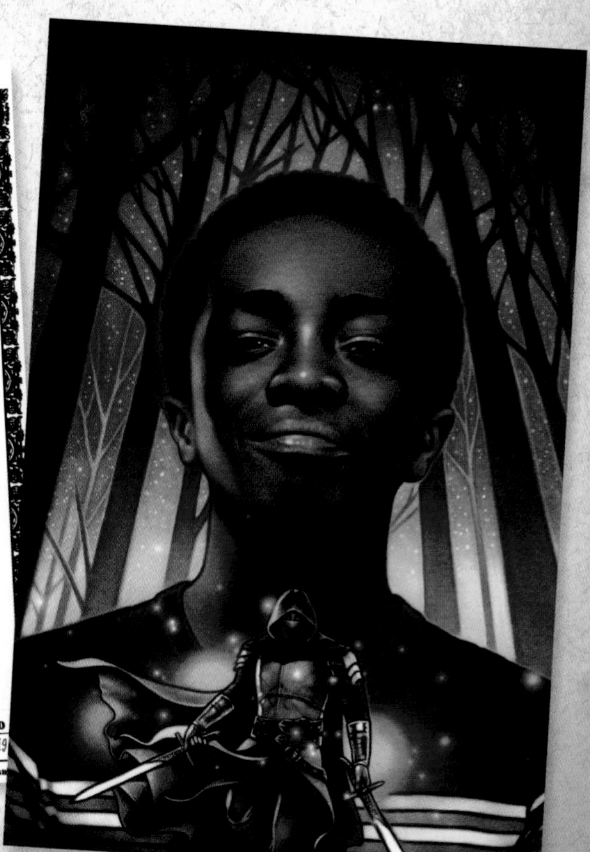

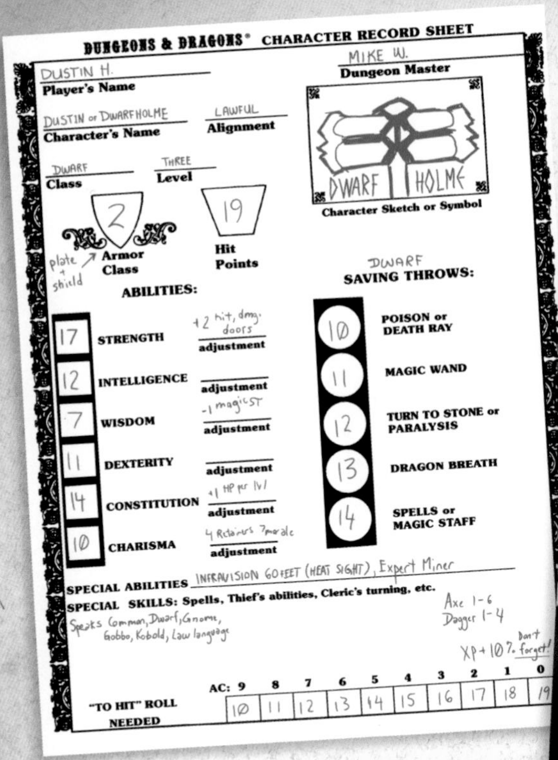
DUNGEONS & DRAGONS® CHARACTER RECORD SHEET

Player's Name: DUSTIN H.

Dungeon Master: MIKE W.

Character's Name: DUSTIN of DWARFHOLME

Alignment: LAWFUL

Class: DWARF

Level: THREE

Character Sketch or Symbol: DWARF HOLME

Armor Class: 2 (plate + shield)

Hit Points: 19

ABILITIES:

Score	Ability	Adjustment
17	STRENGTH	+2 hit, dmg, doors
12	INTELLIGENCE	
7	WISDOM	-1 magic ST
11	DEXTERITY	
14	CONSTITUTION	+1 HP per lvl
10	CHARISMA	4 Retainers 7 morale

DWARF SAVING THROWS:

10	POISON or DEATH RAY
11	MAGIC WAND
12	TURN TO STONE or PARALYSIS
13	DRAGON BREATH
14	SPELLS or MAGIC STAFF

SPECIAL ABILITIES: INFRAVISION 60 FEET (HEAT SIGHT), Expert Miner

SPECIAL SKILLS: Spells, Thief's abilities, Cleric's turning, etc.

Speaks Common, Dwarf, Gnome, Gobbo, Kobold, Law language

Axe 1-6
Dagger 1-4

XP + 10% Don't forget!

AC:	9	8	7	6	5	4	3	2	1	0
"TO HIT" ROLL NEEDED	10	11	12	13	14	15	16	17	18	19

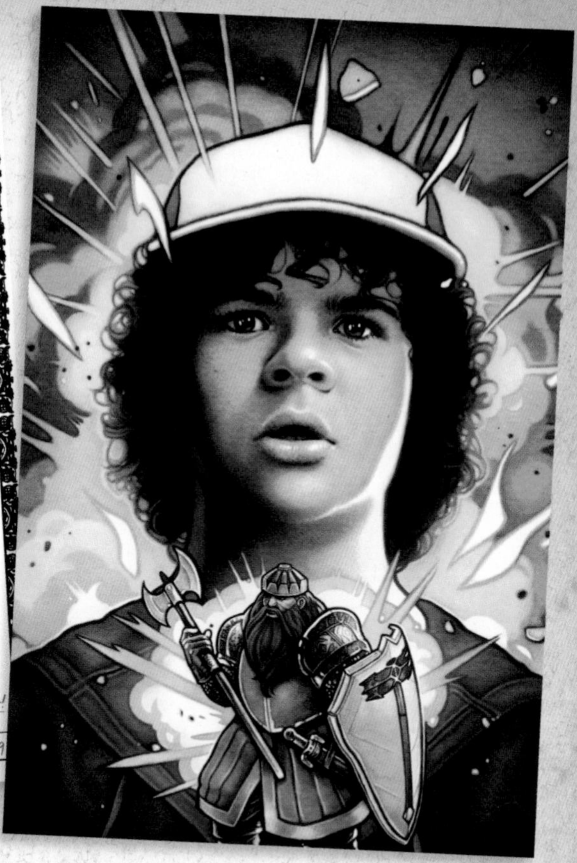

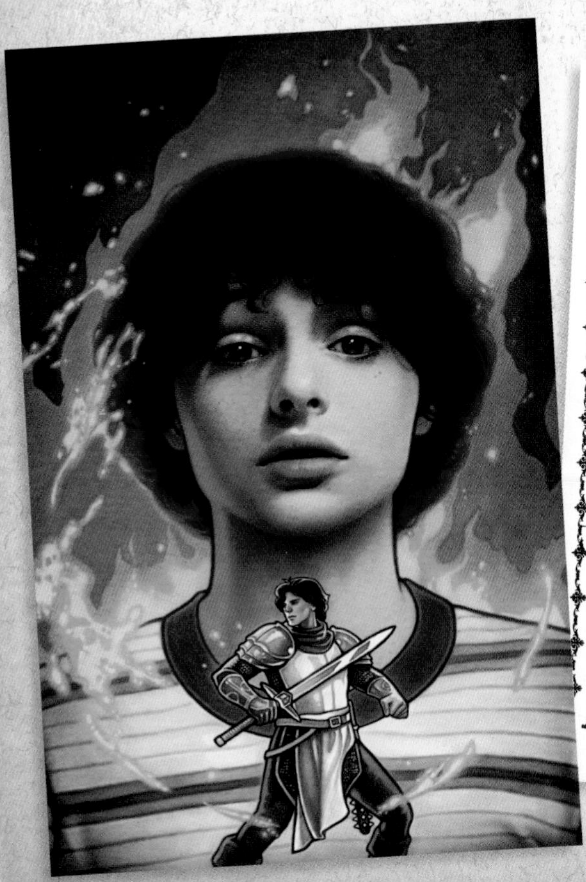

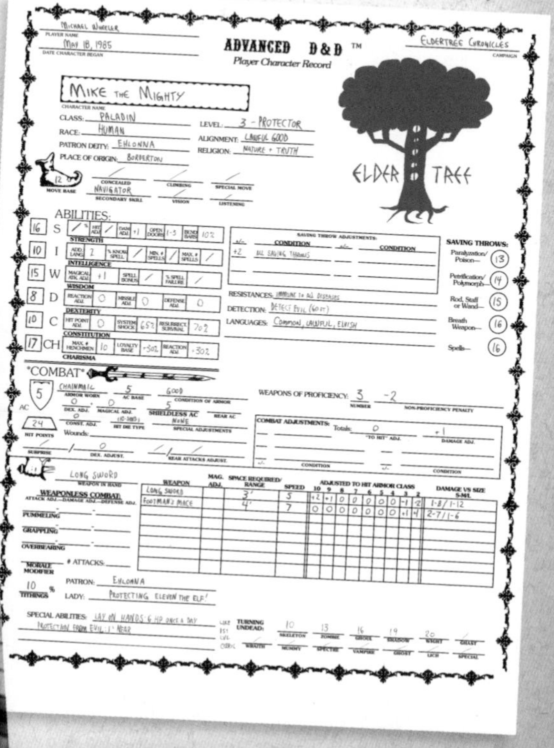
ADVANCED D&D™ Player Character Record

PLAYER NAME: MICHAEL WHEELER

DATE CHARACTER BEGAN: MAY 18, 1985

CAMPAIGN: ELDERTREE CHRONICLES

CHARACTER NAME: MIKE THE MIGHTY

CLASS: PALADIN — LEVEL: 3 - PROTECTOR

RACE: HUMAN — ALIGNMENT: LAWFUL GOOD

PATRON DEITY: EHLONNA — RELIGION: NATURE + TRUTH

PLACE OF ORIGIN: BORDERTON

ELDER TREE

MOVE BASE: 12 — CONCEALED: / — CLIMBING: / — SPECIAL MOVE: /

SECONDARY SKILL: NAVIGATOR — VISION: / — LISTENING: /

ABILITIES:

Score									
16	S (STRENGTH)	%	/	HIT ADJ. /	DAM ADJ. +1	OPEN DOORS 1-3	BEND BARS 10%		
10	I (INTELLIGENCE)	ADD. LANG. 2	% KNOW SPELL /	MIN. # SPELLS /	MAX. # SPELLS /				
15	W (WISDOM)	MAGICAL ATK. ADJ. +1	SPELL BONUS /	% SPELL FAILURE /					
8	D (DEXTERITY)	REACTION ADJ. 0	MISSILE ADJ. 0	DEFENSE ADJ. 0					
10	C (CONSTITUTION)	HIT POINT ADJ. 0	SYSTEM SHOCK 65%	RESURRECT. SURVIVAL 70%					
17	CH (CHARISMA)	MAX. # HENCHMEN 10	LOYALTY BASE +30%	REACTION ADJ. +30%					

SAVING THROW ADJUSTMENTS: +/- CONDITION: +2 ALL SAVING THROWS

RESISTANCES: IMMUNE TO ALL DISEASES

DETECTION: DETECT EVIL (60 FT)

LANGUAGES: COMMON, LAWFUL, ELVISH

SAVING THROWS:

Paralyzation/Poison—	13
Petrification/Polymorph—	14
Rod, Staff or Wand—	15
Breath Weapon—	16
Spells—	16

COMBAT

AC 5 — ARMOR WORN: CHAINMAIL — AC BASE: 5 — CONDITION OF ARMOR: GOOD

DEX. ADJ.: 0 — MAGICAL ADJ.: 0 — SHIELDLESS AC: 5 — REAR AC

HIT POINTS: 24 — CONST. ADJ.: 0 — HIT DIE TYPE: (10-SIDED) — SPECIAL ADJUSTMENTS: NONE

Wounds:

SURPRISE: / — DEX. ADJUST.: 0 — REAR ATTACKS ADJUST.: / / /

WEAPONS OF PROFICIENCY: NUMBER: 3 — NON-PROFICIENCY PENALTY: -2

COMBAT ADJUSTMENTS: Totals: "TO HIT" ADJ.: 0 — DAMAGE ADJ.: +1

WEAPON IN HAND: LONG SWORD

WEAPONLESS COMBAT: ATTACK ADJ.—DAMAGE ADJ.—DEFENSE ADJ.

PUMMELING

GRAPPLING

OVERBEARING

MORALE MODIFIER — # ATTACKS:

WEAPON	MAG. ADJ.	SPACE REQUIRED/RANGE	SPEED	10	9	8	7	6	5	4	3	2	DAMAGE VS SIZE S-M/L
LONG SWORD		3'	5	+2	+1	0	0	0	0	0	-1	-2	1-8/1-12
FOOTMAN'S MACE		4'	7	0	0	0	0	0	0	0	+1	+1	2-7/1-6

TITHINGS: 10 %

PATRON: EHLONNA

LADY: PROTECTING ELEVEN THE ELF!

SPECIAL ABILITIES: LAY ON HANDS: 6 HP ONCE A DAY
PROTECTION FROM EVIL: 1" NEAR

TURNING UNDEAD: LIKE 1ST LVL CLERIC

SKELETON	ZOMBIE	GHOUL	SHADOW	WIGHT	GHAST
10	13	16	19	20	/

WRAITH	MUMMY	SPECTRE	VAMPIRE	GHOST	LICH	SPECIAL
/	/	/	/	/	/	/

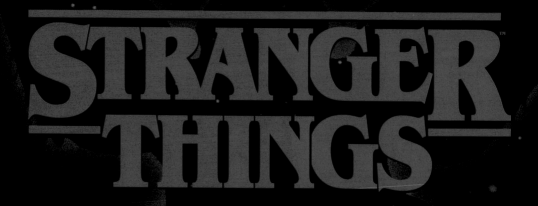

STRANGER THINGS™

THE NOSTALGIA-IGNITING HIT NETFLIX ORIGINAL SERIES COMES TO COMICS!

JODY HOUSER STEFANO MARTINO
KEITH CHAMPAGNE LAUREN AFFE NATE PIEKOS
STRANGER THINGS
THE OTHER SIDE

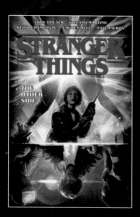

VOLUME 1: THE OTHER SIDE
Jody Houser, Stefano Martino,
Keith Champagne, Lauren Affe
ISBN 978-1-50670-976-5 • $17.99

STRANGER THINGS
SIX
JODY HOUSER EDGAR SALAZAR
KEITH CHAMPAGNE MARISSA LOUISE NATE PIEKOS

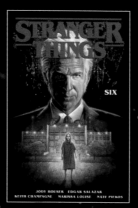

VOLUME 2: SIX
Jody Houser, Edgar Salazar,
Keith Champagne, Marissa Louise
ISBN 978-1-50671-232-1 • $17.99

STRANGER THINGS
INTO THE FIRE
JODY HOUSER RYAN KELLY
LE BEAU UNDERWOOD TRIONA FARRELL NATE PIEKOS

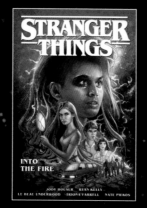

VOLUME 3: INTO THE FIRE
Jody Houser, Ryan Kelly,
Le Beau Underwood, Triona Farrell
ISBN 978-1-50671-308-3 • $19.99

STRANGER THINGS
CAMP
SCIENCE CAMP
JODY HOUSER EDGAR SALAZAR
KEITH CHAMPAGNE MARISSA LOUISE NATE PIEKOS

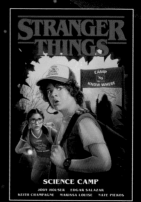

VOLUME 4: SCIENCE CAMP
Jody Houser, Edgar Salazar,
Keith Champagne, Marissa Louise
ISBN 978-1-50671-576-6 • $19.99
COMING MAY 2021!

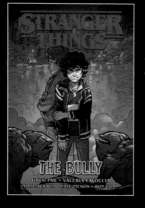

STRANGER THINGS
THE BULLY
GREG PAK • VALERIA FAVOCCIA
DAN JACKSON • NATE PIEKOS • RON CHAN

STRANGER THINGS: THE BULLY
Greg Pak, Valeria Favoccia,
Dan Jackson, Nate Piekos
ISBN 978-1-50671-453-0 • $12.99

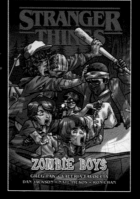

STRANGER THINGS
ZOMBIE BOYS
GREG PAK • VALERIA FAVOCCIA
DAN JACKSON • NATE PIEKOS • RON CHAN

STRANGER THINGS: ZOMBIE BOYS
Greg Pak, Valeria Favoccia,
Dan Jackson
ISBN 978-1-50671-309-0 • $10.99

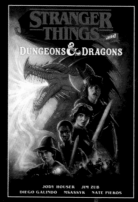

STRANGER THINGS and
DUNGEONS & DRAGONS
JODY HOUSER JIM ZUB
DIEGO GALINDO MSASSYK NATE PIEKOS

STRANGER THINGS AND DUNGEONS & DRAGONS
Jody Houser, Jim Zub,
Diego Gallindo, MsassyK
ISBN 978-1-50672-107-1 • $19.99
COMING JUNE 2021!

DARK HORSE COMICS

DARKHORSE.COM • AVAILABLE AT YOUR LOCAL COMICS SHOP OR BOOKSTORE
To find a comics shop near you, visit comicshoplocator.com
For more information or to order direct, visit darkhorse.com

NETFLIX